Homeland Security and Critical Infrastructure Protection

Homeland Security and Critical Infrastructure Protection

Pamela A. Collins and **Ryan K. Baggett**

PRAEGER SECURITY INTERNATIONAL
Westport, Connecticut • London

Library of Congress Cataloging-in-Publication Data

Collins, Pamela A. (Pamela Ann), 1957–
  Homeland security and critical infrastructure protection /
Pamela A. Collins and Ryan K. Baggett.
       p. cm.
  Includes bibliographical references and index.
    ISBN 978-0-313-35147-1 (hbk. : alk. paper) — ISBN 978-0-313-35148-8
(ebook) 1. National security—United States. 2. Terrorism—United
States—Prevention. 3. Infrastructure (Economics)—United States.
4. Public works—Security measures—United States.
I. Baggett, Ryan K. II. Title.
  HV6432.C645   2009
  363.340973—dc22   2009006255

British Library Cataloguing in Publication Data is available.

Library of Congress Catalog Card Number: 2009006255

ISBN: 978-0-313-35147-1

First published in 2009

Praeger Security International, 88 Post Road West, Westport, CT 06881
An imprint of Greenwood Publishing Group, Inc.
www.praeger.com

Printed in the United States of America

The paper used in this book complies with the
Permanent Paper Standard issued by the National
Information Standards Organization (Z39.48-1984).

10   9   8   7   6   5   4   3   2   1

The authors of this book would like to personally thank a valued friend and colleague for their commitment and dedication to this nation's emergency response community.

Mr. Robert Coullahan has more than 25 years experience in emergency preparedness; domestic preparedness and combating terrorism programs; critical infrastructure protection; systems engineering; and integration and response operations. The authors had the distinct pleasure to work with Mr. Coullahan on the implementation of a national program he developed for the Department of Homeland Security, National Preparedness Directorate, Federal Emergency Management Agency. This program has been instrumental in providing FEMA with the support necessary to provide much needed technical assistance to state and local public safety and emergency response providers.

Mr. Coullahan has a distinguished career in providing program and technical management support of both national and globally-distributed information infrastructure initiatives providing data and decision support services for environmental and disaster research and operations. His experience is based upon his advanced educational attainment, earning his Masters of Science Degree in Telecommunications and a Master of Arts Degree in Security Management from The George Washington University and a Bachelor of Arts degree from the University of California at Irvine. Mr. Coullahan is Board-certified in both emergency management (Certified Emergency Manager) and security management (Certified Protection Professional). He is a Certified Business Continuity Professional and is a certified emergency medical technician (EMT).

He has played a key leadership role on programs of national significance including a Weapons of Mass Destruction (WMD) Biological–Chemical Preparedness study for the National Guard; the White House Y2K Information Coordination Center; and the multiagency Global Disaster Information Network (GDIN) program. Mr. Coullahan has served five years as Vice President and Director of Government & International Programs for an award-winning international information services organization and as work group chairperson for international and public–private initiatives in support of the Emergency Information Infrastructure (EII) and the G7 Global Emergency Management Information Network Initiative (GEMINI), among others.

Mr. Coullahan is also a veteran of the United States Army and has provided service to protecting this country as active and reserve status for nearly a decade. After retiring as Senior Vice President on completion of twenty years of service to a major engineering and science corporation, Robert now serves as the President and Chief Operating Officer for the Readiness Resource Group, which provides technical assistance in programs including: emergency preparedness, homeland security, critical infrastructure protection, business continuity management, executive crisis management training, vulnerability assessments, and capabilities-based planning. Additional information regarding this company can be found at http://www.readinessresource.net/overview.htm.

Mr. Coullahan graciously provided section three of this publication, and the authors dedicate this book to Mr. Robert Coullahan for his lifelong work and tireless commitment to the public safety profession, and more specifically his invaluable dedication and service to the emergency response community to whom we owe a debt of gratitude.

Contents

Preface

This book was written in order to provide a resource on the complex nature of critical infrastructure in the United States. It is anticipated that those reading this text are either new to the subject or perhaps are in a position that requires them to assume certain responsibilities for the critical infrastructure in their community or organization, or simply because they want to understand this issue and its importance to our nation's overall safety and security. The approach taken in the design and layout of the material contained in the book was done so with the notion that those reading it would have available to them a comprehensive primer on critical infrastructure protection.

Since the inception of the Department of Homeland Security (DHS) and their recent five-year anniversary, the publication of documents, guidelines, polices, directives, and legislation has been prolific and would be difficult for any one person to easily access, let alone digest. Therefore, our intent was to provide a book that would contain timely and relevant information that could be viewed in one source by the reader. While the material is intended to be foundational, persons who have worked in homeland security–related positions at the state and local levels, either in the public or private sector, would find this book useful not only as desk reference or resource but as a resource that could enhance their knowledge and understanding of critical infrastructure protection, including the identification of key resources. It would also be useful to persons who want to retool and pursue a career in the growing homeland security field. Finally, for those individuals who are just beginning their professional careers this book provides an invaluable resource in becoming knowledgeable about the DHS, developing an understanding in many of the core components and framers of the DHS, and creating an appreciation for the complexity of this issue and the challenges our nation is facing.

The book is organized to simplify and present in a logical and sequential manner a historical context of homeland security and critical infrastructure protection in the United States. To accomplish this it is divided into three overarching sections beginning with condensed but necessary background information on the DHS, the evolution and history of critical infrastructure in this country, and a review of key legislation, presidential directives, and the approach to assessing our nation's infrastructure. The second section provides a comprehensive look at the federally identified sectors the make up our countries national infrastructure. While much of the data used for the writing of this book are foundational and represent guiding documentation for the DHS, it is still a fluid and dynamic process that is continually under evaluation, assessment, and modification. However, it is important to note that the timing of the book was not accidental and is in step with recent significant revisions and modifications to key guidelines and documents set forth by the DHS. The third and final section of the book provides the reader with the concept of "all hazards," which is fundamental to the understanding of critical infrastructure and the four pillars of homeland security that much of the current body of knowledge is based upon: prevent, prepare, respond, and recover to restore order and overall continuity in our country and our individual communities.

The authors have devoted a great deal of time to ensuring that the data contained in this book are the most current and relevant information available to provide to the reader. They both have been working for the DHS since its inception, providing support through a variety of federally funded programs. They developed this work with the appreciation of the time they have personally spent working in this field and the understanding and experience they have obtained not only in areas related to homeland security but more specifically to the important and complex issue of critical infrastructure protection. It is their hope and desire that this book will make that path much more accessible for others by putting forth in a single resource the information and resources necessary to become conversant and knowledgeable about our nation's critical infrastructure.

Acronyms

AAGNS	Assistant Attorney General for National Security
ACE	Automated Commercial Environment
ACS	Access Control Systems
AFM	Acoustic-Flow Monitor
AGDC	Antarctic Glaciological Data Center
ALS	Advanced Life Support
AMS	American Meteorological Society
AOR	Area of Responsibility
APEC	Asia-Pacific Economic Cooperation
APHIS	Animal Plant Health Inspection Service
ARCSS	Arctic System Science Data Coordination Center
ASCE	American Society of Civil Engineers
ASIS	American Society for Industrial Security
ATA	American Trucking Association
ATF	Bureau of Alcohol, Tobacco, Firearms, and Explosives
ATSA	Aviation and Transportation Security Act
AVO	Alaska Volcano Observatory
BIA	Bureau of Indian Affairs
BIS	Bureau of Industry and Security
BLM	Bureau of Land Management
BOR	Bureau of Reclamation
BZPP	Buffer Zone Protection Program
CARVER	Criticality, Accessibility, Recoverability, Vulnerability Effect, Recognizability
CATV	Cable Television Networks
CBP	Customs and Border Protection

CBRNE	Chemical, Biological, Radiological, Nuclear, and Explosive
CCRI	Climate Change Research Initiative
CCSP	Climate Change Science Program
CCTV	Closed-Circuit Television Systems
CDC	Centers for Disease Control and Prevention
CECA	Consumer Energy Council of America
CERT	Community Emergency Response Team
CFATS	Chemical Facility Anti-Terrorism Standards
CFR	Code of Federal Regulations
CFS	Commercial Facilities Sector
CFTC	Commodity Futures Trading Commission
CHER-CAP	Community Hazards Emergency Response– Capability Assurance Process
CI/KR	Critical Infrastructure/Key Resource
CIA	Central Intelligence Agency
CIPAC	Critical Infrastructure Partnership Advisory Council
CIRES	Cooperative Institute for Research in Environmental Sciences
CJIS	Criminal Justice Information Services Division
CME	Chicago Mercantile Exchange
COG	Continuity of Government
COOP	Continuity of Operations
COOP/COG/ECG	Continuity of Operations/Continuity of Government/Enduring Constitutional Government
CRSR	Congressional Research Service Report
CS&C	Office of Cybersecurity and Communications
CSA	Controlled Substances Act
CSBC	Conference of State Bank Supervisors
CSGCC	Communications Sector Government Coordinating Council
CSSP	Communications Sector Specific Plan
C-TPAT	Customs-Trade Partnership Against Terrorism
CUSEC	Central U.S. Earthquake Consortium
CVO	Cascades Volcano Observatory
CWA	Safe Drinking Water Act
CWC	Chemical Weapons Convention
CWIN	Critical Infrastructure Warning Information Network
DACC	Distributed Active Archive Centers
DEA	Drug Enforcement Administration
DHA	Department of Humanitarian Affairs
DHS	Department of Homeland Security
DHS ODP	DHS Office for Domestic Preparedness
DHS S&T	DHS Science and Technology Directorate
DNDO	Domestic Nuclear Detection Office
DOC	Department of Commerce
DOD	Department of Defense

DOE	Department of Energy
DOI	Department of Interior
DOJ	Department of Justice
DOS	Department of State
DOT	Department of Transportation
EF	Education Facilities
EIA	Energy Information Administration
EMI	Emergency Management Institute
EMP	Electromagnetic Pulse
EMS	Emergency Medical Services
EOC	Emergency Operation Centers
EPA	Environmental Protection Agency
EPCRA	Emergency Planning and Community Right-to-Know Act
ESA	European Space Agency
ESF	Emergency Support Function
ESS	Emergency Services Sector
FAA	Federal Aviation Administration
FBI	Federal Bureau of Investigation
FBIIC	Financial and Banking Information Infrastructure Committee
FCA	Farm Credit Administration
FCC	Federal Communications Commission
FCRA	Fair Credit Reporting Act
FDA	Food and Drug Administration
FDIC	Federal Deposit Insurance Corporation
FedEx	Federal Express
FEMA	Federal Emergency Management Agency
FERC	Federal Energy Regulatory Commission
FHFB	Federal Housing Finance Board
FinCEN	Financial Crimes Enforcement Network
FIRESCOPE	Firefighting Resources of California Organized for Potential Emergencies
FISA	Foreign Intelligence Surveillance Act
FMD	Foot and Mouth Disease
FOIA	Freedom of Information Act
FPS	Federal Protective Service
FRB	Federal Reserve Board
FRE	Federal Rules of Evidence
FSIS	Food Safety and Inspection Service
FS-ISAC	Financial Services Information Sharing and Analysis Center
FSLC	Federal Senior Leadership Council
FSSCC	Financial Services Sector Coordinating Council for Critical Infrastructure Protection and Homeland Security
FWS	Fish and Wildlife Service
GAO	Government Accountability Office
GDP	Gross Domestic Product
GETS	Government Emergency Telecommunications Service

GFS	Government Facilities Sector
GIS	Geographical Information Systems
GNP	Gross National Product
GPS	Global Position System
GSA	General Services Administration
HAZMAT	Hazardous Materials
HHS	Department of Health and Human Services
HITRAC	Homeland Infrastructure Threat and Risk Analysis Center
HPW	High Power Microwave
HSA	Homeland Security Act
HSC	Homeland Security Council
HSIN	Homeland Security Information Network
HSPD	Homeland Security Presidential Directives
HVO	Hawaiian Volcano Observatory
IACP	International Association of Chiefs of Police
IAEM	International Association of Emergency Managers
IAFC	International Association of Fire Chiefs
IAIP	Information Analysis and Infrastructure Protection Directorate
IC	Incident Commander
IC	Intelligence Community
ICAO	International Civil Aviation Organization
ICE	Immigration and Customs Enforcement
ICP	Incident Command Post
ICS	Incident Command System
IED	Improvised Explosive Device
IGP	Office of Intergovernmental Programs
IMF	International Monetary Fund
IMO	International Maritime Organization
IMSI	Incident Management Systems Integration Division
INC	Immigration and Naturalization Services
IND	Improvised Nuclear Device
IPCC	Intergovernmental Panel on Climate Change
ISACS	Information Sharing and Analysis Centers
ISE	Information Sharing Environment
IST	Inherently Safer Technologies
IT	Information Technology
ITDS	International Trade Data System
JFO	Joint Field Office
JIC	Joint Information Center
JICC	Joint Intelligence Community Council
JIS	Joint Information System
LEPC	Local Emergency Planning Committee
LNG	Liquefied Natural Gas
LVO	Long Valley Observatory
MAA	Mutual Aid Agreements
MACS	Multiagency Coordination Systems
MAO	Maximum Allowable Outage
MOA	Memorandums of Agreements

MOS	Metal Oxide Semiconductor
MSRB	Municipal Securities Rulemaking Board
MTS	Maritime Transportation System
NADB	National Asset Database
NAE	National Academies of Engineering
NAIC	National Association of Insurance Commissioners
NARA	National Archives and Records Administration
NARUC	National Association of Regulatory Utility Commissioners
NASA	National Aeronautics and Space Administration
NASD	National Association of Securities Dealers
NASEMSD	National Association of State EMS Directors
NCC	National Counterterrorism Center
NCCT	National Coordinating Center for Telecommunications
NCEP	National Centers for Environmental Prediction
NCP	National Contingency Plan
NCS	National Communications System
NCSD	National Cyber Security Division
NDMC	National Drought Mitigation Center
NDMS	National Disaster Medical System
NEHRP	National Earthquake Hazards Research Program
NEIC	National Earthquake Information Center
NEPA	National Environmental Policy Act
NERC	North American Electric Reliability Council
NFA	National Futures Association
NGDC	National Geophysical Data Center
NGO	Nongovernmental Organizations
NHC	National Hurricane Center
NIC	National Integration Center
NICC	National Interagency Coordination Center
NID	National Inventory of Dams
NIFC	National Interagency Fire Center
NIIMS	National Interagency Incident Management System
NIMS	National Incident Management System
NIOSH	National Institute for Occupational Safety and Health
NIPP	National Infrastructure Protection Plan
NISAC	National Infrastructure Simulation and Analysis Center
NIST	National Institute of Standards and Technology
NLHP	National Landslide Hazards Program
NLIC	National Landslide Information Center
NMI	National Monuments and Icons
NOAA	National Oceanic and Atmospheric Administration
NPD	National Preparedness Directorate
NPS	National Park Service
NRC	Nuclear Regulatory Commission
NRF	National Response Framework

NRP	National Response Plan
NS/EP	National Security/Emergency Preparedness
NSA	National Security Act
NSF	National Science Foundation
NSIDC	National Snow and Ice Data Center
NSSE	National Special Security Event
NSSL	National Severe Storms Laboratory
NTIA	National Telecommunications and Information Administration
NTSB	National Transportation Safety Board
NWS	National Weather Service
NYSE	New York Stock Exchange
OCC	Office of the Comptroller of the Currency
OECD	Organization for Economic Cooperation and Development
OFHEO	Office of Federal Housing Enterprise Oversight
OGT	Office of Grants and Training
OIP	Office of Infrastructure Protection
OMB	Office of Management and Budget
OPS	Office of Protection Services
OSDFS	Department of Education's Office of Safe and Drug-Free Schools
OSHA	Occupational Safety and Health Administration
OSTP	Office of Science and Technology Policy
OTE	Operational Test and Evaluation
OTS	Office of Thrift Supervision
PCCIP	President's Commission on Critical Infrastructure Protection
PCII	Protected Critical Infrastructure Information
PCIS	Partnership for Critical Infrastructure Security
PDD-63	Presidential Decision Directive 63
PDSI	Palmer Drought Severity Index
PKEMAR	Post Katrina Emergency Management Reform
PSTN	Public Switched Telephone Network
PTE	Potential Threat Element
PTWC	Pacific Tsunami Warning Center
R&D	Research and Development
RAM	Risk Assessment Methodologies
RDD	Radiological Dispersal Devices
RDT&E	Research, Development, Test, and Evaluation
RF	Radio Frequency
RFPA	Right to Financial Privacy Act
RMA	Office of Risk Management and Analysis
RMP	Risk Management Program
S&T	Science and Technology Directorate
SAR	Search and Rescue
SAV	Site Assistance Visits
SCADA	Supervisory Control and Data Acquisition
SCC	Sector Coordinating Council
SDR	Subcommittee on Disaster Reduction

SDWA	Safe Drinking Water Act
SEC	Securities and Exchange Commission
SHIRA	Strategic Homeland Infrastructure Risk Assessment
SI	Smithsonian Institution
SIPC	Securities Investor Protection Corporation
SME	Subject Matter Experts
SOHO	Solar and Heliospheric Observatory
SOP	Standard Operating Procedure
SPUC	State Public Utility Commissions
SRO	Self-Regulatory Organizations
SSA	Sector-Specific Agencies
SSP	Sector-Specific Plans
TAFB	Tropical Analysis and Forecast Branch
TCL	Target Capabilities List
TEI/TO	Training and Exercise Integration/Training Operations
TNT	Trinitrotoluene
TPC	Tropical Prediction Center
TSA	Transportation Security Administration
TSB	Technical Support Branch
TSGCC	Transportation Sector Government Coordinating Council
TSP	Telecommunications Service Priority
TWC	Tsunami Warning Centers
UC	Unified Command
UN	United Nations
UNEP	United Nations Environment Program
UPS	United Parcel Service
USACE	U.S. Army Corps of Engineers
USAR	Urban Search and Rescue
USCG	U.S. Coast Guard
USDA	Department of Agriculture
USGCRP	U.S. Global Change Research Program
USGS	U.S. Geological Survey
USNSN	U.S. National Seismograph Network
USPS	United States Postal Service
USSS	United States Secret Service
US-VISIT	United States Visitor and Immigrant Status Indicator Technology
UTL	Universal Task List
UWB	Ultra Wide Band
VBIED	Vehicle-Based Improvised Explosive Devices
VHP	Volcano Hazards Program
WC/ATWC	West Coast/Alaska Tsunami Warning Center
WHO	World Health Organization
WMD	Weapons of Mass Destruction
WMO	World Meteorological Organization
WPS	Wireless Priority Service
WTC	World Trade Center
YVO	Yellowstone Volcano Observatory

Introduction

As we reflect on the horrific and life-changing events of 9/11 and one of the most devastating natural disasters in the United States in terms of lives lost and persons displaced from Hurricane Katrina, the question that remains is whether our critical infrastructures are more secure and better able to withstand and recover from these types of incidents. Further, given the formation of the U.S Department of Homeland Security (DHS) and the billions of dollars spent on strengthening our Nation's infrastructure, can it be firmly stated that the Nation is in a better position to prevent, prepare for, respond to, and recover from a catastrophic event?

According to the Federal Emergency Management Agency (FEMA), considerable accomplishments over the last few years have been achieved, resulting in the improvement of the overall control of our borders, passenger screening, critical infrastructure protection, emergency response, and immigration law enforcement. DHS has also produced a number of key critical infrastructure documents that have set a national tone in these areas, such as the National Strategy for the Physical Protection of Critical Infrastructures and Key Assets.[1] This document identified a set of national goals and objectives that served as "guiding principles" for the protection of infrastructures and key assets that were deemed vital to the United States' national security, governance, public health and safety, economy, and public confidence. Further, the National Infrastructure Protection Plan (NIPP)[2] and supporting Sector-Specific Plans (SSPs) jointly address a coordinated approach for roles and responsibilities in the protection of critical infrastructure and key resources (CI/KR) for federal, state, local, tribal, and private sector security partners. The NIPP also sets national priorities, goals, and requirements for effective distribution of funding and resources intended to ensure the continuity of government, the U.S. economy, and public services in the event of a terrorist attack or other disaster.

This book focuses specifically on how the federal government and the private sector have addressed the issue of protecting this Nation's critical infrastructure and key resources and will identify what steps have been taken to strengthen these while providing a critical analysis of the remaining gaps in these systems. As part of the discussion, we explore the issues surrounding the largest reorganization of the federal government since the formation of the Department of Defense (DOD) in 1947 and provide a thoughtful examination of the process for the formation of a new cabinet-level Department of Homeland Security (DHS). This massive reorganization by the federal government demonstrates an unprecedented commitment, both organizationally and financially, to defend against a specific threat: terrorism. We also provide an overview and a discussion on the Presidential Directives, legislation, policies, and initiatives put into place to secure the Nation's critical infrastructure and key resources.

Additionally, we provide the reader with a comprehensive overview of the national strategy for infrastructure protection along with detailed discussion of the CI/KR sectors to include Energy, Transportation and Shipping, Facilities and National Icons, Environmental, Electronic Transmission, and Public Safety. We use a framework that incorporates the DHS model to prevent, prepare for, respond to, and recover from a national crisis or event, such as a terrorist attack or natural disaster. These four areas represent the DHS framework upon which homeland security is being developed and implemented.

••

DHS Framework

Prevention
Prevention activities may include: heightened inspections; improved surveillance and security operations; public health and agricultural surveillance and testing; immunizations; isolation, or quarantine; and, as appropriate, specific law enforcement operations aimed at deterring, preempting, interdicting, or disrupting illegal activity and apprehending potential perpetrators and bringing them to justice.

Preparedness
Preparedness is a continuous process involving efforts to identify threats, determine vulnerabilities, and identify required resources.

Response
Response refers to the policies and processes for coordinating federal, state, and local support activities that address the short-term, long-term, direct effects of an incident. These activities include immediate actions to preserve life, property, and the environment; meet basic human needs; and maintain the social, economic, and political structure of the affected community.

Recovery

Recovery involves actions needed to help individuals and communities return to normal, when feasible. Recovery actions include the development, coordination, and execution of service and site restoration plans and the reconstitution of government operations and services through individual, private sector, nongovernmental, and public assistance programs.[3]

··

The work is divided into three sections. The first section focuses on the role of prevention, providing the reader with an overview of homeland security and infrastructure protection to include definitions and descriptions of critical infrastructure, specific legislation, and Presidential Directives. The National Infrastructure Protection Plans, the importance and specific roles of both the public and private sectors as part of the national strategy, and how assessments are used to determine the overall effectiveness of the various critical infrastructures are also discussed.

The second section provides a detailed discussion of the seventeen specific critical infrastructure and key resources sectors DHS has formally identified (see Table I.1). This text has collapsed these seventeen different sectors into six over-arching categories, which consist of Energy Systems, Transportation and Shipping, Facilities and National Icons, Environmental, Electronic Transmissions, and Public Safety.

The third section, focuses on the all-hazards approach taken by DHS and includes chapters on Weapons of Mass Destruction (WMD), Natural Disasters (Weather Related and Geological), and Accidents. This section provides an overview of the threats the United States faces while addressing the issues of homeland security and its part of the response and recovery framework. The threats identified for this text also include a discussion on weapons of mass destruction and the likelihood of these being introduced into this country.

Additionally, the recent natural disasters such as Hurricanes Katrina, Rita, and Ike have created a shift in DHS from focusing primarily on terrorism threats to all-hazards threats. This shift has been significant and continues to be debated as to how best to balance the approach to prevention, response, and recovery. This topical discussion also includes how DHS is managing both man-made and natural disasters and the role of FEMA. It will also include information on emergency and disaster planning as well as a review of critical infrastructure

Table I.1 Critical Infrastructure and Key Resources Sectors

Agriculture and Food	Banking and Finance	Chemical
Commercial Facilities	Communications	Dams
Defense Industrial Base	Emergency Services	Energy
Government Facilities	Information Technology	National Monuments and Icons
Nuclear Reactors, Materials, and Waste	Postal and Shipping	Public Health and Healthcare
Transportation Systems	Water	

protection and the complexities involved in identifying and protecting these systems. The discussion provides an overview of how communities and the federal government respond to a national event by examining it from the perspective of the emergency responder, the status of and impacts from issues surrounding interoperability, the incident command system (ICS), and the mandate for communities to become compliant with FEMA's National Incident Management System (NIMS). The Office of Infrastructure Protection (OIP) within the National Protection and Programs Directorate of DHS will also be reviewed to better understand the role they play in developing policy and procedures for successful response by the public safety community.

This section also addresses the response and recovery role by what have been termed "first receivers" and "secondary responders," which refers to the public health system and how it plays a critical role in supporting emergency responders who are often first on the scene. Recovery and the elements necessary to return a community, city, state, or region to normalcy (i.e., restoration of lifelines) after an event such as Hurricanes Katrina and Ike and the slow recovery of the gulf shores region are also discussed. Recovery is examined from an all-hazards approach, which involves how communities rebuild themselves and survive a national catastrophic incident. Specific topics that will be included are emergency assistance and mutual aid agreements, business and government continuity, insurance and risk management, and fear and trauma, with some additional insights to a number of key considerations including forecasting and warning of possible terrorist events and natural disasters, wireless communications systems, and geographical information systems (GIS). Much of this discussion will be supplemented with the use of case studies to illustrate the lessons learned and best practices of prior events.

It is the hope of the authors that this book will provide the reader with a comprehensive overview and analysis of critical infrastructure protection. As part of that discussion, the intent is to provide a primer on what is the DHS and homeland security, how it is structured, and what are the key roles and responsibilities not only of the federal government, but of each state and community throughout the United States.

There has been much enthusiasm for the formation of the DHS and as much criticism of the organization and governance structure in place. The true test of the success of the DHS is not merely measured by the absence of a terrorist event, but by the acceptance and approval of states, communities, and the individuals who make up the cities and towns throughout America. The success is also measured by how we protect and preserve this Nation's critical infrastructure and our ability to prepare for, prevent, respond to, and recover from an event in which we come together collectively to preserve human life and our way of life that is unique and inherent to the United States.

1

The U.S. Department of Homeland Security and Infrastructure Protection

Build a safer, more secure, and more resilient America by enhancing protection of the Nation's CI/KR to prevent, deter, neutralize, or mitigate the effects of deliberate efforts by terrorists to destroy, incapacitate, or exploit them; and to strengthen national preparedness, timely response, and rapid recovery in the event of an attack, natural disaster, or other emergency.[1]

Critical Infrastructure Background

The term "infrastructure," as defined by the *Oxford Pocket Dictionary of Current English*,[2] is the basic physical and organizational structures and facilities (e.g., buildings, roads, and power supplies) needed for the operation of a society or enterprise. Prior to the events of September 11, 2001, the term "infrastructure" primarily referred to the U.S. public works system, which included systems such as roadways, bridges, water and sewer systems, airports, seaports, and public buildings. These earlier references often were put in a context of the concern for their "deteriorating, obsolete, and insufficient capacity."[3]

After the World Trade Center (WTC) and Oklahoma City Federal Building terrorist attacks in the 1990s there was an increased interest on the Nation's infrastructure, and discussions went beyond the concern regarding the adequacy of these systems to a focus on how to better protect them. The term infrastructure was broadened to include this new domestic threat of international and domestic terrorism. On July 15, 1996, President Clinton signed Executive Order 13010, which established the President's Commission on Critical Infrastructure Protection (PCCIP) and expanded the definition of infrastructure to include:

> A framework of interdependent networks and systems comprising identifiable industries, institutions (including people and procedures), and distribution capabilities that provide a reliable flow of products and services essential to the defense and economic security of the United States, the smooth functioning of government at all levels, and society as a whole.[4]

The outcome from the work of the Commission was a final report that led to the creation of a Presidential Decision Directive 63 *(PDD-63)* in May of 1998. The intent of the Directive was to establish a national capability within five years that would provide for the protection of our critical infrastructure from any intentional disruption. At the time the word "critical" referred mostly to the physical and cyber-based systems necessary for minimal operation of the economy and government.[5]

There were no other significant changes to the definition of critical infrastructure until the Uniting and Strengthening America by Providing Appropriate Tools Required to Intercept and Obstruct Terrorism Act of 2001 (Public Law 107-56) (USA PATRIOT Act) and the Homeland Security Act of 2001 were signed into law after the tragic events of September 11, 2001. According to the USA PATRIOT Act, "critical" infrastructure was defined as:

> Systems and assets, whether physical or virtual, so vital to the United States that the incapacity or destruction of such systems and assets would have a debilitating impact on security, national economic security, national public health or safety, or any combination of those matters.[6]

There were also references made to "key assets," which were described as a subset of these critical resources. Key assets were defined as "individual targets whose destruction would not endanger vital systems, but could create local disaster or profoundly damage our Nation's morale or confidence."[7] These key assets include structures and symbols that have historic and symbolic meaning to the United States, such as the Statue of Liberty, which is associated with American freedom. The companion document to this initial reference to the importance of critical infrastructures and key assets was the National Strategy for the Physical Protection of Critical Infrastructures and Key Assets. This document expanded on the discussion of "key assets" to include things such as historical attractions, centers of government and commerce, facilities that are associated with our national economy, i.e., Wall Street, chemical plants, and large, prominent events where large numbers of the public attend, such as the World Series. This document provides a national strategy for reducing the Nation's vulnerability to acts of terrorism by protecting the critical infrastructures and key assets from physical attack by identifying a set of national goals and objectives intended to secure specific infrastructures that are deemed vital to the United States' national security, governance, public health and safety, economy, and public confidence.

This national strategy also sets forth specific objectives intended to maintain public order and provide for continuity of operations (COOP) to include:

1. Identification of those assets determined to be most critical to preserving national health and safety, governance, economic and national security, and public confidence.
2. Provide for a method or system that allows for timely warning of an imminent threat or danger.
3. Once the critical assets and infrastructure are accounted for and proper controls and protection provided, there will then be a focus on other infrastructures that could become terrorist targets.

....

Critical Infrastructure refers to physical and virtual assets and systems that are so vital to the United States that their destruction and/or incapacitation would cause debilitating affects to the Nation's security, economy, public health, public safety, or a combination.

Key Resources are a subset of critical infrastructure whose destruction would greatly affect the Nation's morale and confidence, but would not endanger the operation of vital systems.

....

Terrorism vs. "All-Hazards"

The terms national security and homeland security take on different meanings within the context of DHS. National security refers to efforts on the part of the federal government to protect the United States' "national interests" through our military, foreign policies, and the intelligence community. These agencies focus on protecting our airspace and national borders as well as international operations. Conversely, homeland security refers to efforts not only on the part of the federal government, but also on the states, local authorities, and their communities as well as the private sector to secure the United States against both man-made and natural threats. Further, since 2004, there has been a shift from the more narrow terrorism focus to an inclusive all-hazards approach.

....

National Security refers to efforts to protect and secure national interests through the federal government by means of the military, foreign policy, and the intelligence community (i.e., National Security Agency [NSA] and the Central Intelligence Agency [CIA]).

Homeland Security refers to the efforts of federal, state, and local governments as well as the private sector and private citizens to make the Nation more prepared for and secured against man-made and natural threats.

....

Historically the federal government's role has been to provide response and recovery operational resources for large-scale natural disasters such as floods, hurricanes, and earthquakes. Also, prior to 9/11, terrorism preparedness was a part of the FEMA planning approach to prepare for all types of emergency events. After the attacks, however, federal attention was predominately focused on preparing for terrorist attacks. It was not until after Hurricane Katrina, the wildfires in California, and other large-scale disasters that another shift occurred from terrorism to an all-hazards approach for national preparedness. This transition has been facilitated by the fact that terrorist attacks share common characteristics with natural and accidental disasters. The primary distinction, however, is that DHS prevention capabilities focus on terrorist attacks while natural or accidental disasters are more similar for the elements of response and recovery.

This movement from a more narrow focus on terrorism to a broader focus on all hazards has resulted in DHS developing three major policy initiatives that are intended to create a national, all-hazards coordinated and comprehensive response to large-scale incidents. They include a national response plan, a command and management process, and a national preparedness goal (see Chapter 4: National Incident Management System). DHS was directed through two Homeland Security Presidential Directives (HSPD) -5 and -8 (See Chapter 2: Infrastructure Protection Legislation and Presidential Directives), to develop a balanced approach to both terrorist and all-hazards events in order to create a national domestic all-hazards preparedness goal, consisting of measurable readiness priorities and targets.

Criticisms of Critical Infrastructure and Key Resources

While the efforts of trying to identify and categorize the Nation's critical assets is and of itself a very daunting task, and acknowledging the fact that significant progress has been made in accomplishing this, there has been some criticism of the DHS in the approach and process they have used to conduct this work. According to a Congressional Research Service Report (CRSR) for Congress in 2004,[8] there has been some criticism of the DHS' approach to the identification of critical infrastructures and the fact that they continue to add to or modify the national Critical Infrastructure and Key Resources list. Some of this criticism has come from the private sector, which has called for "clear and stable definitions of asset criticality" in order for them to properly identify and target harden their critical assets. The concern is that if the list continues to shift or change it makes it very difficult for the private sector to adequately prioritize their assets based upon available resources. The private sector is also concerned that if the DHS does not provide criteria regarding "criticality" it would be difficult for the federal government to enforce any potential future security regulations related to critical infrastructure. Also, by the DHS's own admission, in testimony to Congress in 2004, the Assistant Secretary for of the DHS Information Analysis and

Infrastructure Protection Directorate (IAIP), the directorate responsible for the National Asset Database (NADB), stated that "what we have done to identify critical assets in the United States and what the states and local municipalities and cities have done often do not reconcile."[9]

....

Eighty percent of the critical infrastructure in the United States is owned and operated by the private sector.

....

Other criticism from the private sector points to the delay in the DHS providing a draft infrastructure protection plan three years after 9/11 instead of soon after the incident. Even after its anticipated and delayed release, the presented draft plan was not as specific and aggressive as needed concerning those areas in need of immediate improvement and protection, provided what officials have learned about improving critical infrastructure protection within the private sector. The general concern of the owners and operators of critical infrastructure is that the type and breadth of information they are being asked to submit on organizational vulnerabilities is very sensitive and priority information, and if somehow made available to the public or their competitors it could impact public relations and their competitive advantage in the market. There is also the concern that their exposure to liability would increase. The result was a desire by the private sector for the government to adjust the language of the Freedom of Information Act (FOIA) of 1966 (amended 1996, 2002, and 2007). The FOIA is a federal statute that allows individuals the right to request access to government records. FOIA also establishes a presumption that records in the possession of agencies and departments of the Executive Branch of the U.S. government are accessible to the people, except to the extent that the records are protected from disclosure by any of nine exemptions contained in the law or by one of three special law enforcement record exclusions. Released records may contain information withheld or redacted under one of the following nine FOIA exemptions:

1. National defense and foreign relations information that is currently and properly classified as authorized by Executive Order.
2. Pertains solely to the internal rules and practices of the agency.
3. Information that is prohibited from disclosure by another federal law.
4. Applies to information such as trade secrets and commercial or financial information obtained from a person on a privileged or a confidential basis.
5. Applies to inter- and intraagency communications, which are deliberative in nature and involve the decision-making process.
6. Applies to information that would constitute a clearly unwarranted invasion of the privacy of an individual.
7. Records of information compiled for law enforcement purposes, to the extent that the production of those records (A) could reasonably be expected to interfere with enforcement proceedings, (B) would deprive a person of a right to a fair trial or an impartial adjudication, (C) could reasonably be expected to constitute an unwarranted invasion of personal privacy, (D) could reasonably be

expected to disclose the identity of a confidential source, (E) would disclose techniques and procedures for law enforcement investigations or prosecutions, or would disclose guidelines for law enforcement investigations or prosecutions, or (F) could reasonably be expected to endanger the life or physical safety of any individual.

8. Information relating to the supervision of financial institutions.
9. Contains geological or geophysical information concerning wells.

Another type of information request is a personal records request under the Privacy Act of 1974 (Public Law 93-579). A Privacy Act Request is one in which an individual seeks records on themselves that are contained in a file within an agency system of records that is retrievable by the individual's name or personal identifier. All Privacy Act Requests must be submitted in writing and contain the requester's original signature. Privacy Act Requests are processed under both the FOIA and the Privacy Act to allow maximum disclosure to the requester.[10]

The private sector wanted the federal government to craft a specific exemption to the FOIA statute (i.e., a (b)(3) exemption) in order to provide the necessary legal protection for the information that would required to be shared. The idea was that this clause would eliminate agency discretion to disclose protected information for any FOIA request. There was also the concern of how this information would be shared by the DHS with state and local officials as well.

The information gathered from the private and public sectors regarding the Nation's critical infrastructure have been utilized to develop and maintain the National Asset Database (NADB). The NADB contains information on more than 77,000 individual assets, ranging from dams, hazardous materials sites, and nuclear power plants to local festivals, petting zoos, and sporting good stores. The fact that there are such a large number of assets contained in the NADB (i.e., assets generally perceived as having more local importance than national importance) has attracted criticism from the press and from members of Congress. Many critics of the NADB have assumed that it is (or should be) the DHS's list of the Nation's most critical assets and are concerned that, in its current form, it is being used inappropriately as the basis upon which federal resources, including infrastructure protection grants, are allocated. According to the DHS, both of those assumptions are wrong. The DHS characterizes the NADB not as a list of critical assets, but rather as a national asset inventory providing the universe from which various lists of critical assets are produced. As such, the DHS maintains that it represents just the first step in its risk management process outlined in the National Infrastructure Protection Plan (NIPP). The DHS has developed, apparently from the NADB, a list of about 600 assets that it has determined are critical to the Nation. Also, while the NADB has been used to support federal

....

The National Asset Database (NADB) contains information on more than 77,000 individual assets throughout the Unites States.

....

grant-making decisions, according to a DHS official, it does not drive those decisions. In July 2006, the DHS Office of the Inspector General released a report on the NADB. Its primary conclusion was that the NADB contained too many unusual and out-of-place assets and recommended that those judged to be of little national significance be removed from the NADB.[11]

Scope of the United States Critical infrastructure

The DHS has received much of the criticism in the way of the types and scale of the identified critical infrastructure and key assets. The great expanse of this country and the vast infrastructure, however, is often difficult to grasp and compiled in a meaningful and easily understood format. For example, according to the U.S. National Research Council (NRC) the transportation system in the United States alone consists of four million interconnected miles of paved roadways, including 45,000 miles of interstate freeway and 600,000 bridges. The railway system has more than 500 freight railroads and nearly 300,000 miles of track spreading from one end of the country to the other. Additionally, it is estimated that five people use the U.S. rail system for every one person that uses air transportation. As for the United States aviation system, it comprises approximately 500 commercial-service airports and approximately 14,000 smaller general aviation airports.[12] Further, the oil and gas transmissions system is made up of nearly two million miles of pipeline. All of these transportation systems are dependent on other critical infrastructure and key resources to effectively operate, such as bridges, tunnels, dispatch centers, and storage facilities. All of which could become a single point of failure for the rail system.

In addition to transportation, the United States had nearly 2,800 electrical plants across the Nation as recently as 2002, with the largest portion located in the west and north central regions of the country (see Table 1.1).[13]

When discussing power supply, one must also take into consideration the total number of dams in the United States, which is currently estimated at nearly 80,000. These data are maintained by the National Inventory of Dams (NID) and normally apply to dams that are at least fifty feet or more in height, or with a normal storage capacity of 5,000 acre-feet or more, or with a maximum storage capacity of 25,000 acre-feet or more.[14] Dams provide hydroelectric power, which is the process by which a hydraulic turbine converts the energy of flowing water into mechanical energy which in turn, through the use of a hydroelectric generator, converts this mechanical energy into electricity. Hydroelectric dams accounted for approximately six percent of the total United States electricity generated in 2005.[15]

Inland waterways account for nearly nine percent of total domestic freight carried by the U.S Maritime Transportation System (MTS) on its network of inland waterways, which includes the Mississippi River System and the intracoastal and navigable internal waterways of the Atlantic, Gulf, and Pacific Coasts. The inland fleet currently totals more than 33,000 vessels, and more than 770 million tons of freight is transported on the Nation's inland

Table 1.1 Number of Plants at U.S. Electric Utilities by Census Division and State (2002)

Census Division State	Number of Plants
U.S. Total	2,776
New England	**116**
Connecticut	8
Maine	11
Massachusetts	21
New Hampshire	15
Rhode Island	2
Vermont	59
Mid-Atlantic	**98**
New Jersey	6
New York	69
Pennsylvania	23
East North Central	**440**
Illinois	59
Indiana	40
Michigan	134
Ohio	79
Wisconsin	128
West North Central	**539**
Iowa	123
Kansas	96
Minnesota	110
Missouri	91
Nebraska	82
North Dakota	17
South Dakota	20
South Atlantic	**310**
Delaware	6
Florida	69
Georgia	56
Maryland	6
North Carolina	54
South Carolina	51
Virginia	48
West Virginia	20
East South Central	**129**
Alabama	39
Kentucky	30
Mississippi	22
Tennessee	38
West South Central	**245**
Arkansas	33
Louisiana	33
Oklahoma	41
Texas	138

Mountain	**306**
Arizona	36
Colorado	67
Idaho	46
Montana	15
Nevada	21
New Mexico	17
Utah	80
Wyoming	24
Pacific Contiguous	**408**
California	278
Oregon	59
Washington	71
Pacific Noncontiguous	**185**
Alaska	167
Hawaii	18

waterways each year. Of this cargo, the principal commodities carried are coal, oil products, and food and farm products, all bulk cargo. While 75% of the coastwise trade is in Alaskan crude oil and petroleum products, large numbers of containers are shipped in domestic coastwise markets including containerized forest products and livestock. These intermodal waterway systems are an aggregation of state, local, or privately owned facilities and private companies. More than 1,000 harbor channels and 25,000 miles of inland, intracoastal, and coastal waterways in the U.S. serve more than 300 ports and more than 3,700 terminals that handle passenger and cargo movements. For example, annually, the U.S. marine transportation system:

- Moves more than 2 billion tons of domestic and international freight;
- Imports 3.3 billion barrels of oil to meet U.S. energy demands;
- Transports 134 million passengers by ferry;
- Serves 78 million Americans engaged in recreational boating; and
- Hosts more than 5 million cruise ship passengers.

The intercoastal waterways play a critical role in our day-to-day local, state, and national economy through the support of waterborne cargo. These waterway systems, which consist of approximately 9,400 waterway facilities, supports 110,000 commercial fishing vessels and recreational fishing that contribute more than $100 billion to state economies, and the national estimates of their economic impact are in excess of $740 billion to U.S. Gross Domestic Product (GDP). The U.S. waterway system also provides employment for more than 13 million citizens.

Finally, the U.S. airport system accounts for another area of considerable impact on the U.S. economy and consists of more than 5,000 public use airports. The U.S. airline system set an annual record by carrying nearly 770 million scheduled domestic and international passengers in 2007. Table 1.2

Table 1.2 Domestic Scheduled Airline Travel on U.S. Carriers

	MONTHLY			ANNUAL		
	DEC 06	*DEC 07*	*CHANGE %*	*2006*	*2007*	*CHANGE %*
Passengers (in millions)	53.5	53.2	−0.6	658.4	679.1	3.1
Flights (in thousands)	805.0	800.8	−0.5	9708.1	9809.4	1.0

provides both a monthly and annual look at the number of passengers and flights during a 12-month period between 2006 and 2007.[16]

When the overall numbers of passengers and cargo that is moved from one end of this country through the use of the Nation's critical infrastructure is examined, it is staggering to realize what the immediate impact would be to the Nation if even just one of these systems failed.

••

The vast **critical infrastructure system** in the United States includes:

- Four million miles of paved roadways and 600,000 bridges;
- 500 freight railroads and 300,000 miles of track;
- 500 commercial service airports and 14,000 general aviation airports;
- Two million miles of oil and gas transmission pipelines;
- 2,800 electric plants;
- 80,000 dams; and
- 1,000 harbor channels and 25,000 miles of inland, intracoastal, and coastal waterways servicing more than 300 ports and 3,700 terminals.

••

2

....

Infrastructure Protection Legislation and Presidential Directives

Presidential Directives

Since 1947, each presidential administration has adopted and tailored a system for announcing and circulating within the administration presidential directives involving domestic, foreign, and military policies. Presidential

....

Presidential Directives are signed by the president of the United States and issued by the National Security Council.

....

directives establish a policy and may have the force of law. Unlike an executive order, presidential directives are not required to be published in the *Federal Register* or the *Code of Federal Regulations*. Both an executive order and a presidential directive remain effective upon a change in administration, unless otherwise specified in the document, and both continue to be effective until subsequent presidential action is taken.[1]

Presidential Directives are signed or authorized by the President and issued by the National Security Council. The National Security Council was established by the National Security Act of 1947 (PL 235 - 61 Stat. 496; U.S.C. 402), amended by the National Security Act Amendments of 1949 (63 Stat. 579; 50 U.S.C. 401 et seq.). Later in 1949, as part of the Reorganization Plan, the National Security Council was placed in the Executive Office of the President. The National Security Council is the President's principal forum for considering national security and foreign policy matters with his senior national security advisors and cabinet officials. Since its inception under President Harry S. Truman, the function of the National Security

Council has been to advise and assist the President on national security and foreign policies. The National Security Council also serves as the President's principal arm for coordinating these policies among various government agencies.

Following the terrorist attacks on the World Trade Center (WTC) in New York City and the Pentagon in Arlington, Virginia on September 11, 2001, President George W. Bush established, with Executive Order (E.O.) 13228 of October 8, 2001, the Office of Homeland Security and the Homeland Security Council within the Executive Office of the President to assist with the planning and coordination of federal efforts to combat terrorism and maintain the domestic security of the United States.

Later the same month on October 29, 2001, the President issued the first instrument in a new series of directives referred to as the Homeland Security Presidential Directives (HSPDs). The initial directive concerned the organization and operation of the Homeland Security Council, and as of the printing of this text there have been twenty-four subsequent HSPDs. The following provides a brief summary of each HSPD. For a more detailed explanation of these directives, visit the Department of Homeland Security's Website at: http://www.dhs.gov/xabout/laws/editorial_0607.shtm.

••

Despite their common goal and purpose, **Presidential Directives** have been issued under different names by the Presidential administrations.

- National Security Action Memoranda (NSAM): Presidents John F. Kennedy and Lyndon B. Johnson
- National Security Decision Memoranda (NSDM): Presidents Richard M. Nixon and Gerald R. Ford
- Presidential Directive (PD): President James Earl Carter, Jr.
- National Security Decision Directive (NSDD): President Ronald W. Reagan
- National Security Directive (NSD): President George H. W. Bush
- Presidential Decisions Directive (PDD): President William J. Clinton
- National Security Presidential Directive (NSPD): President George W. Bush
- Homeland Security Presidential Directive (HSPD): President George W. Bush[2]

••

Homeland Security Presidential Directives (HSPD)[3]

HSPD-1: Organization and Operation of the Homeland Security Council

Homeland Security Presidential Directive (HSPD)–1 created the Homeland Security Council (HSC) and enumerates its functions. The purpose of the HSC is twofold:

1. To coordinate homeland security–related efforts across executive departments and agencies of all levels throughout the country; and

2. To implement the Department's policies through eleven Policy Coordination Committees.

HSPD-2: Combating Terrorism through Immigration Polices

HSPD-2 created a task force which works aggressively to prevent aliens who engage in or support terrorist activity from entering the United States and to detain, prosecute, or deport any such aliens who are within the United States. HSPD-2 also mandated the creation of the Foreign Terrorist Tracking Task Force to coordinate federal agencies in the implementation of the aggressive policy outlined above. HSPD-2 further enhanced the enforcement capabilities of the Immigration and Naturalization Services (INS) and the Customs Service, as well as implementing measures to combat international student visa abuse. This HSP also mandated coordination with the immigration efforts of both Canadian and Mexican authorities.

HSPD-3: Homeland Security Advisory System

HSPD-3 established a comprehensive and effective means to disseminate information regarding the risk of terrorist acts to federal, state, and local authorities and to the American people. To accomplish this, HSPD-3 created a Homeland Security Advisory System to inform all levels of government and local authorities, as well as the public, to the current risk of terrorist acts. The Homeland Security Advisory System involves a five-level, color-coded Threat Condition indicator to correspond to the current situation. Agency-specific Protective Measures associated with each Threat Condition will allow a flexible, graduated, and appropriate response to a change in the Nation's level of risk.

HSPD-4: National Strategy to Combat Weapons of Mass Destruction

HSPD-4 applied new technologies, increased emphasis on intelligence collection and analysis, strengthened alliance relationships, and established new partnerships with former adversaries to counterterrorist threats in all of its dimensions.

HSPD-5: Management of Domestic Incidents

HSPD-5 enhanced the ability of the United States to manage domestic incidents by establishing a single comprehensive national incident management system. This management system is designed to cover the prevention of, preparation for, response to, and recovery from terrorist attacks, major disasters, and other emergencies. The implementation of such a system would allow all levels of government throughout the Nation to work efficiently and effectively together. The directive further detailed which government officials oversee and have authority for various parts of the national incident management system, as well making several amendments to various other HSPDs.

HSPD-6: Integration and Use of Screening Information

HSPD-6 established the Terrorist Threat Integration Center. HSPD-6 also focused on the use of information about individuals known or suspected to engage in terrorist activities. United States policy is to develop, integrate, and maintain thorough, accurate, and current information about individuals known or appropriately suspected to be or have been engaged in conduct related to terrorism. Such information shall be used to support federal, state, local, territorial, tribal, foreign-government, and private sector screening processes, and diplomatic, military, intelligence, law enforcement, immigration, visa, and protective processes. HSPD-6 is to be implemented in a manner consistent with the provisions of the Constitution and applicable laws, including those protecting the rights of all Americans.

HSPD-7: Critical Infrastructure Identification, Prioritization, and Protection

HSPD-7 established a national policy for federal departments and agencies to identify and prioritize critical infrastructure and key resources within the United States and to protect them from terrorist attacks. The directive defined relevant terms and delivered thirty-one policy statements. These policy statements defined what the directive covered and the roles various federal, state, and local agencies will play in carrying it out.

HSPD-8: National Preparedness

HSPD-8 identified steps for improved coordination in response to incidents. HSPD-8 described the way federal departments and agencies will prepare for such a response, including prevention activities during the early stages of a terrorism incident. HSPD-8 further established policies to strengthen preparedness in the United States in order to prevent and respond to threatened or actual domestic terrorist attacks, major disasters, and other emergencies. HSPD-8 also required a national domestic all-hazards preparedness goal, with established mechanisms for improved delivery of federal preparedness assistance to state and local governments. HSPD-8 also outlined actions to strengthen preparedness capabilities of federal, state, and local entities. HSPD-8 is a companion to HSPD-5.

HSPD-8 Annex 1: National Planning

Annex 1 to HSPD-8 further enhanced the preparedness of the United States by formally establishing a standard and comprehensive approach to national planning. The Annex is meant to provide guidance for conducting planning in accordance with the National Incident Management System (NIMS, 2004) in the National Strategy for Homeland Security (2007). Planning is one of the eight national priorities set forth in the National Preparedness Guidelines, and it is a target capability across all homeland security mission areas.

HSPD-9: Defense of United States Agriculture and Food

HSPD-9 established a national policy to defend the agriculture and food system against terrorist attacks, major disasters, and other emergencies. The United States agriculture and food system is an extensive, open, interconnected, diverse, and complex structure providing potential targets for terrorist attacks. The United States agriculture and food system is vulnerable to disease, pest, or poisonous agents that occur naturally, are unintentionally introduced, or are intentionally delivered by acts of terrorism. HSPD-9 defined policies, including roles and responsibilities, awareness and warning, and vulnerability assessments, to provide the best protection possible against a successful attack on the agriculture and food system.

HSPD-10: Biodefense for the 21st Century

HSPD-10 provided a comprehensive framework for our Nation's Biodefense for the 21st century. The United States has aggressively pursued a broad range of programs and capabilities to confront the biological weapons threat. The results of a comprehensive study of current capabilities provided a blueprint for a future biodefense program that fully integrates the sustained efforts of the national and homeland security, medical, public health, intelligence, diplomatic, and law enforcement communities. The pillars of this national biodefense program are Threat Awareness, Prevention and Protection, Surveillance and Detection, and Response and Recovery. A classified version of HSPD-10 contains specific direction to departments and agencies.

HSPD-11: Comprehensive Terrorist-Related Screening Procedures

HSPD-11 implemented a coordinated and comprehensive approach to terrorist-related screening that supports homeland security, at home and abroad. HSPD-11 builds upon HSPD-6 to accomplish this. HSPD-11 established comprehensive terrorist-related screening procedures in order to more effectively detect and interdict individuals known or reasonably suspected to be engaged in terrorist activities. HSPD-11 enhanced terrorist-related screening through comprehensive, coordinated procedures that detect, identify, track, and interdict people, cargo, and other entities. HSPD-11 further required that the Secretary of Homeland Security submit a report setting forth plans and progress in the implementation of this directive. The report will outline a strategy to enhance the effectiveness of terrorist-related screening activities.

HSPD-12: Policy for a Common Identification Standard for Federal Employees and Contractors

Currently, there are wide variations in the quality and security of identification used to gain access to secure facilities where there is potential for terrorist attacks. In order to eliminate these variations, the intent of HSPD-12 is to enhance security, increase government efficiency, reduce identity fraud, and protect personal privacy by establishing a mandatory government-wide standard for secure and reliable forms of identification issued by the federal government to its employees and contractors (including contractor employees).

HSPD-13: Maritime Security Policy

HSPD-13 established policy guidelines to enhance national and homeland security by protecting U.S. maritime interests. HSPD-13 further established a Maritime Security Policy Coordinating Committee to coordinate interagency maritime security policy efforts. It also underscores the importance of securing the maritime domain, which is defined as "all areas and things of, on, under, relating to, adjacent to, or bordering on a sea, ocean, or other navigable waterway, including all maritime-related activities, infrastructure, people, cargo, and vessels and other conveyances."

HSPD-14: Domestic Nuclear Detection

HSPD-14 established the Domestic Nuclear Detection Office (DNDO) as part of the national effort to protect the Nation from radiological and nuclear threats, which is staffed by representatives from several federal, state, and local government agencies. The DNDO provides a single accountable organization with dedicated responsibilities to develop the global nuclear detection architecture, and acquire and support the deployment of the domestic detection system to detect and report attempts to import or transport a nuclear device or fissile or radiological material intended for illicit use. The mission of the office addresses a broad spectrum of radiological and nuclear protective measures, but it is focused directly on nuclear detection. This includes establishing strong linkages across multiple Departments and levels of government.

HSPD-15: U.S. Strategy and Policy in the War on Terror

While the actual text of HSPD-15 is classified, it has been noted that this directive deals with limiting the bureaucratic hindrances that limit the ability of various federal agencies to combat terrorism. It has also been stated that the directive also attempts to coordinate all elements of the War on Terrorism, including diplomatic, legal, financial, and military components of the war. This coordination works to meet six goals:

1. Deny terrorists the resources they need to operate and survive;
2. Enable partner nations to counter terrorism;
3. Deny proliferation of weapons of mass destruction, recover and eliminate uncontrolled materials, and maintain a capacity for consequence management;
4. Defeat terrorists and their organizations;
5. Counter state and non-state support for terrorism in coordination with other U.S. government agencies and partner nations; and
6. Contribute to the establishment of conditions that counter ideological support for terrorism.

Lastly, the directive states that the military is to play a secondary or support role to other federal agencies in the War on Terror.[4]

HSPD-16: Aviation Strategy

HSPD-16 detailed a strategic vision for aviation security while recognizing ongoing efforts, and directed the production of a National Strategy for Aviation Security and supporting plans. The supporting plans address the following areas: aviation transportation system security, aviation operational threat response, aviation transportation system recovery, air domain surveillance and intelligence integration, domestic outreach, and international outreach. These strategies and supporting plans are described below.

National Strategy for Aviation Security: An overarching national strategy is necessary to optimize the coordination and integration of government-wide aviation security efforts. The Strategy sets forth U.S. government agency roles and responsibilities, establishes planning and operations coordination requirements, and builds on current strategies, tools, and resources. Supporting plans have been drafted by the Departments and Agencies as required by HSPD-16.[5]

Aviation Transportation System Security Plan: This plan seeks to enhance public security and economic growth by promoting global aviation security practices aimed at reducing vulnerabilities associated with the aviation transportation system. It sets forth a risk-based implementation plan for the continued reduction of vulnerabilities within the aviation transportation system. The development of this plan was led by the Secretaries of Homeland Security and Transportation.[6]

Aviation Operational Threat Response Plan: This plan ensures a comprehensive and coordinated U.S. government response to air threats against the United States or U.S. interests. The development of this plan was led by the Secretary of Defense and the Attorney General.[7]

Aviation Transportation System Recovery Plan: Rapid recovery from an attack or similar disruption in the Air Domain is critical to the economic well-being of our Nation. A credible capacity for rapid recovery will minimize an incident's economic impact. This plan includes recommended measures to mitigate the operational and economic effects of an attack in the Air Domain. The development of this plan was led by the Secretaries of Homeland Security and Transportation.[8]

Air Domain Surveillance and Intelligence Integration Plan: In order to have effective knowledge of the threat to the United States and U.S. interests in the Air Domain, the U.S. government must have a plan to coordinate requirements, priorities, and implementation of national air surveillance resources and the means to share this information with appropriate stakeholders. This plan supports an enhanced surveillance capability to detect and deter threats that could lead to an attack on the U.S. aviation transportation system. The development of this plan was led by the Secretary of Defense and the Director of National Intelligence.[9]

Domestic Outreach Plan: The successful implementation of HSPD-16 must include coordination with state and local government authorities and consultation with appropriate private sector persons and entities. This plan ensures that this proper coordination with the private sector and local government authorities takes place. The development of this plan was led by the Secretaries of Homeland Security and Transportation.[10]

International Outreach Plan: U.S. government efforts must be global efforts and developed with the cooperation of other governments and international organizations. This plan is aimed at ensuring the proper coordination with entities abroad. The development of this plan was led by the Secretary of State.[11]

HSPD-17: Nuclear Materials Information Program

While the specifics of HSPD-17 are classified, the goal of this directive is to consolidate information from all sources pertaining to worldwide nuclear materials holdings and their security status into an integrated and continuously updated information management system. This will help the United States understand the gaps in current knowledge and ensure that such information is available to support all appropriate federal departments' and agencies' nonproliferation, counter-proliferation, and counterterrorism efforts. HSPD-17 further requires the development of a national registry for identifying and tracking nuclear material samples that are held throughout the United States to support the information needs of the U.S. government.

HSPD-18: Medical Countermeasures against Weapons of Mass Destruction

HSPD-18 established policy guidelines to draw upon the considerable potential of the scientific community in the public and private sectors to address medical countermeasure requirements relating to Chemical, Biological, Radiological, and Nuclear (CBRN) threats. HSPD-18 addressed the need for preparation against an attack by terrorist forces using a weapon of mass destruction. HSPD-18 further acknowledged that having sufficient resources on hand at all times and at all places is not a realistic possibility. The policy set forth in HSPD-18 is a two-tiered approach for development and acquisition of medical countermeasures. Tier I is a focused development of Agent-Specific Medical Countermeasures, and Tier II concerns the development of a Flexible Capability for New Medical Countermeasures.

HSPD-19: Combating Terrorist Use of Explosives in the United States

HSPD-19 established a national policy, and called for the development of a national strategy and implementation plan, on the prevention and detection of, protection against, and response to terrorist use of explosives in the United States. It is the policy of the United States to counter the threat of explosive attacks aggressively by coordinating federal, state, local, territorial, and tribal government efforts and collaborating with the owners and operators of critical infrastructure and key resources to deter, prevent, detect, protect against, and respond to explosive attacks.

HSPD-20: National Continuity Policy

HSPD-20 established a comprehensive national policy on the continuity of federal government structures and operations and a single National

Continuity Coordinator responsible for coordinating the development and implementation of federal continuity policies. This policy further established the National Essential Functions and prescribed continuity requirements for all executive departments and agencies in order to ensure a comprehensive and integrated national continuity program that will enhance the credibility of our national security posture and enable a more rapid and effective response to and recovery from a national emergency.

HSPD-20 Annex A: Continuity Planning

Annex A of HSPD-20 assigned executive departments and agencies to a category commensurate with their Continuity of Operations/Continuity of Government/Enduring Constitutional Government (COOP/COG/ECG) responsibilities during an emergency. In accordance with HSPD-20, National Continuity Policy, executive departments and agencies are assigned to one of four categories commensurate with their COOP/COG/ECG responsibilities during an emergency. These categories are used for continuity planning, communications requirements, emergency operations capabilities, and other related requirements.

HSPD-21: Public Health and Medical Preparedness

HSPD-21 established a national strategy that will enable a level of public health and medical preparedness sufficient to address a range of possible disasters. It is the policy of the United States to plan and enable provision for the public health and medical needs of the American people in the case of a catastrophic health event through continual and timely flow of information during such an event and rapid public health and medical response that marshals all available national capabilities and capacities in a rapid and coordinated manner.

HSPD-23: National Cyber Security Initiative

While the official text of HSPD-23 has not been released, the U.S. Department of Homeland Security (DHS) stated in a released dated April 8, 2008, that HSPD-23 "formalized a series of continuous efforts designed to further safeguard federal government systems and reduce potential vulnerabilities, protect against intrusion attempts, and better anticipate future threats."[12] The release also defined that "while efforts to protect our federal network systems from cyber attacks remain a collaborative, government-wide effort, the Department of Homeland Security (DHS) has the lead responsibility for assuring the security, resiliency, and reliability of the Nation's Information Technology (IT) and communications infrastructure."[13]

HSPD-24: Biometrics for Identification and Screening to Enhance National Security

HSPD-24 established a framework to ensure that federal executive departments and agencies use mutually compatible methods and procedures in the collection, storage, use, analysis, and sharing of biometric and associated bio-graphic and contextual information of individuals in a lawful and appropriate manner, while respecting their information privacy and other legal rights under United States law.

Legislation, Laws, and Acts

Homeland Security Act of 2002

The Homeland Security Act (HSA) of 2002 (Public Law 107-296), signed into law by President George W. Bush on November 25, 2002, established the Department of Homeland Security (DHS). The primary mission of this newly formed executive department was to prevent terrorist attacks and reduce or minimize damage from a terrorist attack occurring within the United States borders and in the event there was an attack assist in the recovery efforts. The Department's primary responsibilities correspond to the five major functions established by the HSA:

1. Information analysis and infrastructure protection;
2. Chemical, biological, radiological, nuclear, and related countermeasures;
3. Border and transportation security;
4. Emergency preparedness and response; and
5. Coordination with other parts of the federal government, with state and local governments, and with the private sector.

The importance of the HSA to critical infrastructure protection is the establishment of an Under Secretary for Information Analysis and Infrastructure Protection (now the Office for Infrastructure Protection under the National Protection and Programs Directorate). This office was given the responsibility for:

1. Receiving and analyzing law enforcement information, intelligence, and other information in order to understand the nature and scope of the terrorist threat to the American homeland and to detect and identify potential threats of terrorism within the United States;
2. Comprehensively assessing the vulnerabilities of key resources and critical infrastructures;
3. Integrating relevant information, intelligence analyses, and vulnerability assessments to identify protective priorities and support protective measures;
4. Developing a comprehensive national plan for securing key resources and critical infrastructures;
5. Taking or seeking to effect necessary measures to protect those key resources and infrastructures;
6. Administering the Homeland Security Advisory System, exercising primary responsibility for public threat advisories, and providing specific warning information to state and local governments and the private sector, as well as advice about appropriate protective actions and countermeasures; and
7. Reviewing, analyzing, and making recommendations for improvements in the policies and procedures governing the sharing of law enforcement, intelligence,

and other information relating to homeland security within the federal government and between the federal government and state and local governments.[14]

The HSA established the authority for the Secretary of Homeland Security to have access to intelligence and other information from agencies and departments of the United States government for the purpose of fulfilling the mission of information analysis and infrastructure protection. There are three broad categories of information the Secretary has access to, which include reports, assessments, and analytical information.[15]

USA PATRIOT Act of 2001

The Uniting and Strengthening America by Providing Appropriate Tools Required to Intercept and Obstruct Terrorism Act (Public Law 107-56, USA PATRIOT Act), passed by the U.S. Congress in reaction to the terrorist attacks of September 2001, significantly alters a considerable number of laws, including many related to information policy. The Patriot Act allows for greater access to information sharing by law enforcement and intelligence personnel in order to share information that is needed to help connect the dots and disrupt potential terror and criminal activity. The broad information sharing provisions also enhances the ability of the U.S. Customs and Border Protection to screen international visitors and determine whether an apprehended alien presents a threat to security or public safety.

The Patriot Act also enhances DHS investigations into the international movement of illicit funds through money transmittal businesses, bulk cash smuggling, and cyber crimes. The United States Secret Service (USSS), for example, has established fifteen nationwide electronic crimes taskforces and ten working groups to detect and stop computer-based crime. According to the DHS, in 2005 a program entitled Operation Firewall resulted in the USSS arresting twenty-eight individuals in eight states and six countries involved in a global cyber crime network. The apprehended suspects stole nearly 1.7 million credit card numbers.

As a result of their Patriot Act authorities, the U.S. Immigration and Customs Enforcement (ICE) has expanded their investigative strategy to target underlying financial systems that terrorists and other criminal organizations often exploit in raising, moving, and storing illicit funds. ICE seeks to deny criminal organizations access to these systems. For example, new anti-money laundering provisions of the Patriot Act have allowed ICE to launch numerous initiatives to combat the laundering of funds originating from foreign public corruption, bribery, or embezzlement. In 2003, ICE created the Foreign Corruption Task Force in Miami specifically to target funds being laundered in the United States that had been embezzled from foreign governments. The ICE-led task force, which is the only one of its kind in the Nation, seeks to prosecute violators, seize embezzled funds, and repatriate the money to the victimized governments. Using new provisions under the Patriot Act, the ICE also created a nationwide campaign against illegal/unlicensed money transmittal businesses that since 2005 has resulted in the arrest of more than 155 individuals, 142 criminal indictments, over $25 million in illicit profits seized, and several unlicensed money transmittal businesses shut down (see Case Study for example of Patriot Act aided investigations).

....

Case Studies: Examples of Immigration and Customs Enforcement (ICE) Operations Aided by the USA PATRIOT Act

On September 22, 2005, a key player in a scheme to illegally transfer more than $100 million to Pakistan through a New Jersey money transmittal business was sentenced to nearly four years in prison as a result of an investigation by ICE and Internal Revenues Service (IRS) agents. Umer Darr, a Pakistani native and naturalized U.S. citizen, was first arrested in June 2003 along with five other men. ICE agents found that Darr and his associates were affiliated with a money transmitting firm called Access Inc. of USA, which operated out of a small, upstairs apartment of a suburban house. The business kept an unlisted number; did not advertise in the Yellow Pages, and could only be accessed through an unmarked rear door. Yet through this small hidden business, more than $100 million in virtually untraceable funds were illegally moved to Pakistan. Several defendants in this ongoing case have been convicted.

On September 13, 2005, ICE achieved the first ever conviction in the District of Columbia under Title 18 USC Section 1960 of the U.S. Patriot Act. Aissatou Pita Barry, 38, of Silver Spring, Maryland, pleaded guilty to operating an unlicensed money transmitting business that illegally wired more than $15.5 million around the globe on behalf of 5,000 relatively unknown customers. Barry's company, Guinex International, never asked customers about the source of their funds, yet conducted roughly 65,000 transactions on their behalf. Barry and other Guinex employees also provided customers with the numbers of various bank accounts controlled by Barry and instructed customers that they could make deposits directly into those accounts. Barry was in the United States on a Diplomatic Passport that authorized her only to work at the Guinea Embassy.

On July 27, 2005, Ali Abdurahman, 37, pleaded guilty to federal charges of operating an unlicensed money transfer business in California that illegally funneled nearly $2 million to the Middle East and other countries overseas. The charge against Abdurahman is the culmination of a probe by ICE that began more than two years after ICE received a tip from a San Francisco–based investigator for Bank of America regarding suspicious financial transactions in the Orange County area. ICE's investigation revealed that the airport shuttle driver deposited more than $2.4 million into his personal accounts at several local banks. Financial records show he wired more than $1.6 million of those funds overseas, primarily to the United Arab Emirates (UAE). One of Abdurahman's clients was an Ethiopian national named Abubakar Baharun. Baharun, 37, was recently arrested and indicted by a grand jury in Santa Ana in connection with a bank fraud and check-kiting scheme. ICE investigators revealed that Baharun used Abdurahman's money transmitter service to wire the proceeds from his illegal activities to an account in the UAE.

On March 22, 2005, ICE agents arrested Hossein Esfahani, in Lincolnwood, Illinois, on charges of operating an illegal money transmittal business and transferring funds to Iran in violation of the U.S. embargo on Iran. The criminal complaint alleges that Esfahani moved more than $3.75 million to domestic and international locations from his unlicensed money service business in Illinois from 1999 through 2003. The majority of Esfahami's illegal money transmittals were directed to money exchanges in Dubai, United Arab Emirates (UAE). Those Dubai money exchanges, in turn, converted the wired funds into Iranian currency and then directed the funds to recipients throughout Iran, according to the complaint. During the enforcement action, Esfahani resisted arrest and ICE agents found a loaded .22 caliber pistol, which he was not licensed to possess, in his house.

On March 15, 2005, ICE agents arrested Louay Habbal, 45, a naturalized U.S. citizen from Syria, for operating an unlicensed money transmittal business located at his Vienna, Virginia, residence. Habbal was arrested upon his arrival at Dulles International Airport in the United States on a flight from Damascus, Syria. The indictment alleges that Habbal operated a business called Mena Exchange, which received funds from customers nationwide and deposited these funds in bank accounts in Virginia and elsewhere. After taking a portion of these funds as a fee, Mena Exchange transferred more than $23 million to Syria and other nations between November 2001 and July 2004. ICE agents seized more than $100,000 from the company's accounts.

....

The Patriot Act also included far-reaching modifications to the Foreign Intelligence Surveillance Act (FISA) of 1978.[16, 17] A new enhancement of the Patriot Act, entitled the Domestic Security Enhancement Act of 2003,[18] has been drafted by the Department of Justice (DOJ). If it were to become law, it would serve to further expand investigative powers under FISA to collect and analyze information.[19] The changes to the FISA by the Patriot Act, and the potential further changes to FISA that would occur if the Patriot Act Domestic Security Enhancement Act became law, have major implications for information policy.

Another affect on the FISA is the Patriot Act Additional Reauthorizing Amendments Act of 2006 (Public Law 109-178).[20] This act clarifies that individuals who receive FISA orders can challenge nondisclosure requirements, that individuals who receive national security letters are not required to disclose the name of their attorney, that libraries are not wire or electronic communication service providers unless they provide specific services, and for other purposes. The act also amends the FISA to allow a person receiving a production order (an order from the Director of the Federal Bureau of Investigation [FBI] or his designee [Director] to produce any tangible thing, such as a book, document, or record) to challenge its legality by filing a petition with a pool of three district court judges established by the Chief Justice of the United States for such purpose. The act requires the presiding judge of the pool to immediately assign a judge to conduct an initial review of a petition and further requires such judge, within 72 hours of the assignment, to make an initial petition review. The judge is required to immediately deny such petition if it is frivolous and affirm the production or nondisclosure order.

The passage of the Patriot Act and other concurrent reactions to the terrorist attacks of September 11, 2001, reflect a decision by the federal government to view security in terms of "the preservation of the security of the homeland."[21] A more expansive approach to security than the United States has previously taken (national security and internal security), homeland security has led to the creation of a new cabinet level department (U.S. Department of Homeland Security), to the alteration of many laws and judicial traditions, and to a virtual abandonment of "Cold War era barriers between foreign intelligence and domestic law enforcement."[22] Among its many impacts, the Patriot Act modifications of FISA affect the degrees to which and the methods by which law enforcement agencies can collect and analyze personal information.[23]

Pandemic and All-Hazards Preparedness Act of 2006 (Public Law 109-417)[24]

This act requires the Department of Health and Human Services (HHS) to oversee advanced research, development, and procurement of qualified countermeasures and qualified pandemic or epidemic products. It is also the Department that maintains the Strategic National Stockpile (SNS) and provides logistical support for medical and public health aspects of federal responses to public health emergencies. The act also calls for the development and implementation of a near real-time electronic nationwide public health situational awareness capability through an interoperable network of systems to share data and information to enhance early detection of, rapid response to, and management of potentially catastrophic infectious disease outbreaks and other public health emergencies.

There is also requirement to establish a Medical Reserve Corps to provide for an adequate supply of volunteers in a federal, state, local, or tribal public health emergency. To support this system, HHS is called on to link existing state verification systems to maintain a single national interoperable network of systems to verify the credentials and licenses of healthcare professionals who volunteer to provide health services during a public health emergency and encourage states to establish and implement mechanisms to waive the application of licensing requirements applicable to health professionals seeking to provide medical services during a national, state, local, or tribal public health emergency. Finally there is a requirement for the Secretary of Veteran Affairs (VA) to: (1) ensure the readiness of VA medical centers for a public health emergency; (2) organize, train, and equip the staff of such medical centers to support the Secretary of HHS in the event of a public health emergency and incidents covered by the National Response Plan (NRP); and (3) provide medical logistical support to the National Disaster Medical System (NDMS) and the Secretary of HHS as necessary.

Secure Fence Act of 2006 (Public Law 109-367)[25]

The intent of the Secure Fence Act of 2006 was to direct the Secretary of Homeland Security to take appropriate actions to achieve operational control over U.S. international land and maritime borders, including:

1. Systematic border surveillance through more effective use of personnel and technology, such as unmanned aerial vehicles, ground-based sensors, satellites, radar coverage, and cameras; and
2. Physical infrastructure enhancements to prevent unlawful border entry and facilitate border access by U.S. Customs and Border Protection, such as additional checkpoints, all weather access roads, and vehicle barriers. The act defines "operational control" as the prevention of all unlawful U.S. entries, including entries by terrorists, other unlawful aliens, and instruments of terrorism, narcotics, and other contraband.

The act also directs the Secretary to report annually to Congress on border control progress.

USA PATRIOT Improvement and Reauthorization Act of 2005 (Public Law 109-177)[26]

The intent of the USA PATRIOT Improvement and Reauthorization Act of 2005 was to extend and modify authorities needed to combat terrorism and for other purposes. This act has not been amended since the Conference Report was filed in the House on December 8, 2005. This Reauthorization Act repeals the sunset date for (thus making permanent) the surveillance provisions of the USA PATRIOT Act, with the following exception:

- Provides for a four-year extension (through December 31, 2009) of provisions: (1) granting roving surveillance authority under the Foreign Intelligence Surveillance Act of 1978 (FISA) where the Court finds that the actions of the target may thwart the identification of a specified person; and (2) authorizing the Director of the Federal Bureau of Investigation (FBI) to apply for a court order requiring production of tangible things (including books, records, papers, and documents) for foreign intelligence and international terrorism investigations.

Other notable sections within the USA PATRIOT Improvement and Reauthorization Act of 2005 include the following:

- **Section 103:** Amends the Intelligence Reform and Terrorism Prevention Act of 2004 to: (1) extend for four years (through December 31, 2009) provisions revising the definition of an "agent of a foreign power" to include any non-U.S. person who engages in international terrorism or preparatory activities (thus permitting issuance of FISA orders targeting such persons without a showing that they are members or agents of a terrorist group or a foreign power ["lone wolf" provision]); and (2) repeal the sunset date for provisions setting forth additions to the offense of providing material support to terrorists.
- **Section 402:** Amends the International Emergency Economic Powers Act to increase penalties for violating a license, order, or regulation under the Act and also amends the Racketeer Influenced and Corrupt Organizations Act to expand its scope to include offenses relating to illegal money transmitters and felony violations of the Foreign Corrupt Practices Act. This Act authorizes the Department of Homeland Security to investigate violations of money laundering and related offenses.

Intelligence Reform and Terrorism Prevention Act of 2004 (Public 108-458)[27]

The intent of the Intelligence Reform and Terrorism Prevention Act of 2004 was to reform the intelligence community and the intelligence and intelligence-related activities of the United States government, and for other purposes. This act has not been amended since the Conference Report was filed in the U.S. House of Representatives on December 7, 2004. Notable sections within the Intelligence Reform and Terrorism Prevention Act of 2004 are described below in the following sections.

Section 1011

Amends the National Security Act of 1947 to establish a Director of National Intelligence, to be appointed by the President with the advice and consent of the Senate. The Director is required to ensure that timely, objective, and independent national intelligence based upon all available sources is provided to:

1. The President;
2. The heads of departments and agencies of the executive branch;
3. The Chairman of the Joint Chiefs of Staff and senior military commanders; and
4. The Senate and House of Representatives and congressional committees.

This Act gives the Director access to all national intelligence and intelligence related to national security collected by federal entities, unless otherwise directed by the President.

This Act calls for "national intelligence" and "intelligence related to national security" to be redefined to include all intelligence, regardless of the source, that pertains to more than one government agency and involves:

1. Threats to the United States, its people, property, or interests;
2. The development, proliferation, or use of weapons of mass destruction (WMDs); or
3. Any other matter bearing on national or homeland security.

The Act also establishes the National Counterterrorism Center (NCC) to:

1. Analyze and integrate all U.S. intelligence pertaining to terrorism and counterterrorism;
2. Conduct strategic operational planning for counterterrorism activities;
3. Ensure that intelligence agencies have access to, and receive, all intelligence needed to accomplish their missions; and
4. Serve as the central and shared knowledge bank on known and suspected terrorists and international terror groups.

Section 2001

Directs the Director of the FBI to continue efforts to improve the intelligence capabilities of the FBI and to develop and maintain within the FBI a national intelligence workforce. The new requirements call for the FBI Director to:

1. Develop and maintain a specialized and integrated national intelligence workforce of agents, analysts, linguists, and surveillance specialists who are recruited, trained, and rewarded in a manner that creates an institutional culture in the FBI with substantial expertise in, and commitment to, the intelligence mission of the FBI;
2. Establish career positions in national intelligence matters;
3. Recruit agents with backgrounds and skills relevant to the intelligence mission of the FBI;
4. Provide agents with training in intelligence and opportunities for assignments in national intelligence matters; and
5. Make advanced training and work in intelligence matters a precondition to employee advancement.

There is also a requirement to submit to Congress a strategy for combining terrorist travel intelligence, operations, and law enforcement into a cohesive effort to intercept terrorists, find terrorist travel facilitators, and constrain terrorist mobility.

Section 4001

This section of the act requires the Secretary of Homeland Security to develop and implement a National Strategy for Transportation Security and transportation modal security plans; and issue guidance for the use of biometric or other technology that positively verifies the identity of each employee and law enforcement officer who enters a secure area of an airport. It also requires the development of a uniform travel credential for federal, state, and local law enforcement officers that incorporates biometrics and a process for using such credential to verify officer identity for purposes of carrying weapons on board aircraft.

Section 4071

Directs the Secretary of Homeland Security to:

1. Implement a procedure under which the DHS compares information about cruise ship passengers and crew with a terrorist watchlist;
2. Use information obtained by this comparison to prevent identified persons from boarding or to subject them to additional security scrutiny through the use of no transport and automatic selectee lists;
3. Require, by rulemaking, that cruise ship operators provide passenger and crew information for purposes of such comparison; and
4. Establish operating procedures and data integrity measures for no transport and automatic selectee lists.

Subtitle B - Border and Immigration Enforcement

Requires the increase of:

1. The number of full-time Border Patrol agents by not less than 2,000 per fiscal year from FY 2006 through 2010; and

2. The number of full-time immigration and customs enforcement investigators by not less than 800 per fiscal year for the same period.

Section 6402

Private Security Officer Employment Authorization Act of 2004: Allows employers of private security officers who are authorized by regulation to request criminal history record information searches of such security officers through a state identification bureau (authorized employers) to submit fingerprints or other means of positive identification for purposes of such searches. The act requires written consent from employees prior to such searches and employee access to any information received. It also establishes criminal penalties for the knowing and intentional use of information obtained through criminal history record information searches for purposes other than determining an individual's suitability for employment as a private security officer.

Section 6802

This section expands the jurisdictional bases and scope of the prohibition against weapons of mass destruction (WMDs) and the definition of "restricted persons" subject to the prohibition on possession or transfer of biological agents or toxins to include individuals acting for a country determined to have provided repeated support for international terrorism. It also includes chemical weapons within the definition of WMDs. The act adds offenses involving biological weapons, chemical weapons, and nuclear materials to the racketeering predicate offense list. Such as, it is unlawful for any person to knowingly produce, construct (engineer or synthesize in the case of variola virus), otherwise acquire, transfer, receive, possess, import, export, or use, or possess and threaten to use:

1. Missile systems designed to destroy aircraft;
2. Radiological dispersal devices; or
3. Variola virus.

This extends to nuclear materials and makes it unlawful for any person to knowingly manufacture, produce, transfer, acquire, receive, possess, import, export, or use, or possess and threaten to use any atomic weapon. There are penalties for such offenses including fines and imprisonment for twenty-five or thirty years to life.

Section 7301

This section of the act calls for the adoption of a unified incident command system and the enhancement of communications connectivity between and among all levels of government and emergency response providers. It directs the Secretary of Homeland Security to establish a program to enhance public safety interoperable communications at all levels of government and to create an Office for Interoperability and Compatibility within the DHS Directorate of Science and Technology (S&T) to carry out DHS programs relating to SAFECOM and other programs. For more information on SAFECOM visit: http://www.safecomprogram.gov/SAFECOM/.

Post Katrina Emergency Management Reform (PKEMR) Act of 2006[28]

The Post Katrina Emergency Management Reform (PKEMR) Act of 2006 amends the Homeland Security Act of 2002 to make extensive revisions to emergency response provisions while keeping the Federal Emergency Management Agency (FEMA) within the U.S. Department of Homeland Security (DHS). It also sets forth provisions regarding FEMA's mission, which include:

1. Leading the nation's efforts to prepare for, respond to, recover from, and mitigate the risks of, any natural and man-made disaster, including catastrophic incidents;
2. Implementing a risk-based, all-hazards plus strategy for preparedness; and
3. Promoting and planning for the protection, security, resiliency, and post-disaster restoration of critical infrastructure and key resources, including cyber and communications assets.

There is also specific language in the PKEMR Act regarding the role, qualifications, authority, and responsibilities of the Administrator of FEMA, who will:

1. Have not less than five years of executive leadership and management experience, significant experience in crisis management or another relevant field, and a demonstrated ability to manage a substantial staff and budget;
2. Report to the Secretary of Homeland Security without being required to report through any other DHS official;
3. Be the principal emergency preparedness and response advisor to the President, the Homeland Security Council, and the Secretary;
4. Provide federal leadership necessary to mitigate, prepare for, respond to, and recover from a disaster;
5. Develop a national emergency management system capable of responding to catastrophic incidents; and
6. Develop and submit to Congress annually an estimate of the resources needed for developing the capabilities of federal, state, and local governments necessary to respond to a catastrophic incident.

The PKEMR Act also transfers to FEMA all functions of the Under Secretary for Federal Emergency Management and of the Directorate of Preparedness and requires FEMA to be maintained as a distinct entity within the DHS, which establishes within FEMA a Director for Preparedness and a Director for Response and Recovery. In addition to creating two distinct directors, it also calls for the creation of ten regional offices and area offices for the Pacific, for the Caribbean, and for Alaska. These Regional Offices are required to establish multiagency strike teams to respond to disasters, including catastrophic incidents. There is also a requirement to establish a National

Advisory Council on Preparedness and Response, which advises the Administrator of FEMA on all aspects of preparedness and emergency management in an effort to ensure close coordination with its partners across the country. Members are appointed by the Administrator and represent a geographic and significant cross-section of officials from emergency management and law enforcement, and include homeland security directors, adjutants general, emergency response providers from state, local, and tribal governments, private sector, and nongovernmental organizations.

The National Advisory Council was established in June 2007 and is being instituted to ensure effective and ongoing coordination of the federal preparedness, protection, response, recovery, and mitigation for natural disasters, acts of terrorism, and other man-made disasters. Specifically, the Council will focus attention in the development and revision of the national preparedness goal, the national preparedness system, the National Incident Management System (NIMS), the National Response Framework (NRF), and other related plans and strategies. The PKEMR Act also provides for the credentialing of DHS personnel and assets likely to be used to respond to major disasters. It also calls for technical assistance to states and local governments that experience severe weather events, including the preparation of hurricane evacuation studies and plans assessing storm surge estimates, evacuation zones, evacuation clearance times, transportation capacity, and shelter capacity. There is a requirement in the act that each state establish minimum performance requirements for public and community preparedness down to the regional and local level.

3

....

National Infrastructure Protection Plan

Build a safer, more secure, and more resilient America by enhancing protection of the Nation's CI/KR to prevent, deter, neutralize, or mitigate the effects of deliberate efforts by terrorists to destroy, incapacitate, or exploit them; and to strengthen national preparedness, timely response, and rapid recovery in the event of an attack, natural disaster, or other emergency.[1]

Background

The National Infrastructure Protection Plan (NIPP) and supporting Sector-Specific Plans (SSPs) provide a coordinated approach to critical infrastructure and key resources (CI/KR) protection roles and responsibilities for federal, state, local, tribal, and private sector security partners. The NIPP sets national priorities, goals, and requirements for effective distribution of funding and resources, which help to ensure that our government, economy, and public services continue in the event of a terrorist attack or other disaster.[2] Further, Homeland Security Presidential Directive (HSPD)-7 designated the Secretary of Homeland Security as the "principal federal official to lead CI/KR protection efforts among federal departments and agencies, state and local governments, and the private sector" and assigns responsibility for CI/KR sectors to specific Sector-Specific Agencies (SSAs), as noted in Table 3.1.

The NIPP is based on the following fundamental components:

- Strong public-private partnerships to foster relationships and facilitate coordination within and across CIKR sectors;
- Robust multi-directional information sharing to enhance the ability to assess risks, make prudent security investments, and take protective action; and

Table 3.1 Sector Specific Agency Assignments[3]

Sector Specific Agency	Critical Infrastructure/ Key Resources
Department of Agriculture	Agriculture and Food
Department of Defense	Defense Industrial Base
Department of Energy	Energy
Department of Health and Human Services	Public Health and Healthcare
Department of the Interior	National Monuments and Icons
Department of the Treasury	Banking and Finance
Environmental Protection Agency	Drinking Water and Water Treatment Systems
Department of Homeland Security	Chemical
Office of Infrastructure Protection	Commercial Facilities
	Dams
	Emergency Services
	Nuclear Reactors, Materials, and Waste
Office of Cyber Security and Telecommunications	Information Technology
	Telecommunications
	Postal and Shipping
Transportation Security Administration	Transportation Systems
United States Coast Guard	
Immigration & Customs Enforcement	Government Facilities
Federal Protective Service	

- Risk management framework establishing processes for combining consequence, vulnerability, and threat information to produce a comprehensive, systematic, and rational assessment of national or sector risk.

The NIPP further establishes an overall framework for new and existing security programs. It designates seventeen Critical Infrastructure/Key Resource (CI/KR) Sectors and sets a timeline for developing Sector-Specific Plan (SSP) for each of the respective CI/KR Sectors. The SSPs are developed by sector coordinating councils, which comprise industry representatives and U.S. Department of Homeland Security (DHS) personnel. The SSPs are intended to serve as guidance documents for industry in establishing sector-specific protective activities. These plans include descriptions of the sector's information-sharing mechanisms and protocols.

NIPP implementation relies on critical infrastructure information provided by the private sector. Much of this is sensitive business or security information that could cause serious damage to private firms, the economy, public safety, or security through unauthorized disclosure or access. The federal government has a statutory responsibility to safeguard CI/KR protection-related information. The DHS and other federal agencies use a number of programs and procedures, such as the Protected Critical Infrastructure Information (PCII) Program, to ensure that security-related information is properly safeguarded. Other relevant programs and procedures include Sensitive Security Information for transportation activities, Unclassified Controlled Nuclear Information, contractual provisions, classified national provisions, Classified National Security Information, and Law Enforcement Sensitive Information.[4]

Scope

The NIPP considers a full range of physical, cyber, and human security elements within and across all of the Nation's CI/KR sectors. In accordance with the policy direction established in HSPD-7, the National Strategy for the Physical Protection of Critical Infrastructures and Key Assets, and the National Strategy to Secure Cyberspace, the NIPP includes an augmented focus on the protection of CI/KR from the unique and potentially catastrophic impacts of terrorist attacks. At the same time, the NIPP builds on and is structured to be consistent with and supportive of the Nation's all-hazards approach to homeland security preparedness and domestic incident management.

The NIPP addresses ongoing and future activities within each of the CI/KR sectors identified in HSPD-7 and across the sectors regionally and nationally. It defines processes and mechanisms used to prioritize protection of U.S. CI/KR (including Territories and territorial seas) and to address the interconnected global networks upon which the Nation's CI/KR depends. The processes outlined in the NIPP and the SSPs recognize that protective measures do not end at a facility's fence line or at a national border, and are often a component of a larger business continuity approach. Also considered are the implications of cross-border infrastructures, international vulnerabilities, and cross-sector dependencies and interdependencies.

While the NIPP covers the full range of CI/KR sectors as defined in HSPD-7, it is applicable to the various public and private sector security partners in different ways. The framework generally is applicable to all security partners with CI/KR protection responsibilities and includes explicit roles and responsibilities for the federal government, including CI/KR under the control of independent regulatory agencies, and the legislative, executive, or judicial branches. Federal departments and agencies with specific responsibilities for CI/KR protection are required to take actions consistent with HSPD-7. The NIPP also provides an organizational structure, protection guidelines, and recommended activities for other security partners to help ensure consistent implementation of the national framework and the most effective use of resources. State, local, and tribal government security partners are required to establish CI/KR protection programs consistent with the National Preparedness Goal and as a condition of eligibility for certain federal grant programs.

The NIPP considers a broad range of terrorist objectives, intentions, and capabilities to assess the threat to various components of the Nation's

CI/KR. These assessments acknowledge that terrorists may contemplate attacks against the Nation's CI/KR to achieve three general types of effects:

1. **Direct Infrastructure Effects:** Disruption or arrest of critical functions through direct attacks on an asset, system, or network.
2. **Indirect Infrastructure Effects:** Cascading disruption and financial consequences for the government, society, and economy through public and private sector reactions to an attack. An operation could reflect an appreciation of interdependencies between different elements of CI/KR, as well as the psychological importance of demonstrating the ability to strike effectively inside the United States.
3. **Exploitation of Infrastructure:** Exploitation of elements of a particular infrastructure to disrupt or destroy another target or produce cascading consequences. Attacks using CI/KR elements as a weapon to strike other targets, allowing terrorist organizations to magnify their capabilities far beyond what could be achieved using their own limited resources.[5]

••

The **NIPP** focuses on all physical, cyber, and human security elements as well as interconnected global networks as they relate to CI/KR protection in an all-hazards approach.

Further, the NIPP and its implementation is applicable to all security partners, both public and private, that have CI/KR protection responsibilities.

••

In addition to addressing CI/KR protection related to terrorist threats, the NIPP also describes activities relevant to CI/KR protection and preparedness in an all-hazards context. The direct impacts, disruptions, and cascading effects of natural disasters (e.g., Hurricanes Katrina and Ike, the Midwest flooding of 2008, etc.) and man-made incidents (e.g., the Three Mile Island Nuclear Power Plant accident or the Exxon Valdez oil spill) on the Nation's CI/KR are well documented. The recent experience in the wake of Hurricane Katrina, for example, underscored the vulnerabilities and interdependencies of the Nation's CI/KR.

Authorities, Roles, and Responsibilities

The Homeland Security Act of 2002 provides the basis for DHS responsibilities in the protection of the Nation's CI/KR. The act assigns DHS the responsibility to develop a comprehensive national plan for securing CI/KR and for recommending "measures necessary to protect the key resources and critical infrastructure of the United States in coordination with other agencies of the federal government and in cooperation with state and local government agencies and authorities, the private sector, and other entities."[6]

The Homeland Security Act provides the primary authority for the overall homeland security mission and outlines DHS responsibilities in the protection of the Nation's CI/KR. It established the DHS mission, including "reducing the nation's vulnerability to terrorist attacks," major disasters, and other emergencies, and charged the department with the responsibility for evaluating vulnerabilities and ensuring that steps are implemented to protect the high-risk elements of America's CI/KR.[7] Other CI/KR protection-related legislation includes, but is not limited to, the following:

- Public Health Security and Bioterrorism Preparedness and Response
- Maritime Transportation Security Act;
- Energy Policy and Conservation Act;
- Critical Infrastructure Information Act; and
- Federal Information Security Management Act.[8]

Risk Management

America is an open, technologically sophisticated, highly interconnected, and complex nation with a wide array of infrastructure that spans important aspects of U.S. government, economy, and society. The majority of the CI/KR-related assets, systems, and networks are owned and operated by the private sector. In some sectors, however, such as Water and Government Facilities, the majority of owners and operators are government or quasi- governmental entities.

Eighty percent of the **CI/KR** in the United States is owned and operated by the private sector.

The cornerstone of the NIPP is its risk management framework that establishes the processes for combining consequence, vulnerability, and threat information to produce a comprehensive, systematic, and rational assessment of national or sector risk. The risk management framework is structured to promote continuous improvement to enhance CI/KR protection by focusing activities on efforts to:

- Set security goals;
- Identify assets, systems, networks, and functions;
- Assess risk based on consequences, vulnerabilities, and threats;
- Establish priorities based on risk assessments;
- Implement protective programs; and
- Measure effectiveness.

The results of these processes drive CI/KR risk-reduction and risk management activities. The framework applies to the strategic threat environment that shapes program planning, as well as to specific threats or incident situations. DHS, the SSAs, and other security partners share responsibilities for implementing the risk management structure, in collaboration with other security partners.

Risk assessment involves the integration of threat, vulnerability, and consequence information. **Risk management** involves deciding which protective measures to take based on an agreed upon risk-reduction strategy.

National Review

The NIPP risk management framework responds to an evolving risk landscape that must account for changes in that landscape. The 2006 NIPP established the requirement to fully review and reissue the plan every three years to ensure that it is current and relevant to all security partners. As of the writing of this text, the next NIPP review will be conducted in 2009.

Since the NIPP was released in June 2006, the DHS and its security partners have been working to implement the risk management framework and the sector partnership model to protect the Nation's CI/KR. Throughout this implementation, the DHS has engaged the NIPP feedback mechanisms to capture lessons learned and issues that will be revised and updated in future versions of the NIPP. Some of the known changes that will be addressed in the next revision of the NIPP include the following:

- Establishment of Critical Manufacturing as the 18th critical infrastructure and key resources (CIKR) sector;
- Release of the chemical security regulation;
- Publishing of the Sector-Specific Plans (SSPs) and any sector name changes;
- Sector name changes;
- Removal of references to the National Asset Database (NADB) and replacement with information on the Infrastructure Information Collection System and the Infrastructure Data Warehouse;
- Revision of the discussion of risk assessment methodologies;
- Update on the Protected Critical Infrastructure Information (PCII) Program;
- Clarification of NIPP CI/KR Protection Metrics;
- Update on state, local, tribal, and territorial;
- Homeland Security Information Network (HSIN);
- Critical Infrastructure Warning Information Network (CWIN);
- Evolution from the National Response Plan (NRP) to the National Response Framework (NRF); and
- Further information on the National Infrastructure Simulation and Analysis Center (NISAC).

The following text provides a summary of a select few of the above changes being incorporated into the NIPP.

Sector Addition and Naming

On March 3, 2008, DHS formally established the Critical Manufacturing Sector as the 18th CI/KR sector. Following the creation of this sector, the DHS issued the Chemical Facility Anti-Terrorism Standards (CFATS), which required the DHS to identify high-risk chemical facilities, assess their security vulnerabilities, and require those facilities to submit site security plans meeting risk-based performance standards.

There have also been a number of naming convention updates to existing sectors. These changes include:

- "Commercial Nuclear Reactors, Materials and Waste" to "Nuclear Reactors, Materials and Waste;"
- "Drinking Water and Water Treatment Systems" to "Water;" and
- "Telecommunications" to "Communications."

Further, DHS has recognized the Department of Education's Office of Safe and Drug-Free Schools (OSDFS) as the lead for Education Facilities (EF), a subsector of the Government Facilities Sector.

Risk Management Methodologies

There has been an ongoing debate within DHS and other entities regarding Risk Assessment Methodologies. At the writing of this text, there were nearly twenty-five different vulnerability assessment methodologies being used by the federal government. Due to this varied approach to assessing risks and vulnerabilities, the discussion of risk assessment methodologies will be revised within the NIPP to indicate that there are multiple NIPP-compliant risk assessment methodologies.

NIPP Implementation Metrics

Of particular interest to DHS is the ability to "measure" the implementation of many of the requirements set forth in the NIPP. In order to measure an agency's compliance with or performance, the NIPP sets for a number of CI/KR Protection Metrics, which can be classified into the following four metric areas:

- Core metrics represent a common set of measures that are tracked across all sectors.
- Sector-specific performance metrics are a set of measures tailored to the unique characteristics of each sector.
- CI/KR protection programmatic metrics are used to measure the effectiveness of specific programs, initiatives, and investments that are managed by government agencies and sector partners.
- Sector partnership metrics are used to assess the status of activities conducted under the sector partnership.

Organizational Changes

There have been numerous organizational changes within DHS related to roles and responsibilities described throughout the NIPP. For example, the National Protection and Programs Directorate (formerly the Preparedness Directorate) was formed in 2007 to advance the DHS's risk-reduction mission. Reducing risk requires an integrated approach that encompasses both physical and virtual threats and their associated human elements. The National Protection and Programs Directorate is comprised of the following components:

- **Office of Cybersecurity and Communications (CS&C)**: CS&C has the mission to assure the security, resiliency, and reliability of the Nation's cyber and communications infrastructure in collaboration with the public and private sectors, including international partners.

- **Office of Infrastructure Protection (OIP)**: OIP leads the coordinated national effort to reduce risk to our critical infrastructures and key resources (CI/KR) posed by acts of terrorism. In doing so, DHS increases the Nation's level of preparedness and the ability to respond and quickly recover in the event of an attack, natural disaster, or other emergency.
- **Office of Intergovernmental Programs (IGP)**: IGP has the mission of promoting an integrated national approach to homeland security by ensuring, coordinating, and advancing federal interaction with state, local, tribal, and territorial governments.
- **Office of Risk Management and Analysis (RMA)**: RMA leads the DHS's efforts to establish a common framework to address the overall management and analysis of homeland security risk.
- **United States Visitor and Immigrant Status Indicator Technology (US-VISIT)**: US-VISIT is part of a continuum of biometrically-enhanced security measures, such as digital fingerprints and photographs, that begins outside U.S. borders and continues through a visitor's arrival in and departure from the United States.[9]

Special Considerations

CI/KR protection planning involves special consideration for protection of sensitive infrastructure information, the unique cyber and human elements of infrastructure, and complex international relationships.

••

Assets, Systems, and Networks include one or more of the following elements:

- **Physical** – tangible property;
- **Cyber** – electronic information and communications systems, and the information contained therein; and/or
- **Human** – critical knowledge of functions or people uniquely susceptible to attack.

Cyber infrastructure includes electronic information and communications systems, and the information contained in those systems. Computer systems, control systems such as Supervisory Control and Data Acquisition (SCADA) systems, and networks such as the Internet are all part of cyber infrastructure. **Information and communications systems** are composed of hardware and software that process, store, and communicate. Processing includes the creation, access, modification, and destruction of information. Storage includes paper, magnetic, electronic, and all other media types. Communications include sharing and distribution of information.

The **human** element requires:

- Identifying and preventing the insider threat resulting from infiltration or individual employees determined to do harm;
- Identifying, protecting, and supporting (e.g., via cross-training) employees and other persons with critical knowledge or functions; and

- Identifying and mitigating fear tactics used by terrorist agents and disaffected insiders.

Assessing human element vulnerabilities is more subjective than assessing the physical or cyber vulnerabilities of corresponding assets, systems, and networks, and diverse protective programs and actions to address threats posed by employees and to employees need to be put into place across all sectors.

....

Assessment of the NIPP

In July 2007, the U.S. Government Accountability Office (GAO) published a report on a review of nine sector-specific plans (SSP). The GAO review found that some plans were more comprehensive than others when discussing their physical, human, and cyber assets, systems, and functions due to the sectors reporting different views on the extent to which they were dependent on each of these assets. A comprehensive identification of all three categories of assets is important, according to DHS sector-specific plan guidance, because such an asset analysis provides the foundation on which to conduct risk analyses and identify the appropriate mix of protective programs and actions that will most effectively reduce the risk to the Nation's infrastructure. Yet, only one of the plans—drinking water and water treatment systems—included all three categories of assets. For example, because the communications sector limited its definition of assets to networks, systems, and functions, it did not, as required by DHS plan guidance, discuss how human assets fit into existing security projects or are relevant to fill the gaps to meet the sector's security goals. DHS officials said that the variance in the plans can primarily be attributed to the levels of maturity and cultures of the sectors, with the more mature sectors—sectors with preexisting relationships and a history of working relationships—generally having more comprehensive and complete plans than more newly established sectors without similar prior relationships. Lastly, DHS Office of Infrastructure Protection (OIP) officials acknowledged the differences in how comprehensive the plans are, but said that these initial plans are only a first step and that they will work with the sectors to address differences in future updates. Because of the disparity in the plans, it raises questions as to the extent to which the DHS will be able to use them to identify security gaps and critical interdependencies across the sectors in order to plan future protective measures.

Further, while many of the plans included the required elements of the NIPP risk management framework, such as security goals and the methods the sectors expect to use to prioritize infrastructure as well as to develop and implement protective programs and assess threats, risks, and vulnerabilities, there was significant variance in the level of detail and thoroughness of these reports depending on the maturity of the sector and how the sector defined its assets and functions. Additionally, while all of the plans described the threat analyses that the sector conducts, eight of the plans did not describe any incentives the sector would use to encourage owners to conduct voluntary risk assessments, as required by the NIPP. These incentives are important because a number of the industries in the sectors are privately owned and not regulated, and the government must rely on voluntary compliance with the NIPP.

At the time of the GAO review, there were seventeen critical infrastructure sectors. All of these had established government councils, and nearly all sectors had initiated voluntary private sector councils. As expected, each sector organized based upon their unique needs and organizational issues, with some being more successful than others. For example, the report specifically noted that because of the diversity of the public health and healthcare sector collaboration had been difficult. Conversely, the nuclear sector is much more consistent across the Department of Energy (DOE) and has a long history of collaboration. As a result, council activities have ranged from getting organized to refining infrastructure protection strategies. Ten sectors, such as banking and finance, had formed councils prior to development of the NIPP and had collaborated on plans for economic reasons, while others had formed councils more recently. As a result, the more mature councils could focus on strategic issues, such as recovering after disasters, while the newer councils were focusing on getting organized.

Council members reported mixed views on what factors facilitated or challenged their actions. For example, long-standing working relationships with regulatory agencies and within sectors were frequently cited as the most helpful factor. Challenges most frequently cited included the lack of an effective relationship with DHS as well as private sector hesitancy to share information on vulnerabilities with the government or within the sector for fear the information would be released and open to competitors. Based on other reports developed by the GAO, an illustrated lack of trust in DHS and a fear that sensitive information would be released are recurring barriers to the private sector's sharing information with the federal government, to which the GAO has made recommendations to help address these barriers. While all sectors met the December 2006 deadline to submit their sector-specific plans (SSP) to the DHS, the level of collaboration between the sector and government councils on the plans, which the NIPP recognizes as critical to establishing relationships between the government and private sectors, varied by sector.

Lastly, the GAO Report made two key recommendations to the DHS:

- Better definition of DHS critical infrastructure information needs; and
- Better explanation of how this information could be used to attract more users.[10]

4

....

National Incident Management Systems (NIMS)

Introduction and Overview

History has demonstrated that both small- and large-scale emergencies occur every day in the United States. These situations can range from common house fires and automobile accidents to natural and technological disasters. The tragic events of September 11, 2001 coupled with the devastating hurricanes Katrina and Ike demonstrated the need for a comprehensive national approach whereby all responders could work together and communicate effectively. In order to implement this approach, the need for a common national strategy to implement effective incident operations, communications, personnel qualifications, and resource and information management had to operationalize in order for the successful outcome of any incident, large or small. Until 2004, there was no national standard for domestic all-hazards incident response that reached across all levels of government and emergency response agencies.

In 2003, Homeland Security Presidential Directive (HSPD)-5: Management of Domestic Incidents was issued, directing the Secretary of Homeland Security to develop and administer a National Incident Management System (NIMS). The NIMS provides a systematic, proactive approach guiding departments and agencies at all levels of government, the private sector, and nongovernmental organizations to work seamlessly to prevent, protect against, respond to, recover from, and mitigate the effects of incidents.[1] In order for this system to function properly, it had to be applicable across a spectrum of incidents and hazards, regardless of their size or complexity.

Table 4.1 What NIMS Is and Is Not

WHAT NIMS IS:	WHAT NIMS IS NOT:
• A comprehensive, nationwide, systematic approach to incident management, including the Incident Command System, Multiagency Coordination Systems, and Public Information. • A set of preparedness concepts and principles for all hazards. • Essential principles for a common operating picture and interoperability of communications and information management. • Standardized resource management procedures that enable coordination among different jurisdictions or organizations. • Scalable so it may be used for all incidents (from day-to-day to large-scale). • A dynamic system that promotes ongoing management and maintenance.	• A response plan. • Only used during large-scale incidents. • A communications plan. • Only applicable to certain emergency management/ incident response personnel. • Only the Incident Command System or an organizational chart. • A static system.

On March 1, 2004, the first version of the National Incident Management System (FEMA 501) was released. As noted in the document, the NIMS "represents a core set of doctrine, concepts, principles, terminology, and organizational processes to enable effective, efficient, and collaborative incident management at all levels. It is not an operational incident management or resource allocation plan."[2] With this in mind, it is important to understand what NIMS is and is not, as outlined in Table 4.1.

History of Incident Management Systems

After devastating wildfires destroyed much of southern California in the late 1960s, officials in California began to identify common response failures when a multitude of agencies responded to the same incident. Common failures included the inability to determine who was in charge of the incident, not clearly identifiable incident commanders, and a series of conflicts among responder officials with regards to who should be in charge at the incident scene. Furthermore, other officials ranging from federal, state, local, and elected also required a level of command at the scene, with varying degrees of responsibility. In addition to command challenges, there was a lack of interagency coordination with no joint communications systems, a lack of common terminology, and no formal logistics in place.

In response to these challenges, officials created a program called Firefighting Resources of California Organized for Potential Emergencies, better known as FIRESCOPE. This program, consisting of local, state, and federal agencies, "designed a standardized emergency management system to remedy the challenges outlined, which took several years and extensive field testing."[3]

In 1982, the original FIRESCOPE system and other existing incident management systems were combined into a national program called the National Interagency Incident Management System (NIIMS). This system, now referred to by some as the "two-eyed NIMS," became the backbone of a wider-based system for all federal agencies having a role in wildland fire management and served as the basis for the current NIMS. Although many similarities exist between the NIIMS and the NIMS, NIIMS was designed to meet the challenges of wildland fire whereas the design of NIMS was to address the challenges of all hazards or terrorist events. In addition, there is increased emphasis on prevention and preparedness measures in the NIMS framework.

Current NIMS Document

The NIMS document continues to be a "work in progress" as capabilities mature, plans are developed and exercised, and threats against our country are realized. To this end, the Incident Management Systems Integration Division (IMSI), within the National Preparedness Directorate (NPD) of the Federal Emergency Management Agency (FEMA), releases the new version of the NIMS in December 2008. The new version contains several changes based on the input of stakeholders from various responder disciplines. The following significant changes have been noted:

- Reorganization of the document to reflect the normal emergency management process (address preparedness before response);
- Elimination of the perception that NIMS is the only Incident Command System (ICS);
- Expansion of the Preparedness and Resource Management components; and
- Clarification of the concepts within Command and Management, including multiagency coordination and public information.

In the NIMS document, the DHS worked to integrate best practices into a comprehensive framework for use by emergency management/response personnel in an all-hazards context nationwide. NIMS adheres to two overarching principles within this framework: flexibility and standardization. First, the NIMS components are adaptable to any situation, from routine local incidents to those requiring a coordinated federal response. This flexibility facilitates scalability of incident management activities. Secondly, NIMS provides standardized organizational structures to ensure coordination of all responders. This includes standard terminology, which fosters communications in agencies that may have to respond to an incident together. These two principles support the implementation and execution of the five components of NIMS:

1. Preparedness
2. Communications and Information Management
3. Resource Management
4. Command and Management
5. Ongoing Management and Maintenance

The remainder of this chapter will overview these five components with an understanding that each was designed to complement each other in a flexible, systematic manner to provide a common framework for incident management. For more information on these components, view the NIMS document at: http://www.fema.gov/pdf/emergency/nims/nims_doc_full.pdf.

Preparedness

The first component of NIMS, preparedness, is achieved and maintained through a continuous cycle of planning, organizing, training, equipping, exercising, evaluating, and taking corrective action. The effective adoption, implementation, and training of these activities in advance of an incident will greatly increase the chances of successful incident management. One underlying requirement of the preparedness component is a unified approach allowing organizations with diverse experiences and resources to interact effectively towards a common objective. Additionally, organizations must set realistic expectations about the capabilities and resources that they will be able to provide. These expectations are very important in both the credentialing and resource management processes (discussed later in this chapter).

Achieving preparedness is not the job of public emergency responders singularly; rather, preparedness takes support from both the private sector and nongovernmental organizations (NGOs). Everyone must know their role prior to an incident. This role can range from policy (development and formalization of policies and agreements) to coordination or support. Private sector and NGOs are often used to deliver incident-related services and are often the owners and operators of critical infrastructure and key resources. In addition to understanding roles and responsibilities, officials should also know what other preparedness efforts exist that can assist them in the event of an emergency.

As discussed in the introduction of this chapter, the foundation for the NIMS is found in HSPD-5. Other presidential directives, however, are also essential to the preparedness component. For example, HSPD-7: Critical Infrastructure Identification, Prioritization, and Protection establishes policy to identify and prioritize critical infrastructure and key resources. Preparedness plans around these assets should be developed to safeguard this property. Next, HSPD-8: National Preparedness requires the development of a National Preparedness System (NPS), National Preparedness Guidelines, the fifteen National Planning Scenarios, and the Target Capabilities List (TCL).

· ·

HSPD-8 Preparedness Requirements
National Preparedness System (NPS): The NPS provides a way to organize preparedness activities and programs pursuant to the National Preparedness Guidelines (see below). The desired end-state of the NPS is to achieve and sustain coordinated capabilities to prevent, protect against, respond to, and recover from all hazards in a way that balances risk with resources. The NPS provides opportunities for all levels of government, the private sector, nongovernmental organizations, and individual citizens to work together to achieve priorities and capabilities outlined in the National Preparedness Guidelines.

National Preparedness Guidelines (Guidelines): The Guidelines finalize development of the national preparedness goal and its related preparedness tools. The purposes of the Guidelines are to:

- Organize and synchronize national (including federal, state, local, tribal, and territorial) efforts to strengthen national preparedness;
- Guide national investments in national preparedness;
- Incorporate lessons learned from past disasters into national preparedness priorities;
- Facilitate a capability-based and risk-based investment planning process; and
- Establish readiness metrics to measure progress and a system for assessing the nation's overall preparedness capability to respond to major events, especially those involving acts of terrorism.

National Planning Scenarios: The National Planning Scenarios depict a diverse set of high-consequence threat scenarios of both potential terrorist attacks and natural disasters. Collectively, the fifteen scenarios are designed to focus contingency planning for homeland security preparedness work at all levels of government and with the private sector. The scenarios form the basis for coordinated federal planning, training, exercises, and grant investments needed to prepare for emergencies of all types.

Target Capabilities List (TCL): The TCL defines thirty-seven specific capabilities that communities, the private sector, and all levels of government should collectively possess in order to respond effectively to disasters.[4]

· ·

Another closely related federal framework is the National Response Framework (NRF), a guide to how the Nation conducts all-hazards incident management which builds upon NIMS. This framework provides the mechanisms to ensure effective federal support to state, tribal, and local related events. It is important to note that both the NIMS and the NRF are designed to ensure that local jurisdictions retain control over an incident, even when additional resources are requested.

Preparedness Roles
Every citizen has a role to play in community preparedness, as part of an organization, as an individual citizen, or both. Many communities have preparedness organizations that provide coordination to help jurisdictions meet

their preparedness needs. Preparedness organizations should be multijuris-dictional and include both public and private representatives. These organi-zations can take many actions to include, but not limited to, establishing plans, adopting standards and guidelines, resource identification, encourag-ing training opportunities, and conducting after action reviews.

Additionally, it is critical that elected and appointed officials understand their roles and responsibilities during an incident. An uneducated, untrained official could potentially serve as a detriment to an incident and even cause destruction to life or property in extreme cases. In order to serve as an effec-tive element during an incident, elected and appointed officials are encour-aged to take NIMS training, participate in exercises, establish relationships, and maintain awareness of critical infrastructure and key resources within their jurisdictions. During an incident, these individuals are generally not at the scene, but must be able to communicate with the Incident Commander, providing input on policy, direction, and authority.

Lastly, other groups such as NGOs and the private sector can play vital support roles to a community before, during, and after an incident. NGOs, such as community or faith based organizations, should be fully integrated into preparedness efforts. The private sector (utilities, industries, corporations, busi-nesses, etc.) often have response experience and some have valuable resources that can be used in the event of an emergency. Memorandums of Agreements (MOA) should be established with both groups prior to an incident so that all parties are aware of capabilities, expectations, and the roles of others.

Preparedness Elements
One essential step in preparedness planning is to ensure that plans are in place, which effectively outlines how a jurisdiction will coordinate, manage, and support information and resources. These plans must be realistic, scal-able, and applicable to a wide variety of incidents, and should be used as a ba-sis for training and exercised regularly. Additionally, these plans should integrate all relevant entities to facilitate and coordinate management and response. Two specific types of plans that every jurisdiction should develop and maintain is a Continuity of Operations (COOP) and Continuity of Gov-ernment (COG). The planning, testing, training, exercising, and assessment of COOP plans should be implemented across all organizations to ensure the continuance of core capabilities/operations during an incident. Whereas COOP activities support the continuance of business and/or government functions, COG activities address the continuance of constitutional gover-nance ensuring that legislative and/or administrative responsibilities are maintained. In addition to COOP and COG plans, mutual aid and assistance agreements must be put into place.

Mutual aid and assistance agreements are written or oral agreements between and among organizations or jurisdictions that provide a mechanism to quickly obtain emergency assistance in the form of personnel, equipment, materials, and/or other associated services. Although there are several types of agreements, each one should include the elements and provisions.

In addition to plans and agreements, it is critical that procedures and protocols detailing specific actions are implemented in our Nation's jurisdictions. These items could translate into action-oriented checklists during incident response operations. Standard procedure and protocol documents include a standard operating procedure (SOP) or operations manual, a field operations guide, a mobilization guide, and/or a job aid. These protocols allow specific personnel to assess a situation and take immediate actions in order to safeguard life and property. As with plans and agreements, procedures and protocols should be trained and exercised regularly.

Training and exercises should be customized to the responsibilities of the personnel involved in the incident management and allow practitioners to use NIMS concepts and principles as well as become more comfortable using NIMS. Exercises should contain realistic situations and include interaction among both private and public sector, as would be the case in a "real-world" incident. Effective exercises contain a mechanism for incorporating corrective actions into the planning process so that mistakes are less likely to be repeated during an actual event. Two other important elements in preparedness are the standards and guidelines to ensure that the right people show up to an incident with the most effective equipment.

Standards help ensure that personnel possess the minimum knowledge, skills, and experience to effectively and safely execute during an incident. Oftentimes, these standards include training, experience, and physical/medical fitness. The baseline criteria for personnel credentialing, which will allow credentialed personnel to participate in national-level incidents, is currently under development by FEMA's National Integration Center (NIC). Equally important to personnel certification is the assurance that a responders' equipment will perform to certain standards. This assurance will allow for better planning before an incident and rapid scaling and flexibility during an incident.

· ·

NIMS Credentialing Guidelines

Credentialing is the administrative process for validating the qualifications of personnel and assessing their background for authorization and access to an incident involving mutual aid.

As part of the Nation's efforts to strengthen catastrophic response capabilities in line with the NIMS, FEMA's National Integration Center (NIC), Incident Management Systems Integration (IMSI) Division has developed initial minimum criteria for personnel to be deployed using a national credentialing system. For specific job titles, the IMSI Division identified *requisite* and *recommended* baseline criteria for education, training, experience, physical/medical fitness, certification, and licensing. These criteria are intended to complement and support existing credentialing systems. Where national standards do not exist under *requisite* criteria, *recommended* criteria are listed for current and/or future consideration.

The following job titles have been developed by the IMSI Division:

- Animal Emergency Response Job Titles
- Public Works (PW) Job Titles
- Updated PW Job Titles
- Emergency Medical Services (EMS) Job Titles
- Incident Management (IM) Job Titles
- Fire/Hazardous Materials Job Titles
- Search and Rescue (SAR) Job Titles
- Medical and Public Health Credentialing

The above job titles can be viewed and downloaded at: http://www.fema.gov/emergency/nims/rm/job_titles.shtm.[5]

Mitigation

The last component of preparedness is mitigation and provides a foundation in the effort to reduce the loss of life and property and minimize damage to the environment. Risk management, the process for measuring or assessing risk and developing strategies to manage it, is an essential component of mitigation. Example mitigation activities include public education, floodplain management, building code enforcement, implementation of a vital records program, and periodic remapping of hazard or potential hazard zones.

Communications and Information Management

The existence of a flexible communications and information system on which responders can maintain a flow of information during an incident is essential. One component of this system is the establishment of a common operating picture. This process includes the collating and gathering of information in order to make an informed decision during an incident. The common operating picture helps to ensure that management and response personnel are all working from consistent and timely information. These communications must be flexible, reliable, and scalable in order to function in any type of incident. Without communications interoperability, that information may not be relayed to each responder.

Communications interoperability allows responders to communicate within and across agencies and jurisdictions via voice, data, or video on demand, in real time, when needed, and when authorized. In order for interoperability to occur, procedural, technical, and usage must be taken into consideration. Finally, after interoperability is achieved, jurisdictions must ensure that both resiliency and redundancy is built into their communication systems. Resiliency refers to the ability of systems to withstand and continue to perform after damage and/or loss of infrastructure. Redundancy, on the other hand, refers to the ability to communicate through diverse, alternative methods when standard capabilities suffer damage.

Management Characteristics

In an effort to ensure effective management of communications, responders must adhere to standardized communication types. The four types of standardized communications include: Strategic (high-level directions), Tactical (from command to support), Support (support of strategic and tactical communications), and Public Affairs (emergency alerts and warnings). In order to ensure that communications are effective, policy and planning must be implemented. Careful planning should determine what communications systems and platforms will be used, technical specifications of equipment, and what defines essential information. Once these decisions have been made, agreements should be executed outlining the system and platforms the organizations agree to use and share information through during an incident.

Integrated Public Alert and Warning System (IPAWS)

What is IPAWS?

The **Integrated Public Alert and Warning System** (IPAWS) is the Nation's next generation public communications and warning capability. FEMA and the IPAWS Program Management Office (PMO) are working with public and private sectors to integrate warning systems to allow the President and authorized officials to effectively address and warn the public and State and local emergency operations centers via phone, cell phone, pagers, computers, and other personal communications devices.

IPAWS Background

During an emergency, the President, state officials, and local emergency managers need to quickly provide the American public with life-saving information. The current emergency alert system is based on 1990s technology that relied on radio and TV to transmit audio-only alerts. Today, the public uses many different technologies to receive information and are less reliant on TV and radio. For example, many people are not able to watch TV or listen to the radio during the work day, and very few people do so in the middle of the night.

The President issued an executive order two years ago directing DHS to overcome this challenge. In response, FEMA created the IPAWS PMO to oversee the evolution of the alert and warning system. IPAWS will improve public safety through the rapid dissemination of emergency messages to as many people as possible over as many communications devices as possible. To do this, IPAWS expands the traditional alert and warning system to include more modern technologies. At the same time, FEMA is upgrading the alert and warning infrastructure so that no matter what the crisis is, life-saving information will get to the public—day or night, at home, at work, at school, or even on vacation.

What IPAWS Does

The IPAWS improves the reliability, security, and accessibility of public alerts and warnings by transforming today's national emergency alert system from an audio-only system into one that can more reliably and effectively send alerts by voice, text, or video to all Americans, including those with disabilities or who cannot understand English. Through IPAWS, alerts will now flow through multiple devices, such as cell phones, pagers, satellite television/radio, landline phones, desktop computers, personal digital assistants, and road signs. These live or pre-recorded messages may be sent via audio, video, or text in multiple languages, including American Sign Language and Braille.

With the help of the local and state governments and with public participation, IPAWS will use multiple modern technologies to alert the public about an impending or ongoing disaster, enhancing the public's ability to make decisions that could save lives and property. IPAWS supports FEMA's goal to reduce losses of life and property from all hazards by providing timely and accurate information before, during, and after an emergency. With IPAWS, you can get alerts and stay alive.[6]

··

Incident Information

In order for members of an incident command system (ICS) team to make sound decisions, they must have access to a wide variety of information. One example of this information includes incident notification, situation, and status reports. These reports must be standardized to ensure access to critical information such as the specific details of the incident. Next, analytical data, such as public health information, should adhere to collection standards which ultimately equates to more reliable analysis equating to a better informed decision. Last, geospatial information is often communicated during an incident and provides information on geographic locations and characteristics of natural or constructed features or boundaries. As with analytical data, the use of geospatial data standards should be employed to ensure strict attention to detail is maintained.

Communications Standards and Formats

Common terminology, standards, and procedures should be established and detailed in plans and/or agreements. During incident response activities, all participating personnel should follow recognized procedures and protocols and limit radio traffic to messages necessary for the execution of the responder's task. One way to ensure communications are understood by all disciplines is through the use of common terminology. The use of plain language (clear text) increases public safety by ensuring that all those involved will receive information that is timely, clear, acknowledged, and understood by all recipients. In necessary situations, emergency personnel should have a method and system in place to encrypt information so that security can be maintained. A Joint Information System (JIS) and the Joint Information Center (JIC) are important components in maintaining standardized communications.

The JIS integrates incident information in order to provide consistent, accurate, and timely information during the crisis. Meanwhile, the JIC provides a structure for developing and delivering messages, develops and executes public information plans and strategies, advises the ICS team of potential public information challenges that could affect response, and serves as rumor control by dispelling false or inaccurate information.

Resource Management

An effective incident response requires carefully managed resources (personnel, teams, facilities, equipment, and/or supplies). Utilization of standardized resource management concepts such as typing, inventorying, organizing, and tracking will facilitate the overall process. After incident needs are determined, resources can be ordered to facilitate response. Initially, resources will be addressed locally, but as an incident grows, resources may need to be sought from other sources. Resource management is based on several fundamental principles.

First, coordinated planning must be conducted to identify potential resource needs based on a threat and vulnerability assessment. Planning may also include the development of policies to encourage pre-positioned resources, or those items that are moved to an area near the expected incident site. A fundamental component of resource management is the execution of agreements and contracts for services that may be needed during an incident. Next, resources should be categorized by category, kind, and type to facilitate the ordering and dispatch process. Finally, a collection of processes and tools should be implemented to ensure effective identification, ordering, mobilization, and tracking of resources.

These processes should start with logical acquisition procedures including mission tasking, contracting, existing stocks, and making small purchases. Additionally, the employment of a management information system to provide decision support information should be considered. Examples of these systems include resource tracking, transportation tracking, inventory management, and geographical information systems (GIS). As with any technology, efforts should be taken to ensure redundancy in these systems in the event of a system disruption.

....

Emergency Management Assistance Compact (EMAC)

The **Emergency Management Assistance Compact** (EMAC) is a congressionally ratified organization that provides form and structure to interstate mutual aid. Through EMAC, a disaster impacted state can request and receive assistance from other member states quickly and efficiently, resolving two key issues upfront: liability and reimbursement.

EMAC was established in 1996 and stands today as the cornerstone of mutual aid. The EMAC mutual aid agreement and partnership between member states exist because all states share a common enemy: the threat of disaster.

Since being ratified by Congress and signed into law in 1996 (Public Law 104–321), fifty states, the District of Columbia, Puerto Rico, Guam, and the U.S. Virgin Islands have enacted legislation to become members of EMAC. EMAC is the first national disaster-relief compact since the Civil Defense and Disaster Compact of 1950 to be ratified by Congress.

The strength of EMAC and the quality that distinguishes it from other plans and compacts lies in its governance structure, its relationship with federal organizations, states, counties, territories, and regions, and the ability to move just about any resource one state has to assist another state, including medical resources.

The benefits of EMAC include:

- EMAC assistance may be more readily available than other resources.
- EMAC allows for a quick response to disasters using the unique human resources and expertise possessed by member states.
- EMAC offers state-to-state assistance during Governor declared state of emergencies: EMAC offers a responsive and straightforward system for states to send personnel and equipment to help disaster relief efforts in other states. When resources are overwhelmed, EMAC helps to fill the shortfalls.
- EMAC establishes a firm legal foundation: Once the conditions for providing assistance to a requesting state have been set, the terms constitute a legally binding contractual agreement that makes affected states responsible for reimbursement. Responding states can rest assured that sending aid will not be a financial or legal burden, and personnel sent are protected under workers compensation and liability provisions. The EMAC legislation solves the problems of liability and responsibilities of cost and allows for credentials to be honored across state lines.
- EMAC provides fast and flexible assistance: EMAC allows states to ask for whatever assistance they need for any type of emergency, from earthquakes to acts of terrorism. EMAC's simple procedures help states dispense with bureaucratic wrangling.
- EMAC can move resources other compacts can't—like medical resources.[7]

··

The Resource Management Process

The NIMS document outlines a seven-step resource management process that reflects functional considerations, geographical factors, and validated practices. Although each jurisdiction may have specific needs or circumstances, this framework can be used as a foundation in the resource management process. The remainder of this section will provide an overview of this process.

Step 1: Identify Requirements

When an incident occurs, officials should accurately identify (1) what and how much is needed, (2) where and when is it needed, and (3) who will be receiving or using it. These resources can range from equipment, facilities, personnel, or specialized teams. Specific resources for critical infrastructure and key resources (CI/KR) may need to be identified and coordinated through mutual aid agreements (MAA) unique to those sectors. During this process, resource availability may change so it should be coordinated closely. In events such as hurricanes, where catastrophic implications are projected, state and/or federal government may pre-deploy resources so a quick response can be facilitated.

Step 2: Order and Acquire

Resources that cannot be obtained locally are submitted using standardized forms and procedures. Decisions about resource allocation are based on agency protocol and the demands of other incidents that may be occurring simultaneously. It is important to clearly note discrepancies between requested and available resources to the requestor.

Step 3: Mobilize

Several pieces of information must be obtained by response personnel prior to mobilization. This information, includes, but is not limited to:

- Date, time, and place of departure;
- Mode of transportation to the incident;
- Estimated date and time of arrival;
- Reporting location (with contact information);
- Anticipated deployment duration;
- Resource order number;
- Incident number; and;
- Applicable cost and funding codes.

The mobilization process may include planning for deployment based on existing interagency mobilization guidelines, equipping, training, and other logistical considerations.

Step 4: Track and Report

The tracking of resources is conducted before, during, and after an incident. This process maintains accountability for the resource, protects resource safety and security, and enables coordination and movement. Reporting requirements may include reconciliation, accounting, auditing, and inventorying.

Step 5: Recover/Demobilize

Recovery includes the final disposition of resources, including rehabilitation, replenishment, and disposing of, and/or retrograding. Demobilization occurs thereafter and involves the return of the nonexpendable resource to its original location and status. Expendable resources, which must also be accounted for, may be restocked at its point of origin. As part of the Incident Action Plan, a Demobilization Plan will contain specific instructions to efficiently complete the return/reimbursement processes.

Step 6: Reimburse

Whenever applicable, reimbursement provides a mechanism to recoup funds expended for incident-specific activities. These policies/procedures are an integral part of the incident preparedness stage and should be included in preparedness plans, mutual aid agreements (MAA), and assistance agreements.

Step 7: Inventory

Organizations should maintain an accurate and timely inventory of their current resources. The owner of those resources has the final determination of whether those resources are available for others to use during an incident. It is important that inventory systems do not double count a resource (either equipment or personnel) as part of teams for deployment. Deployable resources have different inventory, ordering, and response profiles depending on their potential uses. With regards to personnel, the credentialing process (briefly discussed earlier in the preparedness section) is critical to ensure the right personnel arrive at an incident.

Resource Typing

Resource typing is categorizing, by capability, the resources requested, deployed, and used in incidents. Currently, 16 categories are used in national resource typing:

1. Animals and Agriculture Issues
2. Communications
3. Energy
4. Firefighting
5. Food and Water
6. Hazardous Materials Response
7. Health and Medical
8. Information and Planning
9. Law Enforcement and Security
10. Mass Care
11. Public Information
12. Public Works and Engineering
13. Resource Management
14. Search and Rescue
15. Transportation
16. Volunteers and Donations

Resource users utilize these categories to identify and inventory resources. The NIC is responsible for facilitating the development and issuance of national standards for the typing of resources and ensuring that the typed resources accurately reflect operational requirements.

Command and Management

This section will focus on the three fundamental elements of incident management: Incident Command System (ICS), Multiagency Coordination Systems (MACS), and Public Information. These elements provide standardization through consistent terminology and established organizational structures.

Incident Command System (ICS)

The majority of incidents in this country are managed locally and handled by local emergency responders. Some incidents, however, quickly grow to include a multidisciplinary response, affecting several jurisdictions, and requiring significant additional resources. The ICS system has proven its flexibility, expandability, and scalability in serving as a mechanism for coordinated and collaborative response. "ICS is a widely applicable management system designed to enable effective and efficient incident management by integrating a combination of facilities, equipment, personnel, procedures, and communications operating within a common organizational structure."[8] The system is used by both public and private entities, and is structured into five major functional areas:

1. Command
2. Operations
3. Planning
4. Logistics
5. Finance/Administration

Intelligence/Investigations is an optional sixth area which can be implemented on an "ad hoc" basis.

ICS has been utilized and tested for more than thirty years in incidents small and large, and contains several features which makes its well suited to manage incidents:

- **Common Terminology:** Allows diverse organizations to clearly communicate, including the use of clear text (i.e., text without the use of agency-specific codes or acronyms).
- **Modular Organization:** Based on size and complexity of the incident, as well as the hazard environment created by the incident.
- **Management by Objectives:** Issuance of clear objectives, strategies, assignments, plans, procedures/protocols, and documenting results to measure performance.
- **Incident Action Planning:** Method to capture and communicate the overall incident priorities, strategies, and tactics in both operational and support contexts.
- **Manageable Span of Control:** Should range from three to seven subordinates.
- **Incident Facilities and Locations:** Establishment of operational support facilities in the vicinity of an incident.
- **Comprehensive Resource Management:** Ranges from available or potentially available personnel, teams, equipment, supplies, and facilities.
- **Integrated Communications:** Common communications plan and interoperable communications processes and architectures.
- **Establishment and Transfer of Command:** Clear establishment by an agency with primary jurisdictional authority and a defined process for transferring.
- **Chain of Command and Unity of Command:** Orderly line of authority and a designated supervisor to whom an individual reports.

- **Unified Command:** Allows diverse agencies to work together without affect to authority, responsibility, or accountability.
- **Dispatch/Deployment:** Deployment only when requested by appropriate authority.
- **Information and Intelligence Management:** Gathering, analyzing, sharing, and managing incident-related information and intelligence.

Incident Command

The Incident Commander (IC) is responsible for the overall management of an incident. The Command and General Staff are typically located at the Incident Command Post (ICP). Incident command can be conducted with a single IC or through Unified Command (UC). If the incident occurs in a single jurisdiction and no other functional agencies overlap, a single IC can be used. The IC will develop the objectives under which subsequent planning will take place. If a team effort is required, a Unified Command (UC) can be implemented which will allow all agencies with jurisdictional authority or functional responsibility to jointly provide management at an incident. Each agency maintains its authority, responsibility, or accountability. See Table 4.2 for a comparison between single IC and UC.

Incident Command Organization

Figure 4.1 below displays a traditional incident command system with command and general staff supporting the IC. Below the figure, each function will be highlighted.

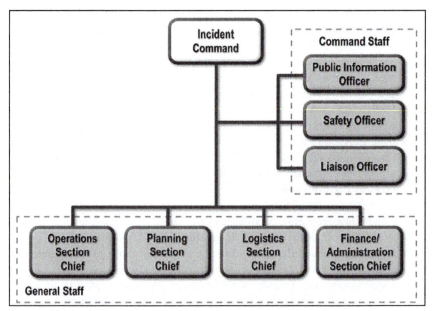

Figure 4.1 Incident Command Organization (Image Courtesy: National Incident Management System (NIMS) – Pre-Decisional DRAFT, 2008)

Table 4.2 Single Incident Commander vs. Unified Command

SINGLE INCIDENT COMMANDER (IC)	UNIFIED COMMAND
The IC is solely responsible (within the confines of their authority) for establishing incident objectives and strategies. The IC is directly responsible for ensuring that all functional area activities are directed toward accomplishment of the strategy.	The individuals designated by their jurisdictional or organizational authorities (or by departments within a single jurisdiction) must jointly determine objectives, strategies, plans, resource allocations, and priorities and work together to execute integrated incident operations and maximize the use of assigned resources.

Command Staff

Public Information Officer: Responsible for interfacing with the public and media and/or with other agencies with incident-related information requirements.

Safety Officer: Monitors operations and advises the IC/UC on all operational safety matters to include health and safety of response personnel.

Liaison Officer: Serves as point of contact for other entities (public and private) to provide input on policies, resources, and other incident-related matters.

General Staff

Operations Section: Responsible for activities which reduce immediate hazards, save lives and property, establishes situational control, and restore normal operations.

Planning Section: Collects, evaluates, and disseminates incident situation information and intelligence to the IC/UC and other management personnel when required.

Logistics Section: Responsible for all service support requirements needed (resources, facilities, security, transportation, supplies, etc.) to facilitate incident management.

Finance/Administration Section: Responsible for activities such as personnel time, maintaining vendor contracts, compensation and claims, and incident cost analysis.

Intelligence/Investigations Section: Responsible for collection, analysis, and sharing of incident-related intelligence. May be a stand-alone unit or embedded with other sections.

Area Command

Area command is an organization established to: (1) oversee the management of multiple incidents that are each being handled by an Incident Command System organization; or (2) to oversee the management of a very large incident that has multiple Incident Management Teams assigned to it. Area

Command has the responsibility to set overall strategy and priorities, allocate critical resources based on priorities, ensure that incidents are properly managed, and ensure that objectives are met and strategies followed.

Multiagency Coordination Systems (MACS)

According to NIMS, MACS consists of a combination of facilities, equipment, personnel, procedures, and communications for the purpose of coordinating and supporting incident management activities. MAC groups and other MAC entities have no incident command or operational responsibilities. Rather, they provide off-scene or "above field level" coordination among impacted organizations.[9] The specific functions of MACS are to:

- Support incident management policies and priorities;
- Facilitate logistical support and resource tracking;
- Inform resource allocation decisions using incident management priorities;
- Coordinate incident-related information; and ;
- Coordinate and resolve interagency and intergovernmental issues regarding incident management policies, priorities, and strategies.[10]

Like NIMS, the National Response Framework (NRF) also addresses the use of MACS to help coordinate activities above the field level. The NRF places special emphasis on systems and organizational structures used by the federal government to facilitate multiagency coordination (e.g., Joint Field Offices, Regional Response Coordination Centers, National Response Coordination Center, etc.).

The NIMS and NRF documents provide the foundation for multiagency coordination doctrine in the United States. Table 4.3 provides other notable resources and voluntary consensus standards that underpin MACS doctrine or emphasize the importance of MACS.

Helping to frame these policy documents and standards are years of practical experience and lessons learned from "real-world" incidents. The after action reports for Hurricane Katrina, for example, site many lessons learned that relate to multiagency coordination.

Implementation of MACS requires written agreements, operational procedures, and protocols. These procedures are often captured in the form of guides, handbooks, and other job aids. For example, the *U.S. Coast Guard Incident Management Handbook* describes MACS in light of the functions fulfilled by the Joint Field Office (JFO) and use of facilities (e.g., Multiagency Command Center) to support interagency coordination and planning. At the state level, the *Florida Incident Field Operations Guide* provides incident management organizations in Florida with guidance for implementing MACS in response to an incident or planned event. See Appendix A to review the MACS section of this guide.

Although the use of the term "multiagency coordination" may be new to many state, tribal, and local entities, it is not new for public safety officials in areas of the country prone to wildfires. Most notably, a large volume of literature exists among Western states and the federal government regarding how

Table 4.3 Key Multiagency Coordination Standards and Resources

Source Document	Description
1. Multiagency Coordination Systems (IS-701), Student Manual, October 2006	The purpose of IS-701 is to introduce MACS and provide examples of how these systems can be used to improve incident response. Among others, the objectives of IS-701 are to: • Define multiagency coordination at the local, state, and federal levels of government; • Define key terms related to MACS; • Identify typical priorities established between elements of the MACS; • Describe the process of acquiring and allocating resources; and • Identify potential coordination and policy issues.
2. NFPA 1561: Standard on Emergency Services Incident Management System, 2008 Edition	This standard establishes the minimum requirements for an incident management system to be used by emergency services to manage all incidents/planned events. Chapter 5 (Functions and Structure of Command) includes one standard that addresses the need for multiagency coordination: *5.7 Multi-Agency Coordination System. When it is deemed necessary to coordinate resources at the regional level, a multi-agency coordination system (MACS) shall be established based upon direction by the authority having jurisdiction to facilitate the coordination and support between agencies or jurisdictions.* Also, the annex to the standard provides additional information about MACS.
3. NFPA 1600: Standard for Disaster/Emergency Management and Business Continuity, 2007 Edition	This standard establishes a common set of criteria for disaster/emergency management and business continuity programs. Although the term "Multi-Agency Coordination Systems" is not referenced in the standard, many MAC elements are located in individual sections, including the following: • 5.6 – Resource Management and Logistics • 5.7 – Mutual Aid/Assistance • 5.9 – Incident Management • 5.12 – Facilities Also, standard 5.12.1 states "[t]he entity shall establish a primary and an alternate emergency operations center, physical or virtual, capable of managing continuity, response, and recovery operations."
4. Standard Guide for the Development and Operation of an Emergency Operations Center (EOC), ASTM International *(under development)*	Once complete, this guide will address issues and concerns in developing, managing, and operating an Emergency Operations Center (EOC). There are no existing standards specific to the development and operation of EOCs. This guide will be applicable in both the public and private sectors by groups and individuals involved in the ownership, management, or operation of an EOC.

they coordinate and allocate resources in responding to incidents. This cooperation was largely necessitated due to the presence of federal land and the high risk of fires.

California organized FIRESCOPE in the 1970s to improve coordination among fire agencies at all levels of government.[11] Since then, the wildfire community has organized national-, regional-, and state-level coordination groups, and has instilled MAC elements into their response and recovery operations. This is evidenced by a wealth of agreements, plans, and procedures, including:

- Planning checklists and considerations;
- Descriptions of MAC Group positions;
- Roles and responsibilities for personnel involved in MAC activities;
- Activation guidance and procedures;
- Use of EOCs and other facilities;
- Meeting objectives, agendas, and reports;
- Mutual aid agreements (MAA); and;
- Demobilization guidance and procedures.

MAC Groups are a common organizational structure for the wildfire community. According to *Multiagency Coordination Systems (IS-701) – Student Manual*, the MAC Group is one of four common ways of organizing a MAC entity.[12] The MAC Group is typically facilitated by a MAC Group Coordinator, and possesses three units:

1. Situation Assessment Unit;
2. Resource Status Information Unit;
3. Joint Information Center (JIC).

The California case study provides an example of this model. See Figure 4.2 below for a sample MAC Group structure.

Public Information
Public information includes the "processes, procedures, and organizational structures required to gather, verify, and coordinate, and disseminate information."[13] All information in the field must be cleared by the IC prior to

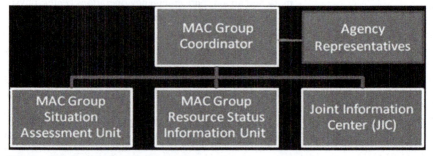

Figure 4.2 Sample MAC Group Structure

release. Table 4.4 displays a sample checklist of responsibilities for the PIO in an ICS structure, which would generally apply to any incident.

Ongoing Management and Maintenance

The NIC is a component of the National Preparedness Directorate (NPD) and is responsible for the direction and oversight of NIMS, supporting routine maintenance and continuous refinement. In this role, the NIC is responsible for NIMS education and awareness, promotion of public and private standards with applicability to NIMS, developing assessment criteria for NIMS components, and integrating NIMS into the national research and development agenda. In addition to these duties, the NIC administers NIMS compliance requirements, facilitates the development of guidance standards, support NIMS training and exercises, and publishes various NIMS-related materials.

In the area of standards, the NIC is responsible for the design and implementation of a credentialing system as discussed earlier in this chapter. The NIC also facilitates the establishment of standards to evaluate the performance, compatibility, and interoperability of incident management equipment and communications systems. Next, the NIC facilitates the development of resource typing and data standards for NIMS information systems.

With regards to training and exercise support, the NIC facilitates the definition of general training requirements and develops training standards and course curriculums to fulfill those requirements. These training requirements

Table 4.4 PIO Major Responsibility Checklist

COMPLETE	PIO MAJOR RESPONSIBILITIES
☐	Determine from the IC whether there are any limits on information release.
☐	Develop material for use in media briefings.
☐	Obtain IC approval of media releases.
☐	Inform the media and conduct media briefings.
☐	Arrange for tours and other interviews or briefings, as required.
☐	Evaluate the need for and, as appropriate, establish and operate a JIS.
☐	Establish a JIC, as necessary, to coordinate and disseminate accurate and timely incident-related information.
☐	Maintain current information summaries and/or displays on the incident.
☐	Provide information on the status of the incident to assigned personnel.
☐	Maintain an Activity Log (ICS 214).
☐	Manage media and public inquiries.
☐	Coordinate emergency public information and warnings.
☐	Monitor media reporting for accuracy.
☐	Ensure that all required agency forms, reports, and documents are completed prior to demobilization.
☐	Have debriefing session with the IC prior to demobilization.

are multidisciplinary, and many courses are available online through the Emergency Management Institute (EMI) in Emmitsburg, Md.

Finally, the NIC is responsible for the development and dissemination of NIMS related publications to the response community. These publications run the gamut from compliance requirements, field operating guides, job aids, computer programs, audio/video resources, and best practice publications. These publications are generally available on the NIMS Website at: http://www.fema.gov/emergency/nims/.

Supporting Technologies

As previously noted, the NIC is committed to the ongoing development of science and technology to further the Nations' ability to manage incidents. These R&D initiatives are coordinated with the DHS Science and Technology Directorate (DHS S&T). These initiatives involve interoperability and compatibility through the use of communication and data standards. Technologies in these areas help improve overall efficiency and effectiveness in all aspects of incident management. Additionally, it is vital for the NIC to acquire the needs of responders for new technologies, procedures, protocols, and standards to facilitate incident management. NIMS provides a mechanism for aggregating and prioritizing these needs and resources.

Additionally, the NIC provides testing and evaluation support to assess technologies against applicable standards. It is noted that many responder agencies do not have the time or resources to comprehensively test NIMS related technologies prior to procurement. This objective component provides product information from a technically proficient and objective entity. All research and development (R&D) planning is based on the operational needs of the entire range of NIMS users.

5

....

Assessments for Infrastructure Protection

Introduction

Every day in this Nation, the products and services that support our standard of living flow to and from our homes, communities, and government. In an effort to ensure these systems and networks that constitute our Nation's critical infrastructure function properly, comprehensive and timely assessments must be conducted at various levels of society. These assessments, which are outlined in both Homeland Security Presidential Directive (HSPD) -7 and -8, provide critical information that help to protect these assets due to their viability in our daily activities.

> The Secretary, consistent with the Homeland Security Act of 2002 and other applicable legal authorities and presidential guidance, shall establish appropriate systems, mechanisms, and procedures to share homeland security information relevant to threats and vulnerabilities in national critical infrastructure and key resources with other federal departments and agencies, state and local governments, and the private sector in a timely manner.[1]

> To the extent permitted by law, the primary mechanism for delivery of federal preparedness assistance will be awards to the States. Awards will be delivered in a form that allows the recipients to apply the assistance to the highest priority preparedness requirements at the appropriate level of government. To the extent permitted by law, federal preparedness assistance will be predicated on adoption of statewide comprehensive all-hazards preparedness strategies. The strategies should be consistent with the national preparedness goal, should

assess the most effective ways to enhance preparedness, should address areas facing higher risk, especially to terrorism, and should also address local government concerns …[2]

To help the reader become more aware of assessments for infrastructure protection, this chapter will overview the general components for critical infrastructure assessments and then examine specific assessments that are currently being utilized for critical infrastructure protection.

General Assessment Framework

As previously noted, the assessment process is the foundation of the critical infrastructure protection lifecycle. A comprehensive assessment provides decision makers with the information necessary to identify the potential threats to which a community is susceptible. This process allows for the identification of scenarios based on realistic assumptions and provides justification for the expenditure of resources.

In this chapter, a common assessment framework, detailed in *Federal Emergency Management Agency (FEMA) 426: Reference Manual to Mitigate Potential Terrorist Attacks Against Buildings*, will be overviewed in the context of critical infrastructure protection. *FEMA 426* was developed to provide guidance to the building science community of architects and engineers in an effort to reduce physical damage to buildings, related infrastructure, and people caused by terrorist assaults. This framework has been utilized by the U.S. Department of Defense (DOD), Department of State (DOS), and the General Services Administration (GSA) to the private sector. This model was selected as the example model for this chapter due to its inclusion of general assessment components as well as its applicability to infrastructure protection.

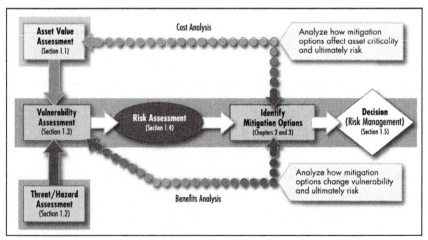

Figure 5.1 Critical Infrastructure Assessment Framework (Courtesy: Federal Emergency Management Agency)

Step One: Asset Value Assessment

The first step of the assessment process is to determine the asset value and the points of contact for that asset. It is useful to begin this process by interviewing representatives who are most familiar with the asset. An asset is defined as a resource, either tangible or intangible, of value requiring protection, such as a building. In order to achieve the greatest risk reduction at the least cost, identifying and prioritizing a building's critical assets is a vital first step in the process to identify the best mitigation measures to improve its level of protection prior to a terrorist attack. Recognizing that people are a building's most critical asset, the process described below will help identify and prioritize infrastructure where people are most at risk and require protection.

An **asset** is a valuable resource that requires protection, which includes people or any other tangible or intangible resource to an organization.

Identifying a building's critical assets is accomplished in a two-step process:

1. Defining and understanding the building's core functions and process; and
2. Identifying the building infrastructure.

First, the core functions and processes necessary for the building to continue to operate or provide services after an attack must be determined. The reason for identifying core functions/processes is to focus the design team on what a building does, how it does it, and how various threats can affect the building. Next, the building infrastructure evaluation will assist with identification and value ranking infrastructure.

After a list of a building's assets or resources of value requiring protection has been identified, they should be assigned a value. Asset value is the degree of debilitating impact that would be caused by the incapacity or destruction of the building's assets. There are many scales that can be used, each with advantages and disadvantages. One example of a quantitative asset value scale is displayed below.

This scale ranges from very high, which means the loss or damage of the building's assets would have exceptionally grave consequences, to very low,

Table 5.1 Quantitative Asset Value Scale

	Asset Value
Very High	10
High	8 to 9
Medium High	7
Medium	5 to 6
Medium Low	4
Low	2 to 3
Very Low	1

which means loss or damage of the building's assets would have negligible consequences or impact.

Step Two: Threat/Hazard Assessment

The next step in the assessment process is the assessment of threats/hazards that may affect the community. Threats and hazards usually fall into two categories: natural (geological, meteorological, and biological) or man-made. With any man-made hazard, it is important to understand the people with the intent to cause harm. For those people, it is essential to understand their weapons, tools, and tactics, realizing that weapons, tools, and tactics can change faster than a building can be modified against the threat.

Threat/hazard assessment information can be sought from federal, state, and local law enforcement, homeland security, and emergency management agencies/departments. For technological hazards, it is also important to gather information from the local fire department and hazardous materials (HAZMAT) unit, and other federal and state environmental protection agencies. These departments, units, and agencies identify critical facilities in vulnerable zones and generate emergency management plans.

•••

A common method to evaluate terrorist threats is to analyze five factors: existence, capability, history, intention, and targeting.

Existence addresses the questions: Who is hostile to the assets, organization, or community of concern? Are they present or thought to be present? Are they able to enter the country or are they readily identifiable in a local community upon arrival?

Capability addresses the questions: What weapons have been used in carrying out past attacks? Do the aggressors need to bring them into the area or are they available locally?

History addresses the questions: What has the potential threat elements done in the past and how many times? When was the most recent incident, where, and against what target? What tactics did they use? Are they supported by another group or individuals? How did they acquire their demonstrated capability?

Intention addresses the questions: What does the potential threat element or aggressor hope to achieve? How do we know this (e.g., published in books or news accounts, speeches, letters to the editor, information)?

Targeting addresses the questions: Do we know if an aggressor (we may not know which specific one) is performing surveillance on our building, nearby buildings, or buildings that have much in common with our organization? Is this information current, credible, and indicative of preparations for terrorist operation (manmade hazards)?

The threat/hazard analysis for any building can range from a general threat/hazard scenario to a very detailed examination of specific groups, individuals, and tactics which the building may need to be designed to repel or defend against.[3]

•••

Step Three: Vulnerability Assessment

After gaining an understanding of the expected threat/hazard capability, the assessor can integrate the information with specific building and site information by conducting a vulnerability assessment. A vulnerability assessment is an in-depth analysis of a building's functions, systems, and site characteristics to identify weaknesses and lack of redundancy, and to determine mitigations or corrective actions that can be designed or implemented to reduce the vulnerabilities. Weaknesses can be found in the system design, physical layout, procedures used, administration of the system, and personnel within the system, management, hardware, and software.[4]

Although there are many different methodologies in conducting these assessments, each methodology contains common elements, such as:

- **Level of Visibility:** What is the perceived awareness of the target's existence and the visibility of the target to the general population, or to the terrorist in particular?
- **Asset Value of Target Site (Individual Asset or Assets Accumulated within Building):** What is the usefulness of the asset(s) to the population, economy, government, company, or organization?
- **Target Value to Potential Threat Element/Aggressor:** Does the target serve the ends of the aggressors identified in the Threat Assessment based on motivations (political, religious, racial, environmental, and special interests)?
- **Aggressor Access to Target:** Does the target have available ingress and egress for a potential aggressor?
- **Target Threat of Hazard:** Are chemical, biological, or radiological materials present in quantities that could become hazardous if released? These quantities could be onsite or in relatively close proximity so that a theft or an accident could render them a hazard to the building or site.
- **Site Population Capacity:** What is the maximum number of individuals at the building or site at a given time? This could be standard worst case occupancy during an average day or peak occupancy at a designated time.
- **Potential for Collateral Damage:** Address potential collateral mass casualties within a 1-mile radius of the target site.

Step Four: Risk Assessment

Risk is the potential for a loss of, or damage to, an asset. It is measured based upon the value of the asset in relation to the threats and vulnerabilities associated with it. Risk is based on the likelihood or probability of the hazard occurring and the consequences of the occurrence. A risk assessment analyzes the threat (probability of occurrence), and asset value and vulnerabilities (consequences of the occurrence) to ascertain the level of risk for each asset against each applicable threat/ hazard.

Risk is the potential loss or damage to an asset that is measured upon the value of the asset and based upon the likelihood of the risk occurring.

The risk assessment provides engineers and architects with a relative risk profile that defines which assets are at the greatest risk against specific threats.

As with previous components, there are numerous methodologies and technologies for conducting a risk assessment. One approach is to assemble the results of the asset value assessment, threat assessment, and vulnerability assessment, and determine a numeric value of risk for each asset and threat/hazard pair in accordance with the following formula:

$$Risk = Asset \times Threat \times Vulnerability$$

Using the results of the asset value, threat, and vulnerability assessments, risk can be computed.

According to Radvanovsky (2006), quantitative approaches estimate a monetary value/cost associated to a risk and its reduction based on several factors:

- Identifying the likelihood that a damaging event or occurrence will happen;
- Identifying costs resulting from potential losses from the event or occurrence; and
- Identifying costs necessary for mitigating actions resulting from those losses.[5]

Quantitative assessments can include features such as graphical outage as well as other graphics to demonstrate levels of risk and allow for easy comparison between assets. Quantitative tools have been criticized, however, on the basis of not providing sufficient detail to explain problematic issues or identifying solutions for these problems.

The increasing difficulty of accurately estimating asset values, especially data and information assets, may lead assessors to utilize a qualitative approach. Qualitative assessments rely on the assessor's judgment causing it to be more subjective in nature when compared to a quantitative approach.

Step Five: Risk Management

The last step of the assessment process is risk management, which is where mitigation efforts are addressed. This step may include implementation of new organizational policies and procedures as well as advance technological, physical, and asset control implementations.[6] Oftentimes, the building regulatory system has addressed natural disaster mitigation (hurricane, tornado, flood, earthquake, windstorm, and snowstorm) through prescriptive building codes supported by well-established and accepted reference standards, regulations, inspection, and assessment techniques. Some man-made risks (e.g., HAZMAT storage) and specific societal goals (energy conservation and life safety) have also been similarly addressed. The building regulation system, however, has not yet fully addressed most manmade hazards or terrorist threats.

The asset owner ultimately has three choices when addressing the risk posed by terrorism:

1. Do nothing and accept the risk.
2. Perform a risk assessment and manage the risk by installing reasonable mitigation measures.
3. Harden the building against all threats to achieve the least amount of risk.

DHS Vulnerability Assessment Methodologies Report

To assist U.S. government departments and agencies in determining their vulnerabilities and allocating their available resources to provide protection from terrorist activity, the U.S. Department of Homeland Security Office for Domestic Preparedness (DHS ODP) developed a comparison of vulnerability assessment methodologies in 2003 to provide a "consumer reports" type of assessment of available methodologies. In developing the report, subject matter experts were convened and developed a listing of the ten most desirable characteristics of a risk assessment methodology:

1. Clearly identify the infrastructure sector being assessed.
2. Specify the type of security discipline addressed, e.g., physical, information, operations.
3. Collect specific data pertaining to each asset.
4. Identify critical/key assets to be protected.
5. Determine the mission impact of the loss or damage of the asset.
6. Conduct a threat analysis and perform assessment for specific assets.
7. Perform a vulnerability analysis and assessment to specific threats.
8. Conduct analytical risk assessment and determine priorities for each asset.
9. Be relatively low cost to train and conduct.
10. Make specific, concrete recommendations concerning countermeasures.

In sum, forty-four private methodologies were considered in the study with several conclusions. First, the most robust methodologies do not solely focus on one sector of the economy. Second, the quality of the assessor in all cases is very important. Next, while all methodologies determined some measure of risk, often implicitly, few actually calculated a numerical value for that risk. Last, the training required to accurately use one of these methodologies varied greatly in time and cost.

National Infrastructure Protection Plan Risk Management Framework

The National Infrastructure Protection Plan (NIPP) Risk Management Framework establishes the processes for combining consequence, vulnerability, and threat information to produce a comprehensive, systematic, and rational assessment of national or sector risk. The goals of the framework include:

- Defining specific outcomes, conditions, end points, or performance targets that constitute an effective protective posture;

- Development of an inventory of the assets, systems, and networks, including those located outside the United States, that constitute this Nation's critical infrastructure and key resources;
- Determination of risk by combining potential direct and indirect consequences of a terrorist attack or other hazards, known vulnerabilities to various potential attack vectors, and general or specific threat information;
- Aggregation and analysis of risk assessment results to develop a comprehensive picture of asset, system, and network risk, and establish priorities based on risk and determine protection and business continuity initiatives that provide the greatest mitigation of risk;
- Selection of sector-appropriate protective actions or programs to reduce or manage the risk identified and secure the resources needed to address priorities; and
- Utilization of metrics and other evaluation procedures at the national and sector levels to measure progress and assess the effectiveness of the national critical infrastructure/key resources (CI/KR) protection program in improving protection, managing risk, and increasing resiliency.[7]

The NIPP Risk Management Framework is applied on an asset, system, network, or function basis, depending on the characteristics of the individual CI/KR sectors. Information gathered during this process helps determine adjustments to specific CI/KR protection activities.

American Society for Industrial Security International General Security Risk Assessment Guideline

The General Security Risk Assessment Guideline, developed by American Society for Industrial Security (ASIS) International, implements a seven-step process creating a methodology for security professionals by which security risks at a specific location can be identified and communicated, along with appropriate solutions. The guideline also includes definitions of terms, a process flow chart, illustrative material in appendices, and references/bibliography.

As noted above, the guideline identifies seven steps for conducting a general security risk assessment:

1. **Understand the organization and identify the people and assets at risk.** *Assets* include people, all types of property, core business, networks, and information.
2. **Specify loss risk events/vulnerabilities.** Risks or threats are those incidents likely to occur at a site, either due to a history of such events or circumstances in the local environment.
3. **Establish the probability of loss risk and frequency of events.** *Frequency of events* relates to the regularity of the loss event. *Probability of loss risk* is a concept based upon considerations of such issues as prior incidents, trends, warnings, or threats, and such events occurring at the enterprise.
4. **Determine the impact of the events**. The financial, psychological, and related costs associated with the loss of tangible or intangible assets of an organization.

5. **Develop options to mitigate risks**. Identify options available to prevent or mitigate losses through physical, procedural, logical, or related security processes.
6. **Study the feasibility of implementation of options**. Practicality of implementing the options without substantially interfering with the operation or profitability of the enterprise.
7. **Perform a cost/benefit analysis**.

Within the appendices of the guideline, each step of the seven-step practice includes examples and other relevant information to guide the practitioner in developing a better understanding of the underlying principles to be applied in the assessment.[8]

CARVER

CARVER is a target analysis and vulnerability assessment methodology used by the military services and the intelligence community. CARVER is an acronym which stands for:

Criticality: Identify critical assets, single points of failure or "choke points."
Accessibility: Determine ease of access to critical assets.
Recoverability: Compare time it would take to replace or restore a critical asset against maximum acceptable period of disruption.
Vulnerability: Evaluate security system effectiveness against adversary capabilities.
Effect: Consider scope and magnitude of adverse consequences that would result from malicious actions and responses to them.
Recognizability: Evaluate likelihood that potential adversaries would recognize that an asset was critical.

CARVER + Shock

CARVER + Shock is an offensive targeting prioritization tool adapted from the military version (CARVER) for use in the food industry. The tool can be used to assess the vulnerabilities within a system or infrastructure to an attack. By conducting a CARVER + Shock assessment of a food production facility or process, the user can determine the most vulnerable points in their infrastructure, and focus resources on protecting the most susceptible points in their system.

As has been previously mentioned, CARVER is an acronym. For this methodology, a seventh attribute, Shock, has been added to the original six to assess the combined health, economic, and psychological impacts of an attack within the food industry. The attractiveness of a target can then be ranked on a scale from one to ten that has been developed for each of the seven attributes. Conditions that are associated with lower attractiveness (or lower vulnerability) are assigned lower values (e.g., one or two), whereas, conditions associated with higher attractiveness as a target (or higher vulnerability) are assigned higher values (e.g., nine or ten). Evaluating or scoring the various elements of the food sector infrastructure of interest for each of the CARVER + Shock attributes can help identify where an attack is most likely to occur in that infrastructure.

Federal agencies, such as the Food Safety and Inspection Service (FSIS) and the Food and Drug Administration (FDA), have used the CARVER + Shock method to evaluate the potential vulnerabilities of farm-to-table supply chains of various food commodities, as well as individual facilities or processes. These evaluations are carried out during face-to-face meetings of representatives from a particular segment of the food processing industry and federal and state food safety agencies, and generally take two to three days. Using a scale from one to ten for each of the seven CARVER + Shock attributes, the participants score the "target attractiveness" of each segment, or "node," on a process flow diagram of the commodity or facility being evaluated (on the one to ten scale previously discussed). The individual scores for each CARVER + Shock attribute are then added together, so that each node in the diagram can have a total score ranging from seven to ten.[9]

Sandia National Laboratories Security Risk Assessment Methodologies

Another example of a risk assessment methodology has been developed by Sandia National Laboratories to assess risk at various types of facilities and critical infrastructures. The methodology is based on the traditional risk equation:

$$Risk = P_A * (1 - P_E) * C$$

Within the formula, P_A is the likelihood of adversary attack, P_E is security system effectiveness, $1 - P_E$ is adversary success, and C is consequence of loss of the asset.

The process begins with a characterization of the facility, including identification of the undesired events and the respective critical assets. Guidance for defining threats is included, as well as for using the definition of the threat to estimate the likelihood of adversary attack at a specific facility. Relative values of consequence are estimated. Methods are also included for estimating the effectiveness of the security system against the adversary attack. Finally, risk is calculated. In the event that the value of risk is deemed to be unacceptable (too high), the methodology addresses a process for identifying and evaluating security system upgrades in order to reduce risk.

Based on the formula, Sandia National Laboratories have developed several Risk Assessment Methodologies (RAM) to include:

- RAM-D (Dams);
- RAM-T (Electrical Utility Transmission Systems);

- RAM-W (Municipal Water Systems);
- RAM-C (Communities);
- RAM-CF (Chemical Facilities);
- RAM-P (Prisons); and
- RAM-E (Pipelines, Electric Power Generation).

While non-nuclear sites, facilities, and critical infrastructures may not require the highest levels of security used at nuclear weapons sites, the approach is the same. The foundation of a risk assessment methodology is the evaluation and design of an integrated performance-based system. Therefore, each specific RAM comprises the following major steps:

- Planning;
- Threat Assessment;
- Site Characterization;
- Consequence Assessment;
- System Effectiveness;
- Risk Analysis; and
- Risk Management and Reduction.[10]

Summary

This chapter outlined a general framework for the assessment of critical infrastructure. This approach, starting with asset value assessment and ending with risk management, provided a high-level overview of a proven system. It should be noted that each of the steps listed do not represent a stand-alone process, but are one part of an overall system. Next, a DHS assessment of vulnerability assessment methodologies was overviewed and the four primary conclusions of the study identified. Finally, the chapter overviewed several different risk assessment models. These models, each with similarities and differences, are derived from both the public and private sectors. In short, this chapter was developed in an effort to provide the reader with a general understanding of the assessment process and reinforce the importance of assessments in critical infrastructure protection lifecycle.

6

....

Energy Systems: Fossil Fuels, Nuclear Reactors, and Hydroelectric Power

Introduction: Critical Infrastructure Energy Systems

This chapter examines the current state and condition of U.S. energy systems infrastructure to include the processing and distribution of fossil fuels such as oil, coal, and natural gas. Nuclear reactors and hydroelectric power generated from dams and the ability of our U.S. electric grid system to adequately support the growing demands for energy consumption are also discussed.

There has been considerable discussion regarding the United States' growing dependence on fossil fuels such as oil, coal, and natural gas. A disruption in one part of the energy infrastructure can easily cause disruptions throughout the entire system. Oil is the largest single source of the energy used in the world today, with natural gas a close second followed by coal. Petroleum represents nearly 40% of the world's primary energy source and roughly 50% of all of the fuel for our global transportation system. In the next 25 to 30 years, oil consumption is estimated to increase by nearly 60%.

The Middle East holds 58% of the world's oil reserves and 42% of the natural gas reserves. The growth in demand for energy will be dominated by non–Organization for Economic Cooperation and Development (OECD) countries, primarily China and India. World excess capacity in oil production will diminish and has already fallen to less than half the level of the 1990s. Table 6.1 provides estimates of the amount of oil remaining at known oil fields.

Table 6.2 provides an overview of the worldwide oil production capability, oil consumption, oil exporters, and oil importers by country as estimated in 2006. As noted in the table, Saudi Arabia is the top producer of oil and the United States is the top consumer and importer of oil.

Table 6.1 Estimated Oil Reserves

ESTIMATED OIL RESERVES	
RESOURCE CATEGORY	ESTIMATED QUANTITY (BILLION BARRELS)
Conventional Oil:	
Known fields produced	896
Known fields future production	871
New fields future production	133
Deep eater future	60
Polar future	30
Gas liquids	400
Total Conventional:	**2900**
Unconventional Oil:	
Heavy Oil	300

Table 6.3 provides a projected picture of the level of production by type and by region. These scenarios,[1,2] produced by the U.S. Department of Energy, Energy Information Administration, project that U.S. oil use increase is 7.8%, but in reality what we have seen is that U.S. petroleum increased 16% from 1990 to 2000. Using these figures and future projections beginning from 1990, the estimated increase exceeds 50% by 2020.

This risk analysis suggests that regardless of the estimates used and over a wide range of possible assumptions, the peaking of conventional oil production is a serious and timely issue. The peaking of conventional oil production, other than in the Middle East and North Africa, appears to be nearly certain before 2030 and, if more conservative estimates are correct, may have already occurred.

Various studies conclude that when peaking occurs it will take most developed countries twenty to twenty-five years to react or respond and make adjustment to energy consumption and response. If efforts were taken to move to alternative sources of energy, it would take the U.S. petroleum-based distribution infrastructure system more than twenty years to distribute a non-petroleum based energy source. Therefore, while there is a growing interest and desire in the United States to seek alternative energy sources, we will have to rely on these existing systems and the infrastructure necessary to distribute them as we undergo a transition to other cleaner and more sustainable sources of energy.

Fossil Fuel Infrastructure

The U.S. fossil fuel distribution system begins when the oil is transferred to freighters that transport it from the point of origin, which is most likely the Middle East, and deliver it to one of the U.S. ports. To provide some perspective on the amount of oil that is moving through these international waters

Table 6.2 Top World Oil Producers, Consumers, Exporters, and Importers (2006)[3,4]

	TOP WORLD OIL PRODUCERS			TOP WORLD OIL CONSUMERS			TOP WORLD OIL EXPORTERS			TOP WORLD OIL IMPORTERS	
RANK	COUNTRY	PRODUCTION	RANK	COUNTRY	PRODUCTION	RANK	COUNTRY	PRODUCTION	RANK	COUNTRY	PRODUCTION
1	Saudi Arabia	10,719	1	United States	20,588	1	Saudi Arabia	8,651	1	United States	12,220
2	Russia	9,668	2	China	7,274	2	Russia	6,565	2	Japan	5,097
3	United States	8,367	3	Japan	5,222	3	Norway	2,542	3	China	3,438
4	Iran	4,146	4	Russia	3,103	4	Iran	2,519	4	Germany	2,483
5	China	3,836	5	Germany	2,630	5	United Arab Emirates	2,515	5	South Korea	2,150
6	Mexico	3,706	6	India	2,534	6	Venezuela	2,203	6	France	1,893
7	Canada	3,289	7	Canada	2,218	7	Kuwait	2,150	7	India	1,687
8	United Arab Emirates	2,938	8	Brazil	2,183	8	Nigeria	2,146	8	Italy	1,558
9	Venezuela	2,802	9	South Korea	2,157	9	Algeria	1,847	9	Spain	1,555
10	Norway	2,785	10	Saudi Arabia	2,068	10	Mexico	1,676	10	Taiwan	942

daily, in 2007 the total world oil production amounted to approximately 85 million barrels per day (bbl/d) and around one-half, or more than 43 million bbl/d of oil, was moved by tankers on fixed maritime routes. The international energy market is dependent upon reliable transport. The blockage of a chokepoint, even temporarily, can lead to substantial increases in total energy costs. In addition, chokepoints leave oil tankers vulnerable to theft from pirates, terrorist attacks, and political unrest in the form of wars or hostilities as well as shipping accidents, which can lead to disastrous oil spills.

Energy security is a prevalent topic in today's environment of sustained high prices, rapidly rising demand, and active energy geopolitics. The topic holds as much importance as national security, thus drawing the attention of international security specialists. Unfortunately, at this point policies to secure the free flow of abundant energy resources are primarily economic.

....

Questions Concerning Energy Policies

- What role, if any, do individual and institutional security specialists, international security organizations, such as NATO, or national defense organizations and militaries, have to play in comprehensive energy security policies of the West?
- How do intelligent security policies affect the market and investment environment?
- What is the interface between public and commercial security interests?
- How can the security community succeed in doing more good than harm?
- When do major threats to energy flows indeed constitute national security matters?

....

A hearing held by the House Subcommittee on International Terrorism and Nonproliferation (ITNP), entitled Terrorist Threats to Energy Security (2005), issued the following opening statement:

The possibility of energy terrorism—attacks on the world's energy infrastructure—does not generate the same attention as potential chemical, biological, and nuclear terrorism. But, the economic implications of such attacks are potentially enormous. Many believe that a "terror premium" is now factored into the price of a barrel of oil, which is nearly $60. Some suggest that oil terrorism is emerging as a major threat to the global economy. Combating this threat should be part of our complex goal of improving our nation's energy security.

Because of U.S. energy demands, and the global nature of energy markets, terrorists can strike at us most anywhere in the world. Oil markets are tight, with little spare capacity today, and demand is increasing. There is strong evidence that a relatively small disruption to oil production throughout the world could spike world energy prices, severely harming the American economy. We have taken steps to improve the security of the energy infrastructure in the U.S. since 9/11. But, unfortunately terrorist attacks abroad could hurt us as if they were committed here at home.

Al-Qaeda and others seem to be thinking this way. Al-Qaeda documents call for "hitting wells and pipelines that will scare foreign companies from working there and stealing Muslim treasures." Last February, a message posted on an al-Qaeda-affiliated Website, entitled "Map of Future al-Qaeda Operations," stated that terrorists would make it a priority to attack Middle East oil facilities.

The vulnerability of Saudi Arabia to energy terrorism is a particular concern. By far, Saudi Arabia is the world's most important oil producing country, being the largest exporter and the only country with significant excess production capacity. Saudi intelligence reportedly disrupted an attack against the Ras Tanura refinery—the largest in the world—in 2002. Over the last few years, there have been several deadly attacks on Western oil workers, including Americans. These attacks disrupted oil markets and drove up insurance premiums. It is worth noting that some Saudis support these terrorist attacks by their financial support for Wahhabism abroad.[5]

Another critical infrastructure in the distribution of oil and natural gas are the thousands of miles of pipelines, which carry one-half of the world's oil and most of its natural gas. These pipelines are generally built above ground, making them common targets for terrorists and insurgents. Pipelines have been attacked in Chechnya, Turkey, Nigeria, Columbia, and elsewhere, costing local governments billions of dollars. In Iraq, pipeline attacks have been pervasive. It is estimated that pipeline sabotage has cost Iraq more than $10 billion in oil revenues, despite the high priority coalition forces have put on pipeline protection. There is concern that the insurgents who have been attacking Iraqi pipelines have gained a measure of expertise, which will be transferred elsewhere.

Global shipping chokepoints are vulnerabilities in the world's energy system. The Strait of Malacca is one of the world's busiest sea-lanes, through which half the world's oil supplies and two-thirds of its liquefied natural gas transit to energy-dependent Northeast Asia. The narrow and shallow Straits have a long history of piracy, and today well-established terrorist groups operate in the region, including Jemaah Islamiya, who is known for killing hundreds of civilians in the Bali car bombing in October of 2002. Some believe several troubling scenarios are possible, such as a terrorist hijacking of an oil or liquefied natural gas (LNG) tanker, which can be turned into a floating bomb to be detonated in a busy seaport.

Getting oil from an oil well to the refinery and from there to the service station requires a complex transportation and storage system. Millions of barrels of oil are transported every day in tankers, pipelines, and trucks. This transportation system has always been the Achilles heel of the oil industry, but has increased in significance even more so since the emergence of global terrorism.

Terror organizations have planned several attacks against oil tankers in the Arabian Gulf and the Horn of Africa. According to Federal Bureau of Investigation (FBI) Director Robert Mueller, there have been a number of attacks on ships that have been thwarted. In June 2002, a group of al-Qaeda operatives suspected of plotting raids on British and American ships and tankers passing through the Strait of Gibraltar were arrested by the Moroccan government. Unfortunately, not all the attacks have been prevented. In

Table 6.3 Important World Oil Transit Chokepoints

NAME	2006 EST. OIL FLOW (bbl/d)	WIDTH AT NARROWEST POINT	OIL SOURCE ORIGIN	PRIMARY DESTINATION	PAST DISTURBANCES	ALTERNATIVE ROUTES
The Strait of Hormuz	16.5 to 17 million	21 miles	Persian Gulf Nations including Saudi Arabia, Iran, and United Arab Emirates	Japan, the United States, Western Europe, other Asian Countries	Sea mines were installed during the Iran–Iraq War in the 1980s. Terrorists threats post September 11, 2001.	145-mile-long East–West Pipeline through Saudi Arabia to Red Sea.
The Strait of Malacca	15 million	1.7 miles	Persian Gulf Nations, West Africa	All Asia/Pacific consumers, including Japan and China	Disruptions from pirates are a constant threat, including a terrorist attack in 2003. Collisions and oil spills are also a problem. Poor visibility from smoke haze.	Reroute through Lombok or Sunda Strait in Indonesia. Possible pipeline construction between Malaysia and Thailand.
The Suez Canal/ Sumed Pipeline	4.5 million	1,000 feet	Persian Gulf Nations, especially Saudi Arabia, and Asia	Europe and the United States	Suez Canal was closed for eight years after Six–Day War in 1967. Two large oil tankers ran aground in 2007 suspending traffic.	Reroute around the southern tip of Africa (the Cape of Good Hope); additional 6,000 miles.

(Continued)

Table 6.3 (*Continued*)

Name	2006 Est. Oil Flow (bbl/d)	Width at Narrowest Point	Oil Source Origin	Primary Destination	Past Disturbances	Alternative Routes
Bab-el-Mandab	3.3 million	189 miles	The Persian Gulf	Europe and the United States	U.S.S. *Cole* attack in 2002.	Northbound traffic can use the East–West oil pipeline through Saudi Arabia or reroute around the southern tip of Africa (the Cape of Good Hope); additional 6,000 miles.
The Turkish Straits	2.4 million	0.5 miles	Caspian Sea Region	Western and Southern Europe	Numerous past shipping accidents due to the straits sinuous geography. Some terrorists threats were made after September 11, 2001.	No clear alternative. Potential pipelines discussed including a 173-mile pipeline between Russia, Bulgaria, and Greece.
The Panama Canal	0.5 million	110 feet	The United States	The United States and other Central American Countries	Suspected terrorist target.	Reroute around Straits of Magellan, Cape Horn, and Drake Passage; additional 8,000 miles.

October 2002, al-Qaeda carried out an attack where a boat packed with explosives rammed and badly holed a French supertanker off Yemen. Given the fact that half of America's oil is imported, terror organizations like al-Qaeda and its affiliates can disrupt the free flow of crude oil into the U.S. by cutting oil transportation routes. Disruption of oil flows through any of these routes could have a significant impact on global oil prices.

There is no doubt that al-Qaeda is intent on hurting the West economically by interrupting the flow of oil to American, European, and Asian markets. Al-Qaeda leaders have vowed numerous times to cut the "economic lifelines" of the world's industrialized societies. Such attacks would not only disrupt life in the West, but also weaken and perhaps topple Gulf oil monarchies heavily dependent on oil revenues for their survival.

One vulnerable area is the tankers that are used to transport the oil. Tankers are too slow and cumbersome to maneuver away from attackers; they do not have any protection and have nowhere to hide. There are approximately 4,000 tankers plying the world's oceans, and any one of them could be attacked in the high seas or while passing through narrow straits in hazardous areas like the Persian Gulf and Southeast Asia. Geography forces the tankers, carrying much of the world's oil supply, to pass through one or more of three narrow straits—the entrances to the Red Sea (Bab-el-Mandab), the Persian Gulf (Strait of Hormuz), and the Strait of Malacca between Indonesia and Malaysia. A quarter of the world trade passes through the Strait of Malacca, including half of all sea shipments of oil bound for East Asia and two-thirds of global LNG shipments.

Located between Oman and Iran, the Strait of Hormuz connects the Persian Gulf with the Gulf of Oman and the Arabian Sea. Hormuz is the world's most important oil chokepoint due to its daily oil flow of 16.5 to 17 million barrels, which is roughly two-fifths of all seaborne traded oil. At its narrowest point the Strait is twenty-one miles wide, and consists of two-mile wide channels for inbound and outbound tanker traffic, as well as a two-mile wide buffer zone.

The majority of oil exported from the Strait of Hormuz travels to Asia, the United States, and Western Europe. Currently, three-quarters of all Japan's oil needs pass through this Strait. Most of the crude exported through the Strait travels long distances by Very Large Crude Carriers (VLCC), which can carry more than two million barrels of oil per voyage.

Closure of the Strait of Hormuz would require use of longer alternate routes at increased transportation costs. Alternate routes include the 745-mile-long Petroline, also known as the East–West Pipeline, across Saudi Arabia. The East–West Pipeline has a capacity to move five million bbl/d. The Abqaiq-Yanbu natural gas liquids pipeline, which also crosses Saudi Arabia to the Red Sea, has a 290,000-bbl/d capacity. Other alternate routes could include the deactivated 1.65-million bbl/d Iraqi Pipeline that runs across Saudi Arabia (IPSA), or the 0.5-million bbl/d Tap-line to Lebanon. Oil could also be pumped north to Ceyhan in Turkey from Iraq.

Bab-el-Mandab is eighteen miles wide at its narrowest point, making tanker traffic difficult and limited to two 2-mile-wide channels for inbound and outbound shipments. Closure of the Strait could keep tankers from the Persian Gulf from reaching the Suez Canal or Sumed Pipeline, diverting them around the southern tip of Africa. This would effectively engage spare tanker capacity, and add to transit time and cost.

These straits are all controlled by Muslim countries where terrorists are known to operate. They are so narrow that a single burning supertanker and its spreading oil slick could block the route for other tankers, hence rocking the entire global oil market for several weeks at the very least.

The risks to our energy supply are frighteningly real, and there is a limit to our ability to deal with them. Only by increasing our energy independence would we be able to minimize the need to transport oil across the globe and thus reduce our vulnerability to these types of attacks. The impact of choke-points can also apply to the complex system of pipelines, through which about 40% of world's oil flows. They run over thousands of miles and across some of the most volatile areas in the world. A simple explosive device could puncture a pipeline, rendering it inoperable. Due to their length, they are very difficult to protect. This makes pipelines potential targets for terrorists. For example, in the summer of 2001, a terror attack was committed on an oil pipeline that feeds Saudi Arabia's Ras Tanura terminal, which is the biggest oil-loading point in Saudi Arabia.

New threats to the security of oil supplies directly affect oil prices. Maritime insurers, for example, have already begun to sharply raise the premiums charged to cover tankers in risky waters. Premiums insurers charge tankers passing through Yemen waters tripled since the supertanker attack in Yemen in 2002. For a typical supertanker carrying about two million barrels of oil, the rate rose to $450,000 a trip from $150,000, adding about fifteen cents a barrel to the delivered cost of the oil; and that is just for the ship—the cargo is insured separately. Terror attacks in other locations will carry premium increases in their wake. The increasing costs of securing pipelines, oil terminals, and tankers are all reflected in the price of gasoline.

Once the oil finally reaches a U.S. port, it then moves into our infrastructure system, which is made up of pipelines, rail cars, and fuel tankers. The system is quite complex, as illustrated below.

Much of the oil that is distributed throughout the country comes in from the Gulf Coast ports, as detailed below.

The largest-diameter lines transport the consolidated natural gas stream to onshore compression stations, dehydration and separation facilities, processing plants, and eventually the Minerals Management Service. The Minerals Management Service estimated that 3,050 of the Gulf's 4,000 platforms and 22,000 of the 33,000 miles of gulf pipelines were in the direct path of either Hurricane Katrina or Rita.

Platforms in shallow water (less than 1,000 feet) are generally fixed platforms, compliant towers, or tension leg platforms that are attached to the seafloor. Typically five to twenty wells are drilled from production platforms, and there are approximately 4,000 platforms in the Gulf of Mexico.

The damage from Hurricanes Katrina and Rita caused the biggest disruption to operations that the industry has ever seen. Hurricane Katrina, which was a Category Five Storm (winds greater than 155 miles per hour), destroyed forty-four platforms and damaged twenty others. It also damaged at least 100 pipelines in federal waters, thirty-six of which were large diameter lines (greater than ten inches), which resulted in the shut-in of at least eight natural gas processing plants.

The offshore and onshore service industry supporting Outer Continental Shelf (OCS) natural gas production and deliveries was also devastated by the hurricanes. Docks and fleets were destroyed, electric power was lost on a wide-scale basis, and transportation fuels were not available for boats, helicopters, and ground transportation that were vital to the recovery of transmission lines for delivery to end users.

Nuclear Reactor Infrastructure

Nuclear power accounts for approximately 20% of the Nation's electrical use, provided by 104 commercial nuclear reactors licensed to operate in the United States. The Nuclear Reactors, Materials, and Waste (Nuclear) Sector includes: nuclear power plants; non-power nuclear reactors used for research, testing, and training; nuclear materials used in medical, industrial, and academic settings; nuclear fuel fabrication facilities; decommissioning reactors; and the transportation, storage, and disposal of nuclear material and waste.

....

The **U.S. Department of Energy,** through the National Nuclear Security Administration (NNSA), works to enhance national security through the military application of nuclear energy. This is achieved through the provision of safe, militarily effective nuclear propulsion plants to the U.S. Navy and the safe and reliable operation of those plants. The NNSA also maintains and enhances the safety, reliability, and performance of the United States nuclear weapons stockpile.

....

There were a total of 104 commercial nuclear generating plants operating in the United States in 2007. These nuclear facilities produce a total of 97,400 megawatts of electricity, which is approximately 20% of the Nation's total electric energy consumption. Electricity from these nuclear power plants, located in thirty-one states, supplies one of every five U.S. homes and businesses, and nuclear power plants provide nearly 75% of the electricity that comes from non-emitting sources of electricity. The United States is the world's largest supplier of commercial nuclear power.

The U.S. Department of Energy (DOE) projects that U.S. electricity demands will rise 25% by 2030. That means the United States would need hundreds of new power plants to provide electricity for our homes and continued economic growth. Maintaining nuclear energy's current 20% share of generation would require building three reactors every two years starting in 2016, based on DOE forecasts.

Figure 6.1 Operating Nuclear Plants in the United States (Image Courtesy: U.S. Nuclear Regulatory Commission)

The impact of this growing demand on electricity and nuclear energy is best illustrated by a power outage that occurred in 2003. The Northeast Blackout of 2003 was a massive widespread power outage that occurred throughout parts of the Northeastern and Midwestern United States, and Ontario, Canada on Thursday, August 14, 2003, at approximately 4:15 PM EDT.[6]

The outage also affected nine nuclear power plants that had to shut down due to the power outage. They had to halt production because the electrical power grid used to supply energy to the Northeast region failed. The nuclear start-up process typically takes approximately five hours if the plant is in a "stand-by" rather than a "shutdown" mode. The nine U.S. nuclear power plants affected by the blackout were functioning properly, but due to the electrical grid infrastructure they were unable to supply the electricity needed to these areas. The following nine nuclear power plants shut down due to instability in the electricity grid: Indian Point 2 and 3 in New York; Perry (Ohio); Fermi (Michigan); Ginna (New York); FitzPatrick (New York); Oyster Creek (New Jersey); and Nine Mile Point 1 and 2 (New York).

The fact that the U.S. electric grid infrastructure is in need of modernization is also supported by a DOE/Energy Information Administration (EIA) report published in 2004. This report concluded that the data collections relied on by the federal government to monitor reliability have not kept pace with the ascendancy of transmission in a restructuring industry. The government does not have the electrical models (power flow models) and data necessary to verify that existing and planned transmission capability is adequate to keep the lights on. The industry's reported plans for assuring reliable operation in the future are not necessarily those analyzed in the power flow analyses that industries submit to the Federal Energy Regulatory Commission

(FERC). Investment in the high-voltage grid for metering, monitoring, communications, software, and computation is unknown. Neither the industry nor the government has data adequate to allow rigorous cost-benefit analyses of transmission-related investments to enhance reliability.[7]

••

The **U.S. power transmission system** is in urgent need of modernization. Growth in electricity demand and investment in new power plants has not been matched by investment in new transmission facilities. Maintenance expenditures have decreased 1% per year since 1992. Existing transmission facilities were not designed for the current level of demand, resulting in an increased number of 'bottlenecks,' which increase costs to consumers and elevate the risk of blackouts.[8]

••

The problem is compounded by the fact that while the federal government acknowledges that the electrical grid infrastructure is outdated and the actual condition of this system is unknown, the EIA reported an increase in the production of energy, which correlates to increase use and demand. The total U.S. net generation of electricity was approximately 3.9 billion kilowatt hours in 2003 with production increasing to net generation of 4.16 trillion kilowatt hours in 2006. Figure 6.2 depicts the percentage of electricity by type of fuel source with coal representing nearly 50% of the fuel used to generate our countries energy needs.

To distribute that power, the U.S. electric transmission grid consists of nearly 160,000 miles of high-voltage (230 kilovolts and greater) transmission lines. In 1999, America's electric utilities spent more than $3 billion maintaining and operating these links to customers, and $2.3 billion on construction expenditures (including replacements, additions, and improvements).[9]

Despite these investments, the state of the grid remains a cause for deep concern among experts. The Consumer Energy Council of America (CECA), a national association of utility officials, state regulators, and consumer advocates, warned that support for new investment in the transmission grid is declining. The CECA noted that investment in the transmission grid was at a low of $83 million per year from 1975 to 1999. It increased to $286 million annually from 1999 through 2003. Although the investment increases are good, total U.S.

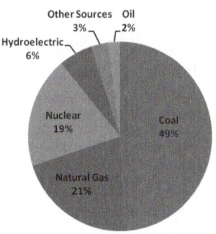

Figure 6.2 Net Generation of Electricity in 2007

transmission capacity decreased by approximately 19% per year between 1992 and 2002. Investment in transmission lines during the next 10 years is expected to be $3 billion to $4 billion per year, while the line-miles of transmission added will be only one-third the rate of electricity demand. In addition, transmission maintenance expenditures have decreased at a rate of one percent annually since 1992, which can affect the reliability of the system.

In 2002, the DOE was equally blunt:

> There is growing evidence that the U.S. transmission system is in urgent need of modernization. The system has become congested because growth in electricity demand and investment in new generation facilities have not been matched by investment in new transmission facilities. Transmission problems have been compounded by the incomplete transition to fair and efficient competitive wholesale electricity markets. Because the existing transmission system was not designed to meet present demand, daily transmission constraints or "bottlenecks" increase electricity costs to consumers and increase the risk of blackouts.[10]

Those fears were realized in the Northeast Blackout of 2003. A series of power plants and transmission lines went offline because of instability in the transmission system in three states. The loss of these plants and transmission lines led to greater instability in the regional power transmission system, and within four hours there was a rapid cascade of additional plant and transmission line outages and widespread power outages. The blackout affected as many as 50 million customers in the United States and Canada, as well as a wide range of vital services and commerce. Air and ground transportation systems shut down, drinking water systems and sewage processing plants stopped operating, manufacturing was disrupted, and several emergency communications systems stopped functioning. The lost productivity and revenue have been estimated to be in the billions of dollars.

In a letter to Congress in February 2004, the North American Electric Reliability Council (NERC), a consortium of public and private power producers that seeks to enforce compliance with voluntary reliability standards, was blunt in its assessment of the performance of the North American transmission grid:

> NERC's analysis of the actions and events that led to the blackout showed that several violations of NERC operating policies contributed directly to the August [2003] outage. This is yet another clear signal that voluntary compliance with reliability rules is no longer adequate, and underscores the urgent need for Congress to authorize the creation of a mandatory reliability system that provides for the establishment and enforcement of reliability rules by an independent, industry-led electric reliability organization, subject to oversight by the Federal Energy Regulatory Commission (FERC) within the United States.[11]

Not all utilities own transmission lines (that is, they are not vertically integrated), and no independent power producers or power marketers own

Figure 6.3 U.S. Power Grids (Image Courtesy: U.S. Department of Energy)

transmission lines. Over the years, these transmission lines have evolved into three major national networks (power grids), which also include smaller groupings or power pools. The three networks are the Eastern Interconnect, the Western Interconnect, and the Texas Interconnect, as illustrated below. The Texas Interconnect is not interconnected with the other two networks (except by certain direct current lines). The other two networks have limited interconnections to each other. Both the Western and the Texas Interconnect are linked with different parts of Mexico. The Eastern and Western Interconnects are completely integrated with most of Canada or have links to the Quebec Province power grid. Virtually all U.S. utilities are interconnected with at least one other utility by these three major grids; the exceptions are utilities in Alaska and Hawaii. The interconnected utilities within each power grid coordinate operations and buy and sell power among themselves. Within each of these power grids, different types of equipment and facilities are owned by many different entities.[12] The major networks consist of extra-high-voltage connections between individual utilities designed to permit the transfer of electrical energy from one part of the network to another. These transfers are restricted, on occasion, because of a lack of contractual arrangements or because of inadequate transmission capability.

Over 9,500 miles of new high-voltage transmission lines were built during the 1990s (nearly a 7% increase). Most of that construction emphasized 230 kilovolts (kV) as the primary voltage used for transmission, but preference for this voltage is projected to drop. Overall, new investment is not at the same level as in the past, yet some 345 kV projects have been undertaken.[13]

Over the past 10 years, utilities have been reluctant to put major investment into transmission lines without knowing how deregulation would affect these assets. Therefore, the growth of the grid was slow and remains so. While the level of new transmission lines being constructed is low, the upgrading of existing transmission assets for a number of utilities is a major effort. Upgrades would provide the fastest and most economical approach to improvement of the grid, but there is a limit to the improvements that can be made using this approach.[14]

Thus, the future of the U.S. transmission network is uncertain and is a continuing concern. Overall, use of the transmission system is growing without significant additions of new construction or upgrades. Approval of new projects and the acquisition of new rights-of-way have been difficult. Many customers oppose having new transmission facilities built nearby. These transmission facilities support interstate commerce, but the sighting and approval are generally a state and local governmental responsibility. In addition, the prelude to deregulation created and continues, to some degree, to cause limited investment in the transmission system.[15]

In the event of the loss of power from the electricity grid, like the event in 2003, the Nuclear Regulatory Commission (NRC) requires that nuclear power plants have dual onsite electric power systems and dual offsite power sources to assure that systems and components will function to safely shut down the plant. Backup power typically is provided by diesel generators, and more than sufficient fuel supplies for the generators are present onsite as well. When the entire grid collapses as it did during the Northeast Blackout in 2003, safety systems are powered by the back-up onsite systems.

Nuclear power plant's electronic security systems also have independent back-up power to keep them functioning. Beyond that, nuclear power plants are protected by a paramilitary security force of 7,000 highly trained, well-armed officers, nearly two-thirds of whom have prior military, law enforcement, or industry security experience. Power plant structures also are protected by a combination of robust structural plant designs and redundant physical barriers.

According to the DHS, nuclear power plant security has been strengthened during the past six years through a commitment of more than $2 billion. This includes the addition of thousands of security officers, better weaponry and detection equipment, and a finely integrated response strategy with federal, state, and local resources. The entirety of the Nation's nuclear security infrastructure is independently tested and evaluated by the NRC. Nuclear power plants have a clear security advantage in that the structures that house reactors and critical operating and safety systems are built to withstand extreme natural events, such as hurricanes, tornadoes, and floods. Concentric security perimeters include physical barriers to protect against unauthorized entry and vehicle intrusion, and security zones are patrolled by well-trained, highly armed officers who may use protective steel defensive positions located throughout the plant if challenged. In the inner-most security zone, access to vital areas is strictly controlled using biometrics and other technologies. Security areas are also constantly monitored using state-of-the-art detection equipment.

The Nuclear Energy industry was one of the first among the critical infrastructure sectors to volunteer for comprehensive security reviews involving federal, state, and local resources that could be called upon in the event of a credible threat at a nuclear power plant. Each nuclear plant has undergone a series of exercises, which includes mock terrorist attacks of the plant by specially trained adversary forces that are skilled in offensive tactics. These adversary teams comprise full-time, highly trained security experts that test each plant's security capability to the exacting standards required by the federal government. The NRC independently evaluates both the performance of the adversary team and the industry's security capabilities and strategies during the force-on-force exercises.

The need for greater investment in the Nation's energy infrastructure is evidenced by a DOE forecast that as much as 334,000 megawatts of new electricity generating capacity will be needed by 2025. While U.S. nuclear power plants in 2004 achieved another record year of electricity production—788.5 billion kilowatt-hours of electricity—there are limits on the amount of additional electricity output existing nuclear power plants can produce.[16]

Hydroelectric Infrastructure

Of the renewable energy sources that generate electricity, hydropower is the most often used. One of the reasons for this is that in the United States the dependence on renewable energy is limited, and the primary source for this type of energy is hydroelectric power generated from dams. This type of energy accounted for 7% of total U.S. electricity generation and 73% of generation from renewables in 2005.

Hydropower is one of the oldest sources of energy and was used thousands of years ago to turn a paddle wheel for purposes such as grinding grain. Our Nation's first industrial use of hydropower to generate electricity occurred in 1880, when 16 brush-arc lamps were powered using a water turbine at the Wolverine Chair Factory in Grand Rapids, Michigan. The first U.S. hydroelectric power plant opened on the Fox River near Appleton, Wisconsin, on September 30, 1882. Until that time, coal was the only fuel used to produce electricity. Because the source of hydropower is water, hydroelectric power plants must be located on a water source. Therefore, it was not until the technology to transmit electricity over long distances was developed that hydropower became widely used.

More than one-half of the total U.S. hydroelectric capacity for electricity generation is concentrated in three States: Washington, California, and Oregon. Approximately 27% is generated in Washington at the Nation's largest hydroelectric facility—the Grand Coulee Dam. It is important to note that only a small percentage of all dams in the United States produce electricity. Most dams were constructed solely to provide irrigation and flood control.[17]

7

....

Transportation Sector – Marine, Road, Rail, and Aviation

Sector Overview

This chapter will provide the reader with an overview of the Transportation Systems and the Postal and Shipping sectors critical infrastructure and key resources. A significant portion of the content for this chapter was taken from the Transportation Systems: Critical Infrastructure and Key Resources Sector-Specific Plan as input to the National Infrastructure Protection Plan.[1]

The Transportation Systems Sector-Specific Plan (SSP) is one of the seventeen sector plans required by the National Infrastructure Protection Plan (NIPP), which implements the requirements of Homeland Security Presidential Directive 7 (HSPD) -7, Critical Infrastructure Identification, Prioritization, and Protection (December 13, 2003). Under HSPD-7, the Nation's critical infrastructure and key resources (CI/KR) are organized into sectors with certain federal agencies designated as Sector-Specific Agencies (SSAs). These agencies are responsible for coordinating the protection activities of the sectors' security partners to prepare for and respond to threats that could have a debilitating effect on security or economic well-being. The U.S. Department of Homeland Security (DHS) is the SSA for the Transportation Systems Sector. The Secretary of Homeland Security has assigned this responsibility to the Transportation Security Administration (TSA) and the U.S. Coast Guard (USCG) for the maritime mode of the Transportation Systems Sector. The DHS, through the TSA and the USCG, in collaboration with the Department of Transportation (DOT) and its modal administrations, and in close cooperation with their federal, state, local, tribal, and private industry security partners, shares the responsibility for developing, implementing, and updating the Transportation Systems SSP and the supporting modal implementation plan annexes. The transportation network is critical to the Nation's way of life and economic vitality. Ensuring its security is the mission charged to all sector partners, including government (federal, state, regional, local, and tribal) and private industry stakeholders.

Every day, the transportation network connects cities, manufacturers, and retailers, moving large volumes of goods and individuals through a complex network of approximately 4 million miles of roads and highways, more than 100,000 miles of rail, 600,000 bridges, more than 300 tunnels and numerous seaports, 2 million miles of pipeline, 500,000 train stations, and 500 public-use airports.

The Transportation Systems Sector consists of six key subsectors, or modes:

1. **Aviation** includes aircraft, air traffic control systems, and approximately 450 commercial airports and 19,000 additional airfields. This mode includes civil and joint use military airports, heliports, short takeoff and landing ports, and seaplane bases.
2. **Maritime Transportation System** consists of about 95,000 miles of coastline, 361 ports, more than 10,000 miles of navigable waterways, 3.4 million square miles of Exclusive Economic Zone to secure, and intermodal landside connections, which allow the various modes of transportation to move people and goods to, from, and on the water.
3. **Highway** encompasses more than four million miles of roadways and supporting infrastructure. Vehicles include automobiles, buses, motorcycles, and all types of trucks.
4. **Mass Transit** includes multiple-occupancy vehicles, such as transit buses, trolleybuses, vanpools, ferryboats, monorails, heavy (subway) and light rail, automated guideway transit, inclined planes, and cable cars designed to transport customers on local and regional routes.
5. **Pipeline Systems** include vast networks of pipeline that traverse hundreds of thousands of miles throughout the country, carrying nearly all of the nation's natural gas and about 65 percent of hazardous liquids, as well as various chemicals.
6. **Rail** consists of hundreds of railroads, more than 143,000 route-miles of track, more than 1.3 million freight cars, and roughly 20,000 locomotives.

The Transportation Systems Sector is highly complex because of a number of reasons. One reason is sheer scale—the sector is composed of hundreds of thousands of assets, links, and nodes spread across the six modes. Some assets, such as airports or rail yards, are stationary. Others, such as hazardous materials (HAZMAT) trucks or commercial airplanes, are mobile and may be used as weapons, as well as targets. These assets are widely distributed geographically, in both rural and urban areas, covering all fifty states and territories. Secondly, the Transportation Systems Sector consists of numerous and diverse stakeholders, including federal, state, and local government agencies, as well as private owner/operators. Owner/operators across the modes may face different decision incentives and constraints. A third reason for the

The **Transportation Sector** is a very large, complex, and interdependent network of hundreds of thousands of stationary and mobile assets that are geographically disperse and owned and operated by numerous stakeholders.

complexity that characterizes the Nation's transportation network is interconnectedness and supply chain implications among the assets and systems which it comprises. The security challenge faced by the 21st century transportation community is due, in large part, to the interconnected, interdependent network that has been created to meet the demands of the economy and of the citizens. Over the past two decades, the sector, like most other infrastructures, has expanded and altered its business models on a global scale to take advantage of the so-called "network effect."[2] While these changes have significantly enhanced the efficiency and effectiveness of the sector, they have also resulted in a more complicated operating model. The result is a transportation network that becomes more and more complex and interdependent each year.

Transportation Systems Sector Security Goals and Objectives

Goal 1: Prevent and deter acts of terrorism using or against the transportation system

Terrorist attacks may seek to directly disrupt transportation systems, or they may use transportation systems to carry out larger attacks against the American people. The primary goal of the Transportation Systems Sector is to prevent and deter criminal and terrorist attacks before they happen without disrupting the free flow of commerce or compromising civil liberties.

Objectives

- Implement flexible, layered, and effective security programs using risk management principles;
- Increase vigilance of travelers and transportation workers; and
- Enhance information and intelligence sharing among Transportation Systems Sector security partners.

Goal 2: Enhance resilience of the U.S. transportation system

The resilience of a transportation system can be improved by increasing its ability to accommodate and absorb damage from natural disasters or terrorist attacks without catastrophic failure.

Objectives

- Manage and reduce the risk associated with key nodes, links, and flows within critical transportation systems to improve overall network survivability. Many transportation systems contain a small number of critical assets that, if attacked, could result in catastrophic failure. These assets can take the form of a node, a link, or a flow.

- Enhance the capacity for rapid and flexible response and recovery to all-hazards events. Response and recovery activities traditionally include first-responder actions and the plans, training, and exercises that support them. Response and recovery activities can also include pre-establishing re-routing procedures, emergency suppliers, and evacuation processes.

Goal 3: Improve the cost-effective use of resources for transportation security

Minimizing unnecessary duplication of efforts, improving coordination, and aligning resources to the highest risks all help the Transportation Systems Sector improve the cost-effective use of resources.

Objectives

- Align sector resources with the highest priority transportation security risks using both risk and economic analyses as decision criteria.
- Ensure robust sector participation in the development and implementation of public sector programs for CI/KR protection.
- Ensure coordination and enhance risk-based prioritization of Transportation Systems Sector security Research, Development, Test, and Evaluation (RDT&E) efforts.
- Align risk analysis methodologies with NIPP Baseline Criteria for assessment methodologies. The NIPP Baseline Criteria states that risk analysis methodologies should be credible, documented, transparent, reproducible, and accurate, and they should enable sector leaders to make sound, cost-effective security decisions.

Transportation Systems Sector Government Coordinating Council (GCC)

There are a number of offices and agencies within the DHS that have responsibilities that directly or indirectly contribute to transportation network security. Additionally, agencies outside of the DHS also have responsibilities and interests in the Transportation Systems Sector. Please note that at the time of the writing of this text the DHS was undergoing considerable reorganization, and some of these agencies listed below may no longer exist or may have been subsumed into other divisions. These changes are in part due to the Post-Katrina Emergency Management Reform Act signed into law in October 2006. This Act called for reorganization of the department's preparedness functions, eliminating the Preparedness Directorate. The law was intended to prevent future federal disaster response failures like those after Hurricane Katrina. The result was a reconstituted Federal Emergency Management Agency (FEMA) that expanded its reach to include many of the

Preparedness Directorate's activities under FEMA's umbrella and elevating FEMA's administrator to the undersecretary level. Below are descriptions of Transportation Systems Sector GCC members.

Transportation Security Administration

The Transportation Security Administration (TSA) was created under the Aviation and Transportation Security Act (ATSA), which gave TSA responsibility for security in all modes of transportation. As part of its security mission, TSA is responsible for assessing intelligence, enforcing security-related regulations and requirements, ensuring the adequacy of security measures at transportation facilities, and carrying out other transportation security responsibilities. Under HSPD-7, TSA was designated as the SSA for the Transportation Systems Sector by DHS.

U.S. Coast Guard

The U.S. Coast Guard (USCG) is a multi-mission maritime service and one of the nation's five Armed Services. Its mission is to protect the public, the environment, and U.S. economic interests in the Nation's ports and waterways, along the coast, on the high seas, or in any maritime region, as required, to support national security. In the event of a maritime incident, USCG will often act in a first-responder capacity. USCG also serves as the SSA for the Maritime transportation mode. The DHS, with the USCG as its executive agent, has the primary responsibility for maritime homeland security, including coordinating mitigation measures to expedite the recovery of infrastructure and transportation systems in the maritime domain, with the exception of Department of Defense (DOD) installations.

Training and Exercise Integration/Training Operations (TEI/TO)

This new FEMA office was formerly the Office of Grants and Training (OGT). The mission of Training and Exercises Integration/Training Operations (TEI/TO) is to provide first responders with high-quality training that enhances their skills for preventing, protecting, responding to, and recovering from man-made and natural catastrophic events. TEI/TO serves the Nation's first responder community, offering more than 125 courses to help build critical skills that responders need to function effectively in mass consequence events. TEI/TO primarily serves state, local, and tribal entities in ten professional disciplines, but has expanded to serve private sector and citizens in recognition of their significant role in domestic preparedness. Instruction is offered at the awareness, performance, and management and planning levels. Students attend TEI/TO courses to learn how to apply the basic skills of their profession in the context of preparing, preventing, deterring, responding to, and recovering from acts of terrorism and catastrophic events.

National Preparedness Directorate

The National Preparedness Directorate (NPD) was established on April 1, 2007, as a result of the Post-Katrina Emergency Management Reform Act of

2006 to oversee coordination and development strategies necessary to prepare for all-hazards. As part of this mission, NPD provides policy and planning guidance that builds prevention, protection, response, and recovery capabilities. NPD programs leverage training courses, policy development, exercises, and technical assistance to build emergency capabilities. Additionally, NPD is developing methods to assess levels of emergency preparedness within individual jurisdictions and throughout the nation.

Department of Transportation
The U.S. Department of Transportation (DOT) has the responsibility for promoting safety, including hazardous materials security, through advocacy, regulation, enforcement, grants, and other means. DOT modal administrations manage many transportation programs that directly affect the protection of critical transportation infrastructure. As stated in HSPD-7, the DOT and the DHS will collaborate on all matters related to transportation security and transportation infrastructure protection in order to balance security requirements with the safety, mobility, and economic needs of the Nation and be prepared to respond to emergencies that affect the viability of the sector.

Department of Energy
As SSA for the Energy Sector, the U.S. Department of Energy (DOE) is responsible for ensuring the security of the nation's energy CI/KR. DOE is a member of the Transportation Systems Sector GCC in its capacity as the lead federal agency responsible for energy. Energy commodities are transported by pipelines, ships, barge, rail, and tanker trucks—assets and systems that cross over into the responsibility of the Transportation Systems Sector.

Department of Defense
The U.S. Department of Defense (DOD) is responsible for defending the Nation from external threats and owns a wide spectrum of support resources that could be requested during a transportation security incident. The DOD has equities in the security of the commercial aspects of the Transportation Systems Sector and has policy devoted to the security of DOD shipments. The DOD, as a member of the Transportation Systems Sector GCC, is involved with the collaboration to determine transportation security policies and decisions.

Department of Justice
The U.S. Department of Justice (DOJ) acts to reduce criminal and terrorists threats, and investigates and prosecutes actual or attempted attacks on, sabotage of, or disruptions of CI/KR in collaboration with the DHS.

Federal Bureau of Investigation
The Federal Bureau of Investigation (FBI) is the principal investigative arm of the DOJ and the lead federal agency for investigations of terrorist acts or

terrorist threats by individuals or groups inside of the United States or directed at U.S. citizens or institutions abroad, where such acts are within the federal criminal jurisdiction of the United States. Within the Transportation Systems Sector, the FBI acts to reduce terrorist threats, as well as investigate and prosecute actual or attempted terrorist attacks on, sabotage of, or disruption of CI/KR. The FBI investigates and prosecutes general criminal violations within the transportation system as directed by statute.

Customs and Border Protection

U.S. Customs and Border Protection (CBP) plays a key role in transportation security and protects against external threats that seek entry into the United States. CBP accomplishes this wide-ranging responsibility by reviewing and verifying cargo manifests, inspecting containers and persons, patrolling the Nation's land borders, and patrolling airways and marine ports. CBP officers are stationed at airports and seaports as well. CBP is also involved in security efforts pertaining to cross-border rail, trucking, and pipeline transportation.

Department of Commerce

The U.S. Department of Commerce (DOC) has many component agencies involved with transportation security-related activities, such as the National Institute of Standards and Technology (NIST), the National Oceanic and Atmospheric Administration (NOAA), the National Telecommunications and Information Administration (NTIA), and the Bureau of Industry and Security (BIS). The BIS advances U.S. national security, foreign policy, and economic interests for the DOC, and plays a critical role in developing, promoting, and implementing policies that ensure a strong, technologically superior defense industrial base. BIS activities include regulating the export of sensitive goods and technologies in an effective and efficient manner; enforcing export control, anti-boycott, and public safety laws; cooperating with and assisting other countries on export control and strategic trade issues; assisting U.S. industry to comply with international arms control agreements; and monitoring the viability of the U.S. defense industrial base and seeking to ensure that it is capable of satisfying U.S. national and homeland security needs.

State and Local Security Partners

In addition to the federal partners identified above, DHS and the Transportation Systems Sector work closely with state and local agencies who are often first on the scene of a transportation security incident. It is the responsibility of federal officials to work closely with regional preparedness organizations to coordinate recovery efforts and restore public confidence following an attack. These agencies also work in close proximity to the owners or operators of the Nation's transportation infrastructure. Public safety agencies, such as law enforcement, fire/rescue, and emergency medical services (EMS), continue to be an integral part of gathering transportation security information and sharing it with the private sector owners and operators.

One of the key lessons learned from the September 11, 2001, attacks were the gaps in the global transportation network resulting in a number of very critical security vulnerabilities. The Transportation Systems Sector recognizes the need to engage with international partners to:

- Identify and understand threats, assess vulnerabilities, and determine potential impacts to the global transportation system;
- Exchange and share effective practices to deter, understand, and prevent future attacks; and
- Promote measures that safeguard the movement of people, goods, and services through international transportation systems.

Examples of this cooperation are the Security and Prosperity Partnership of North America (SPP), which establishes ongoing working groups, including representatives from various federal agencies and Canadian and Mexican ministries to further North American security goals, and the International Maritime Organization (IMO), a specialized agency of the United Nations, which is responsible for measures to improve the safety and security of international shipping and to prevent marine pollution from ships. TSA has taken a leadership role in coordinating such relationships. Asia-Pacific Economic Cooperation (APEC) is the premier forum for facilitating economic growth, cooperation, trade, and investment in the Asia-Pacific region, and TSA played a key role in launching the Aviation Security Sub-Group in APEC. Many security enhancement efforts are already underway; however, the Transportation Systems Sector, through the leadership of TSA, has identified several key strategic focus areas. These areas are:

- Assisting the International Civil Aviation Organization (ICAO) in the area of compliance and enforcement to ensure that aviation security vulnerabilities are identified through the Universal Security Audit Program;
- Increasing international focus on the need for pipeline, freight rail, and mass transit standards and/or best practices;
- Enhancing the ability of key international partners to identify terrorists and/or the instruments of terrorism by sharing technological expertise, lessons learned, and developing new advanced approaches;
- Strengthening international security baseline standards by actively participating in standard-setting organizations;
- Providing effective mechanisms for sharing and reporting information to foreign authorities and stakeholders through expert-level working groups, private conferences, bilateral meetings, and speeches; and
- Minimizing disruptions to the flow of passengers and commerce through regular consultations with international partners to discuss differences in policy or approach, working toward harmonization of measures.

Strengthening transportation security across all modes of the global transportation network requires strong collaboration worldwide to protect the traveling public from terrorism and reduces the potential for a disruption in the flow of commerce.

Private Sector and Other Infrastructure Owners and Operators

Approximately 80% of the critical infrastructure in the United States is privately owned and operated. This of course includes a majority of the transportation systems in this country. Therefore, the federal government must leverage industry's efforts in protecting critical assets through an effective public–private partnership. Challenges most frequently cited in establishing these relationships are the lack of an effective relationship with DHS as well as private sector hesitancy to share information on vulnerabilities with the government or within the sector for fear the information would be released and open to competitors. There appears to be a lack of trust in the DHS, and fear that sensitive information would be released are recurring barriers to the private sector's sharing information with the federal government. The DHS has acknowledged these barriers and continues to overcome these obstacles by the ongoing work of developing and updating private sector response plans.

The Private Sector Office is part of the Office of Policy which is responsible for developing and integrating DHS-wide policies, planning, and programs in order to better coordinate DHS' prevention, protection, response, and recovery missions. This office is responsible for:

- Advising the Secretary on the impact of the Department's policies, regulations, processes, and actions on the private sector.
- Creating and fostering strategic communications with the private sector to enhance the primary mission of the Department to protect the American homeland.
- Interfacing with other relevant federal agencies with homeland security missions to assess the impact of these agencies on the private sector.
- Creating and managing private sector advisory councils composed of representatives of industries and associations designated by the Secretary to: (a) Advise the Secretary on private sector products, applications, and solutions as they relate to homeland security challenges; and (b) Advise the Secretary on homeland security policies, regulations, processes, and actions that affect the participating industries and associations.
- Working with federal laboratories, federally funded research and development centers, other federally funded organizations, academia, and the private sector to develop innovative approaches to address homeland security challenges to produce and deploy the best available technologies for homeland security missions.
- Promoting existing public–private partnerships and development of new public–private partnerships to provide for collaboration and mutual support to address homeland security challenges
- Assisting in the development and promotion of private sector best practices to secure critical infrastructure.
- Coordinating industry efforts regarding department functions to identify private sector resources that could be effective in supplementing government efforts to prevent or respond to a terrorist attack.
- Consulting with the various DHS elements and Department of Commerce on matters of concern to private sector, including travel and tourism industries.

Moreover, in the recently completed DHS Strategic Plan for years 2008 through 2013, there is a specific section devoted to critical infrastructure referred to as Strategic Goal #3 Protect and Strengthen the Resilience of the Nation's Critical Infrastructure and Key Resources. The goal states that DHS will lead the effort to mitigate potential vulnerabilities of the Nation's critical infrastructure and key resources to ensure its protection and resilience. The goal also states that efforts will be taken to foster mutually beneficial partnerships with public and private sector that own and operate a majority of the critical infrastructure and key resources.

Transportation Systems Sector Risk Views

The national transportation network is a large, multifaceted, interdependent mix of links, nodes, flows, processes, agreements, rules, relationships, and regulations. To describe it as complex would be an understatement. The DHS suggest that to better grasp this complexity, stakeholders within the Transportation Systems Sector may want to consider using thematic perspectives or risk views. These risk views are distinct and complementary ways of evaluating transportation infrastructure and defining transportation systems. They are not mutually exclusive, nor is it presumed that the data collected in these views will be collectively exhaustive. Instead, the risk view structure supports a scalable system analysis capability, allowing for the examination of how risk manifests in the system. Risk views are the first step in defining the boundaries of a system, establishing relationships within the system, and identifying interdependencies. For more information regarding risk and vulnerability refer to Chapter 5: Assessments for Infrastructure Protection. The initial set of risk views includes:

- **Modal:** Traditional industry delineation (i.e., Aviation, Maritime, Mass Transit, Highway, Freight Rail, Pipeline). All assets within a mode can be collectively evaluated as a system.
- **Geographic:** All assets within a geographic boundary (e.g., New York State or the city of Los Angeles). This view may be used most often by state, local, and tribal government partners.
- **Functional:** All assets that, taken together, perform a specific function or service (e.g., supplying fuel to the Northeast). This view is supply chain–focused and may be used, for example, by the USCG, CBP, interagency hazardous materials (HAZMAT) transportation working groups, and private sector partners.
- **Ownership:** All assets that fall under a defined set of decision rights, recognized by federal, state, local, and tribal governments (e.g., all assets owned and operated by the New York Mass Transit Authority can be evaluated as a system).

Since 9/11, Congress and the administration, including many federal agencies, have increasingly sought to take a longer-term view of homeland security, recognizing, among other things, that a variety of transportation and border security initiatives are needed, such as improving the mechanisms for screening foreign travelers before they enter the country legally by air, land, or sea ports, and tracking their entry and exit. More recent efforts by terrorists to disrupt society—notably, the alleged attempt by terrorists to bring liquid explosives on board aircraft bound for the United States and terrorist attacks on passenger rail systems in Madrid and London—have further highlighted the need for effective information sharing, proactive planning, and effective risk analysis, in order to identify and mitigate risks to people, national assets, and economic sectors and prioritize resources to address them.

Maritime Transportation System Security

Maritime Transportation System consists of about 95,000 miles of coastline, 361 ports, more than 10,000 miles of navigable waterways, 3.4 million square miles of Exclusive Economic Zone to secure, and intermodal landside connections, which allow the various modes of transportation to move people and goods to, from, and on the water. The DHS established HSPD-13: National Strategy for Maritime Security specifically to address issues unique to maritime transportation. This Directive establishes policy guidelines to enhance national and homeland security by protecting U.S. maritime interests.

HSPD-13 underscores the importance of securing the maritime domain, which is defined as "all areas and things of, on, under, relating to, adjacent to, or bordering on a sea, ocean, or other navigable waterway, including all maritime-related activities, infrastructure, people, cargo, and vessels and other conveyances."[3] In other words, the maritime domain for the United States includes all of our national coastline, the Great Lakes, and all navigable inland waterways such as the Mississippi River and the Intracoastal Waterway. Further, in today's economy the oceans have increased importance, allowing all countries to participate in the global marketplace. More than 80% of the world's trade travels by water, creating a vast global maritime link. About half the world's trade by value, and 90% of the general cargo, is transported in containers.

There are thirty megaports/cities that make up the world's primary, interdependent trading system, encompassing Asia, North America, and Europe. Through a handful of international straits and canals pass 75% of the world's maritime trade and half its daily oil consumption. The infrastructure and systems that span the maritime domain, owned largely by the private sector, have increasingly become both targets of and potential conveyances for dangerous and illicit activities. Moreover, much of what occurs in the maritime domain with respect to vessel movements, activities, cargoes, intentions, or ownership is often difficult to discern. The oceans are increasingly threatened by illegal exploitation of living marine resources and increased competition over nonliving marine resources. Although the global economy continues to increase the value of the oceans' role as highways for commerce and providers of resources, technology and the forces of globalization have lessened their role as barriers. Thus, this continuous domain serves as a vast, ready, and largely unsecured medium for an array of threats by nations, terrorists, and criminals.

The United States depends on physical networks such as the marine transportation system. The ports, waterways, and shores of the maritime domain are lined with military facilities, nuclear power plants, locks, oil refineries, levees, passenger terminals, fuel tanks, pipelines, chemical plants, tunnels, cargo terminals, and bridges. Ports in particular have inherent security vulnerabilities: they are sprawling, easily accessible by water and land, close to crowded metropolitan areas, and interwoven with complex transportation networks. Port facilities, along with the ships and barges that transit port waterways, are especially vulnerable to tampering, theft, and unauthorized persons gaining entry to collect information and commit unlawful or hostile acts.

The DHS is the lead agency for the overall national effort for maritime security. The federal government has three primary responsibilities in regard to this national effort:

1. To produce and distribute timely and accurate threat advisory and alert information and appropriate protective measures to state, local, and tribal governments and the private sector via a dedicated homeland security information network (HISN);
2. To provide guidance and standards for reducing vulnerabilities; and
3. To provide active, layered, and scalable security presence to protect from and deter attacks.

Since private industry owns and operates the vast majority of the Nation's critical infrastructure and key resources, owners and operators remain the first line of defense for their own facilities. They are responsible for increasing physical security and reducing the vulnerabilities of their property by conducting routine risk management planning, as well as investing in protective measures—e.g., staff authentication and credentialing, access control, and physical security of their fixed sites and cargoes—as a necessary business function.

As security measures at ports of entry, land-border crossings, and airports become more robust, criminals and terrorists will increasingly consider the lengthy U.S. coastline with its miles of uninhabited areas as a less risky alternative for unlawful entry into the United States. The United States must therefore patrol, monitor, and exert unambiguous control over its maritime borders and maritime approaches. At-sea presence deters adversaries and lawbreakers, provides better mobile surveillance coverage, adds to warning time, allows seizing the initiative to influence events at a distance, and facilitates the capability to surprise and engage adversaries well before they can cause harm to the United States.[4]

As of November 2007, the CBP set up security requirements for Customs-Trade Partnership Against Terrorism (C-TPAT), which enables international trade companies to decrease the burden of CBP inspections of their goods in exchange for verification of their own security measures. C-TPAT members are in eight of the nine trade sectors, including sea carriers, highway carriers, rail carriers, air carriers, foreign manufacturers, U.S. customs brokers, U.S. and foreign maritime port authorities and terminal operators, and long-haul highway carriers in Mexico. CBP is also in the process of setting up final security criteria for freight consolidators/ocean transportation intermediaries and non-vessel operating common carriers, the final C-TPAT trade sector. Further, the program will focus its efforts on strengthening the partnership with member companies at both the macro and micro levels and leveraging corporate influence throughout the international supply chain in FY 2009. In doing so, the C-TPAT program will continue to ensure compliance with the requirements of the SAFE Port Act to include certifying security profiles within ninety days of submission and conducting validations within one year of certification and revalidations within four years of initial validation. This will require roughly 3,800 to 4,500 on-site validation visits worldwide in fiscal 2009, according to DHS estimates.[5]

U.S. Highway System Security

The U.S. highway system consists of four million interconnected miles of paved roadways, including 45,000 miles of interstate freeway and 600,000 bridges. These networks also contain many other fixed facilities such as terminals, navigation aids, switch yards, locks, maintenance bases, and operation control centers.

The primary issue regarding the critical infrastructure of U.S. highways is the vast expanse of these systems and the ability of many vehicles to bypass federal and state inspection points. This is of concern because of the amount of cargo that is shipped over our highways annually.

CBP has the dual goals of preventing terrorists and terrorist weapons from entering the United States and also facilitating the flow of legitimate trade and travel. Approximately 90% of the world's cargo moves by container. Addressing the threat posed by the movement of containerized cargo across U.S. borders has traditionally posed many challenges for the CBP, in particular balancing the bureau's border protection functions and trade enforcement mission with its goal of facilitating the flow of cargo and persons into the United States. The CBP has said that the large volume of imports and its limited resources make it impossible to physically inspect all oceangoing containers without disrupting the flow of commerce, and it is unrealistic to expect that all containers warrant such inspection.

In response, the DHS introduced the Highway Watch Program in 2005. This program is in cooperation with the American Trucking Association (ATA) and is intended to train highway professionals to identify and report safety and security concerns on our Nation's roads. The program will provide training and communications infrastructure to prepare hundreds of thousands of transportation professionals to respond in the event that they or their cargo are the target of a terrorist attack and to share valuable intelligence with the DHS if they detect potential threats. The rationale of having such a program is that drivers of tractor trailers are in a unique position to be alert to a possible terrorist attack because of the vast amount of miles they travel over U.S. highways. This program is designed to train them for what to look for and how to respond appropriately, how to take safety precautions, and how to report suspicious activity.

CBP has also implemented a program to address the threats associated with cargo coming over the border and onto U.S. highways. This new program, referred to as the Automated Commercial Environment (ACE) program, is a new cargo processing system to modernize the targeting, inspection, enforcement, border security, revenue collection, and trade statistics processes for all cargo entering and leaving the United States. The Automated Commercial Environment (ACE) will be replacing the current Automated Commercial System.

The enhanced ACE program provides an electronic truck manifest, a primary officer interface (the screens CBP officers use), and an expedited importation processing. The officer interface consolidates more than seven separate cargo release systems to provide CBP officers with a comprehensive view of enforcement and transaction history data to enhance enforcement capabilities while simultaneously expediting the movement of trade. The release provides for the automated manifest processes of determining the admissibility of cargo, conveyance, and equipment arriving in the United States. The release interfaces with the Automated Targeting System to provide selectivity data to CBP primary officers, and other authorized users, to target high-risk transactions and to record and track information associated to potential or actual noncompliance. ACE is being integrated with the International Trade Data System (ITDS) to support the international trade data needs of each of the federal agencies with international trade responsibilities. The international trade processes supported by this initiative include data collection, processing, use, dissemination, and storage. Ultimately, ACE will become the central data collection system for the federal agencies that, by law, require international trade data. In addition, ACE will serve as the single point of access for this data.

Rail and Mass Transit System Security

Rail and Mass Transit Surface transportation systems are extremely vulnerable to terrorist attack, as evidenced by the attacks on passenger rail facilities in Madrid, London, and India. Passenger rail, bus, highway, and ferry systems are inherently difficult to secure in the United States because of their open accessibility (typically, many entry and exit points), high ridership (nearly nine billion transit trips per year on buses and subways), and extensive infrastructure (roughly 11,000 track miles of transit rail and 3,000 stations, 3.8 million miles of roads nationwide, and more than 600,000 bridges and tunnels). The freight rail networks extend for more than 300,000 miles, and commuter and urban rail systems cover some 10,000 miles. There are 94,000 private railroad crossings used by both freight and passenger trains. These railway crossings are probably one of the more vulnerable aspects of the railway system in the United States. The U.S. rail transit system is a vital component of the Nation's transportation system.

While the majority of mass transit systems in the Nation are owned and operated by state and local governments and private industry, securing these systems is a shared responsibility among federal, state, and local partners. More robust information exchange, threat detection, and preparedness measures must be undertaken to ensure the security and resilience of the surface transportation system. The Transportation Systems Sector Specific Plan (SSP) published by the DHS in May 2007 brings together federal, state, and local government partners and regional mass transit stakeholders to create a "a secure, resilient transit system that leverages public awareness, technology, and layered security programs while maintaining the efficient flow of passengers."[6] To help accomplish this, the DHS has made millions of funding dollars available through the initiatives such as the Transportation Security Grant Program, Homeland Security Grant Program, Trucking Industry Security Grant Program, and Urban Area Security Initiatives.

Aviation Transportation System Security

The U.S. aviation system has some 500 commercial-service airports and another 14,000 smaller general aviation airports scattered across the country. Although the Nation cannot expect to eliminate all risks of terrorist attack upon commercial aviation, agencies have made progress since 9/11 to reduce aviation-related vulnerabilities and enhance the layers of defense directly exploited by the terrorist hijackers. In general, these efforts have resulted in better airline passenger screening procedures designed to identify and prevent known or suspected terrorists, weapons, and explosives from being allowed onto aircraft. Nevertheless, the Nation's commercial aviation system remains a highly visible target for terrorism, as evidenced by recent alleged efforts to bring liquid explosives aboard aircraft.

HSPD-16: National Strategy for Aviation Security details a strategic vision for aviation security while recognizing ongoing efforts, and directs the production of a national strategy for aviation security and supporting plans. The supporting plans address the following areas:

- Aviation transportation system security;
- Aviation operational threat response;
- Aviation transportation system recovery;
- Air domain surveillance and intelligence integration; and
- Domestic and international outreach.

Over the past five years, the security of the aviation sector has been significantly strengthened through the efforts of the federal government working with state, local, and tribal governments, the international community, and the private sector. Together these partners continue to implement a broad range of aviation security measures through innovative initiatives and by leveraging preexisting capabilities to provide the Nation with an active, layered aviation security, and defense. Such measures include:

- A federalized Transportation Security Officer workforce that screens passengers and baggage traveling on passenger aircraft;
- Hardened cockpit doors to prevent unauthorized access to the flight deck;
- Federal Air Marshals who fly anonymously on commercial passenger aircraft to provide a law enforcement presence;
- Enhanced explosives and threat detection technology deployed in hundreds of airports;
- Airspace and air traffic management security measures; and
- A cadre of canine explosives detection teams screening baggage, cargo, and, increasingly, carry-on items.

Other important security activities include:

- Thousands of pilots who voluntarily participate in the Federal Flight Deck Officer program, which permits trained pilots to carry firearms;
- Flight crew members, including flight attendants, who have voluntarily taken the Transportation Security Administration's (TSA) Advanced Flight Crew Self-Defense course;
- Other federal, state, local, and tribal law enforcement officers who travel armed as part of their normal duties;
- Establishment of a program to collect and analyze suspicious events;
- Efforts to streamline operational coordination on incidents both in the air and on the ground;
- Daily vetting of thousands of crew members and passengers on flights to and from the United States; and
- Improvement of surveillance and intelligence sharing.

In addition, the Nation's air defense mission has been transformed by expanding surveillance and air interdiction efforts inward to counter terrorist air threats, as well as by continuing traditional air defense activities against the threats from hostile nation-states.

The Aviation Transportation System comprises a broad spectrum of private and public sector elements, including aircraft and airport operators, more than 19,800 private and public use airports, and a dynamic system of facilities, equipment, services, and airspace. The Aviation Transportation System continues to grow rapidly, as more and more passengers regularly choose to fly. On a daily basis, thousands of carrier flights arrive, depart, or overfly the continental United States, while each year millions of tons of freight and thousands of tons of mail are transported by air in the United States.

Some of the Nation's aviation infrastructure is owned and operated by state, local, and tribal governments. State governors and/or homeland security agencies, in addition to local and tribal governments, hold a leadership position to address specific aviation security needs or issues and response. During extraordinary circumstances, the federal government may assume lead security responsibility. Typically, except for cross-border traffic, lead responsibility will remain with the states, localities, or tribes. Specific responsibilities of state, local, and tribal governments are discussed in the NIPP and corresponding Transportation Systems SSP. State, local, and tribal governments are currently working with the federal government to identify critical transportation assets, conduct the necessary vulnerability assessments, and develop security plans to protect those assets. They are also developing their response and recovery capabilities to address terrorist attacks and other disruptive incidents, and to meet the National Preparedness Goal. The private sector also has ownership of substantial segments of the Nation's aviation transportation infrastructure. Therefore, an effective national aviation security strategy must be supported by a private sector that internalizes a strong security culture, embedding best practices and government requirements into day-to-day operations. It is the responsibility of private sector owners to conduct and execute business continuity planning, integrate security planning with disaster recovery planning, and to actively participate with federal, state, local, and tribal governments to improve security in the aviation sector.

There is also the need for international cooperation, which is critical to ensuring that lawful private and public activities in the air domain are protected from attack and hostile or unlawful exploitation. Such collaboration is fundamental to worldwide economic stability and growth, and it is vital to the interests of the United States. It is only through such an integrated approach among all aviation partners, governmental and nongovernmental, public, and private, that the United States can improve the security of the air domain.[7]

··

Aviation Transportation System: Suggested Readings

The following strategy and supporting plans have been drafted as required by HSPD-16.

National Strategy for Aviation Security. (http://www.dhs.gov/xlibrary/assets/ laws_hspd_aviation_security.pdf)

Aviation Transportation System Security Plan. Seeks to enhance public security and economic growth by promoting global aviation security practices aimed at reducing vulnerabilities associated with the aviation transportation system. It sets forth a risk-based implementation plan for the continued reduction of vulnerabilities within the aviation transportation system. The development of this plan was led by the Secretaries of Homeland Security and Transportation. (http://www.dhs.gov/xlibrary/assets/hspd16_transsystemsecurityplan.pdf)

Aviation Operational Threat Response Plan. Ensures a comprehensive and coordinated U.S. Government response to air threats against the United States or U.S. interests. The development of this plan was led by the Secretary of Defense and the Attorney General. (http://www.dhs.gov/xlibrary/assets/hspd16_opthreatresp plan.pdf)

Aviation Transportation System Recovery Plan. Rapid recovery from an attack or similar disruption in the Air Domain is critical to the economic well-being of our Nation. A credible capacity for rapid recovery will minimize an incident's economic impact. The ATSR Plan includes recommended measures to mitigate the operational and economic effects of an attack in the Air Domain. The development of this plan was led by the Secretaries of Homeland Security and Transportation.

Air Domain Surveillance and Intelligence Integration Plan. In order to have effective knowledge of the threat to the United States and U.S. interests in the Air Domain, the U.S. Government must have a plan to coordinate requirements, priorities, and implementation of national air surveillance resources and the means to share this information with appropriate stakeholders. The ADSII Plan supports an enhanced surveillance capability to detect and deter threats that could lead to an attack on the U.S. aviation transportation system. The development of this plan was led by the Secretary of Defense and the Director of National Intelligence. (http://www.dhs.gov/xlibrary/assets/hspd16_domsurvintelplan.pdf)

Domestic Outreach Plan. The successful implementation of NSPD-47/HSPD-16 must include coordination with State and local government authorities and consultation with appropriate private sector persons and entities. The DO Plan ensures that this proper coordination with the private sector and local government authorities takes place. The development of this plan was led by the Secretaries of Homeland Security and Transportation. (http://www.dhs.gov/xlibrary/assets/hspd16_domoutreachplan.pdf)

International Outreach Plan. U.S. Government efforts must be global efforts and developed with the cooperation of other governments and international organizations. The IO Plan is aimed at ensuring the proper coordination with entities abroad. The development of this plan was led by the Secretary of State. (http://www.dhs.gov/xlibrary/assets/hspd16_intloutreachplan.pdf)

Postal and Shipping Sector

The Postal and Shipping Sector is an integral component of the U.S. economy, employing more than 1.5 million people and earning revenues of more than $148 billion per year. The Postal and Shipping Sector moves hundreds of millions of messages, products, and financial transactions each day. Postal and shipping activity is differentiated from general cargo operations by its focus on small- and medium-size packages and by service from millions of senders to millions of destinations. The sector is highly concentrated, with a handful of providers holding roughly 96% of the market share. Sector-specific assets include:

- High-volume automated processing facilities;
- Tens of thousands of local delivery units;
- Many and varied collection, acceptance, and retail operations;
- Mail transport equipment; and
- Information and communications networks.

....

Beyond physical and cyber assets, the most crit- ical **Postal and Shipping Sector** asset is public trust because of their trusted access to almost all public and private facilities to collect and distribute the Nation's postal commerce.

....

The Postal and Shipping Sector has many dependencies and interrelationships with a wide range of other sectors, including its potential role as a threat vector to other sectors and the general public. The Banking and Finance, Government Facilities, Commercial Facilities, and Public Health and Healthcare sectors all rely heavily on the Postal and Shipping Sector for the shipment and delivery of critical documents and packages. The Postal and Shipping Sector itself relies on:

- The Transportation Systems Sector for the movement of mail and packages by air, road, or rail, as well as being a major customer of the sector;
- The Energy Sector for power, as well as being a customer of the sector; and
- The Information Technology and Communications sectors for supporting logistics operations and automatic identification and sorting.

All of these sectors are working together to ensure that their efforts support each other.[8]

Postal and Shipping Sector Coordinating Council (SCC)

The Postal and Shipping Sector[9] has formed a Sector Coordinating Council (SCC) comprising the major industry providers (United Parcel Service [UPS™], United States Postal Service [USPS®], Federal Express [FedEx®], and DHL) to work with the DHS and other federal agencies to ensure that the efforts of the private sector are informed by federal activities and vice versa. This council also serves as a critical mechanism for ensuring that the concerns and perspectives of the private sector are considered in federal actions. The SCC's members are believed to represent the majority of the Nation's postal and shipping industry.

In addition to the SCC, several federal agencies have come together to form the Postal and Shipping Government Coordinating Council (GCC), which includes:

- Transportation Security Administration (TSA);
- DHS Office of Infrastructure Protection (OIP);
- U.S. Customs and Border Protection (CBP);
- DHS Mail Management Program;
- DHS Office of Grants and Training;
- U.S. Department of Health and Human Services (HHS) Centers for Disease Control and Prevention (CDC); and
- Food and Drug Administration (FDA).

The objective of the GCC is to:

- Promote effective government coordination of postal and shipping security strategies;

- Identify gaps and activities;
- Establish policies and standards, program metrics, and performance reporting criteria; and
- Foster effective communications and partnerships across government and between government and the private sector.

CI/KR Protection Issues

The Postal and Shipping Sector delivers to virtually any national or international location. Accordingly, postal and shipping personnel have trusted access to almost all public and private facilities in their roles as collectors and distributors of the Nation's postal commerce. To ensure ease of access to and use of the system for its customers, the sector maintains an extremely large number of collection points at which parcels and letters can be inserted for delivery. These collection facilities present a vast array of relatively anonymous entry points at which terrorists could insert dangerous materials for delivery to intended targets. This combination of ubiquitous, trusted personnel access to other sectors, an extraordinary number of points to anonymously insert material, and the potential for delivery to diverse recipients potentially makes the Postal and Shipping Sector an attractive vector that terrorists may use to attack persons or critical infrastructure in other sectors.

Protective Programs

Within the Postal and Shipping Sector, protective programs primarily occur on two distinct levels: (1) overarching, sector-wide protective programs led by TSA as the SSA; and (2) protective programs that are driven by industry partners and, for the most part, performed voluntarily by asset owners and operators. High-priority sector-wide programs include:

- **Exercises.** The Postal and Shipping Sector has conducted several exercises in partnership with private sector stakeholders.
- **Information Sharing.** The Postal and Shipping Sector has established a portal on the Homeland Security Information Network (HSIN). This facilitates and enables information sharing between the SSA and private sector security partners, among federal government agencies (GCC membership), between government and the private sector, and across other critical infrastructure sectors.
- **Vulnerability Assessment Tool.** The Postal and Shipping Sector is in the process of developing a vulnerability self-assessment tool, specifically tailored to the unique characteristics of the sector.
- **Site Assistance Visits (SAVs).** In conjunction with DHS, the SSA performs site assistance visits (SAVs) at key Postal and Shipping Sector stakeholder facilities. The SAVs are carried out at the invitation of and in full cooperation and coordination with major security partners.
- **Strategic Homeland Infrastructure Risk Assessment (SHIRA).** The Postal and Shipping Sector has been an active participant in SHIRA to represent the status of vulnerability in the Nation's infrastructure more accurately.

In addition, the U.S. Postal Service (USPS) has also implemented protective programs and other initiatives to increase the security of the Postal and Shipping Sector and to reduce vulnerabilities. These programs and initiatives include:

- Biological detection systems in 272 processing and distribution centers;
- A facility risk-rating model;
- Facility security surveys;
- Commercial mailer reviews;
- Observation of mail conditions;
- Airport Mail Security Review Program;
- Aviation Mail Security Program;
- Personnel Screening Review Program;
- Financial Security Review Program; and
- Security Force Assessment Survey.

The sector's other private sector security partners are also implementing protective initiatives and programs, although the specifics of these efforts are generally considered proprietary and of a commercially sensitive nature. General examples of such programs include:

- Physical vulnerability mitigation measures, such as perimeter fencing, additional security measures for the handling and storage of hazardous materials, and closed-circuit surveillance systems;
- Cyber security measures, such as encryption and sophisticated package tracking systems; and
- Personnel security measures, such as access control, metal detectors, and identification verification requirements.

Summary

While much attention has been focused on mitigating the specific risks of 9/11, other critical assets ranging from passenger rail stations to power plants are also at risk of terrorist attack. Deciding how to address these risks—setting priorities, making trade-offs, allocating resources, and assessing social and economic costs—is essential. Thus, it remains vitally important for the DHS to continue to develop and implement a risk-based framework to help target where and how the Nation's resources should be invested to strengthen security. The government also faces strategic challenges that potentially affect oversight and execution of new and ongoing homeland security initiatives. Lastly, three challenges in particular—information sharing, risk management, and transforming the DHS as a department—are areas needing urgent attention.

8

....

Facilities and National Icons

Introduction

Terrorism and other forms of destructive attacks have been present internationally and within nations themselves for centuries, from the fable of the
Trojan horse to real murderous cults in first-century Palestine.[1] In order to
protect the way of life that Americans have come to expect and rightfully
deserve, it is imperative that our Nation carefully plans for terrorism, natural
disasters, and other types of attacks to which the United States has fallen victim. No one sector is immune to the effects of these events, and each carries
dire consequences if an event does occur.

This chapter will focus on three specific critical infrastructure/key
resource (CI/KR) sectors:

1. Commercial Facilities Sector (CFS);
2. Government Facilities Sector (GFS); and
3. National Monuments and Icons (NMI) Sector.

These sectors all contain infrastructure that has great functional as well as
symbolic roles to play in American culture. The information presented under
each sector is primarily drawn from government publications, with key components identified for a high level overview.

Commercial Facilities Sector (CFS)

Approximately 80% of the Nation's critical infrastructure is owned by the
private sector, making the development of trusted partnerships between the

federal government and the private sector across all sectors critical to ensure the protection of these assets. Facilities associated with the Commercial Facilities Sector (CFS) operate on the principle of open public access, meaning that the general public can move freely throughout these facilities without the deterrent of highly visible security barriers. The majority of the facilities in this sector are owned and operated by the private sector, with minimal interaction with the federal government and other regulatory entities. Commercial facility owners and operators must be responsible for assessing and mitigating their specific facility vulnerabilities and practicing prudent risk management and mitigation measures.

The CFS consists of the following eight subsectors:

1. Public Assembly (e.g., arenas, stadiums, aquariums, zoos, convention centers);
2. Sports Leagues (e.g., professional sports leagues and federations);
3. Resorts (e.g., casinos);
4. Lodging (e.g., hotels, motels, conference centers);
5. Outdoor Events (e.g., theme and amusement parks, fairs, campgrounds, parades);
6. Entertainment and Media (e.g., motion picture studios, broadcast media);
7. Real Estate (e.g., office and apartment buildings, condominiums, self-storage); and
8. Retail (e.g., retail centers and districts, shopping malls).[2]

. . . .

Largest Commercial Facilities in the United States

Sporting Facility:
Indianapolis Motor Speedway
Speedway, IN
Seating Capacity of 250,000
http://www.indianapolismotorspeedway.com

Casino:
Foxwoods Resort Casino
Ledyard, CT
340,000 square feet of gaming space
http://www.foxwoods.com

Hotel:
MGM Grand Hotel and Casino
Las Vegas, NV
5,044 guest rooms
http://www.mgmgrand.com

Shopping Mall:
Mall of America
Bloomington, MN
520 stores
http://www.mallofamerica.com

Tallest Building:

Sears Tower

Chicago, IL

1,450 feet (110 stories)

http://www.searstower.com

....

In 2006, the U.S. Government Accounting Office (GAO) reported that the disparity of among the subsector stakeholders has made forming a Sector Coordinating Council (SCC) a challenge due to the varied and often unrelated stakeholders nationwide. This sector encompasses owners and operators of stadiums, raceways, casinos, and office buildings that have not previously worked together. In addition, the industries constituting the CFS did not function as a sector prior to the National Infrastructure Protection Plan (NIPP) and did not have any prior association with the federal government. As a result, the CFS SCC exerted a great deal of effort on identifying key stakeholders and agreeing on the scope of the SCC and its membership. As a result, the council established eight sub-councils to allow the disparate members to organize in a meaningful way.[3]

Threats to Commercial Facilities

In January 2007, the Homeland Infrastructure Threat and Risk Analysis Center (HITRAC) issued a report on the DHS's knowledge and analysis of current terrorist threats to CFS assets within the United States. It also described known terrorist goals and motives, their potential application to the CFS, vulnerabilities associated with CFS facilities and assets, and the potential consequences of an attack. Several key findings were issued in the report:

1. DHS continues to receive credible, specific, and corroborated reports indicating terrorist threats to the CFS.
2. Al-Qaeda continues to pose the greatest terrorist threat to the CFS. Al-Qaeda desires to strike the United States again, and an attack against CFS assets could meet its targeting strategy of mass casualties, economic damage, and psychological impact.
3. Sunni extremists and homegrown radicals also pose a threat to this sector. Homegrown radicalization is an emerging and dynamic phenomenon that may spur individuals to attack CFS assets.
4. Terrorist casing reports uncovered in July 2004 on financial institutions in the New Jersey–New York area and in Washington, D.C. provide the greatest insight to date into al-Qaeda's targeting strategy against high-profile financial institutions and the commercial facilities that house them, as well as the surveillance techniques and methods of operations.
5. The CFS is marked by its vast size and diversity of subsector assets. Several characteristics, such as open public access and proximity to the assets of other sectors that also are potential targets, challenge the development and implementation of protective measures for the sector.

The report noted that the September 11, 2001 attacks demonstrated that mitigating the most significant risks to commercial facilities probably lies outside the scope of what most owners and operators can do. With that said, it was noted that owners and operators of CFS assets do have the capability to protect against the prevailing threats against the sector—suicide bombers and vehicle-based improvised explosive devices (VBIED). Protective measures include equipment, personnel, and procedures designed to protect a facility against threats and to mitigate the effects of an attack. Implementation of protective measures involves the commitment of resources in the form of people, equipment, materials, time, and money.

Government Facilities Sector (GFS)

U.S. citizens regularly interact with government at all levels and depend on the provision of various government services, all of which are supported by an array of facilities owned, leased, or operated by government entities. Ensuring the continuity of these functions and services through protection of their associated government assets is vital to homeland security. The Government Facilities Sector (GFS) includes a wide variety of buildings, owned or leased by federal, state, territorial, local, or tribal governments, located domestically and overseas. Many government facilities are open to the public for business activities, commercial transactions, or recreational activities. Others not open to the public contain highly sensitive information materials, processes, and equipment. This includes general-use office buildings and special-use military installations, embassies, courthouses, national laboratories, and structures that may house critical equipment and systems, networks, and functions.

In addition to physical structures, the sector considers cyber elements that contribute to the protection of sector assets (e.g., access control systems [ACS] and closed-circuit television systems [CCTV]) as well as the protection of individuals who possess tactical, operational, or strategic knowledge or perform essential functions. Diverse in function, size, and location, these facilities are differentiated from other CI/KR sectors because they are uniquely governmental.[4, 5]

Government Facilities Sector-Specific Agency

The Federal Protective Service (FPS) is the Sector-Specific Agency (SSA) for the GFS, which is building on its traditional role as protector of facilities owned and leased by the GSA. As the SSA, the FPS coordinates activities for the GFS in conjunction with its Government Coordinating Council (GCC) to identify, assess, and enhance the protection of government facilities determined to be nationally critical. The GCC, chaired by FPS, is the primary coordination point with representatives from government entities with the responsibility for the protection of government facilities. Because of its inherently governmental focus, security partners are limited to representatives from federal, state, local, or tribal government entities involved in the protection of owned or leased facilities. The FPS also represents the sector on the NIPP Federal Senior Leadership Council (FSLC) and through similar coordinating mechanisms established by other CI/KR sectors (such as the GFS Education Facilities [ED] subsector that enables the FPS to work in close coordination with the Department of Education with regard to schools).

The ability to increase situational awareness and readiness through real-time information exchange is essential for the protection of government facilities. The GFS uses a secure Web-based portal, FPS Link, to collaborate and share information with sector security partners. Information sharing is achieved with the portal through the processes detailed below.

- FPS receives information from federal, state, and local governments and continuously monitors open sources of information.
- This information is analyzed for relevance to government facility protection and shared with sector security partners based on the information's time and security sensitivity.
- Tactical information is relayed immediately to government facility owners and operators, law enforcement, and emergency operations centers through alerts, secure messaging, and a live synchronized chat, enabling quick and coordinated actions.
- Operational and strategic information is shared through compartmentalized collaboration tools including forum discussions, online briefings and surveys, a document library, and a community calendar.

Government Facilities Sector-Specific Plan

The Government Facilities Sector-Specific Plan (SSP) details the means by which the NIPP risk management framework is implemented in the sector. It provides guidance to sector security partners to enhance the steady state of preparedness across all government facilities. It is specifically tailored to:

- Address unique characteristics and risk landscapes of the sector;
- Define sector security partners and their roles, responsibilities, and authorities;
- Establish (or document existing) procedures for sector interaction, information sharing, coordination, and partnership;
- Describe the sector-specific mechanisms used to identify assets, understand threats, assess vulnerabilities and consequences, and prioritize investments based on costs and benefits so that they are applied where they offer the greatest mitigation of risk; and
- Provide consistency for protective programs and investments across the sector.

Government Facilities Sector-Specific Plan Goals

The GFS sector recently released its Sector-Specific Plan (SSP), which provides a framework from which to categorize, assess, and protect government facilities necessary for the daily operation of the nation. The GFS SSP establishes five overarching goals.

Goal 1: Implement a long-term government facility risk management program;

Goal 2: Organize and partner for government facility protection;

Goal 3: Integrate government facility protection as part of the homeland security mission;

Goal 4: Manage and develop the capabilities of the GFS; and

Goal 5: Maximize efficient use of resources for government facility protection.

As part of the GFS, the ED Subsector envisions as its goal that all schools and institutions of higher education have comprehensive emergency management plans to deal with all hazards that address the four phases of emergency management—prevention/mitigation, preparedness, response, and recovery.[6]

Government Facilities Sector Security Challenges

George Mason University produces monthly Critical Infrastructure Protection reports which outline various issues in the complex world of CI/KR protection. In the July 2007 issue, the authors discussed the challenges associated with the GFS. Specifically, they stated that the sheer size and scope of the GFS poses a challenge in providing for infrastructure protection efforts, noting that the federal government alone manages more than 3 billion square feet of space and more than 650 million acres of land. Additionally, it was noted that the sector also covers the facilities owned and operated by the more than 87,000 municipal governments across the Nation, as well as U.S. embassies, consulates, and military installations located all over the world. As such, these facilities face a full range of both natural and man-made hazards. Government facilities represent attractive and strategically important targets for both domestic and international terrorist groups as well as criminals. These assets are often targeted because they provide unique services, often perform sensitive functions, and/or have significant symbolic value. Indeed, the most significant terrorist attacks against Americans have targeted government facilities. Because of the high-profile nature of the sector, government facilities operate within a very dynamic risk environment.[7]

National Monuments and Icons (NMI) Sector

As outlined in the National Monuments and Icons (NMI) SSP, the NMI Sector encompasses a diverse array of assets located throughout the United States and its Territories. Many of these NMI assets are listed on either the National Register of Historic Places or the List of National Historic Landmarks. NMI Sector assets that are categorized as "National Critical:"

- Are monuments, physical structures, or objects;
- Are recognized both nationally and internationally as representing the Nation's heritage, traditions, and/or values or are recognized for their national, cultural, religious, historical, or political significance; and
- Serve the primary purpose of memorializing or representing significant aspects of our Nation's heritage, traditions, or values and to serve as points of interest for visitors and educational activities.

NMI assets are primarily physical structures. Included as part of each asset are the operational staff and visitors who may be impacted by a terrorist attack or all-hazards incident. Sector assets do not include famous people or technology applications, although they may contain holdings of significant importance to the Nation's history. There are minimal cyber and telecommunications issues associated with this sector due to the nature of the assets. Some information technology (IT) or telecommunications systems may be used at a few of the assets, and these will be considered during the process of conducting the vulnerability assessment and implementing protective programs as appropriate.

Certain national holidays, such as the Fourth of July, Memorial Day, and Labor Day, represent an especially important factor for this sector, when visitation at selected NMI assets is particularly high. Although a diverse array of NMI assets are scattered across the United States and its territories, this SSP focuses primarily on identifying, prioritizing, assessing, and protecting National Critical NMIs that may be attractive targets for terrorists.

. . . .

There are seventy-five **National Monuments** in the National Park Service system, with a total area of 2,157,574 acres. There are also twenty-one additional National Monuments managed by the National Oceanic and Atmospheric Administration (NOAA), Armed Forces Retirement Home, Bureau of Land Management (BLM), U.S. Fish and Wildlife Service (USFWS), and U.S. Forest Service (USFS).[8]

. . . .

National Monuments and Icons Sector-Specific Plan

The Department of Interior (DOI), as the SSA, will confer with other SSAs and Government Coordinating Councils (GCCs) during the asset identification process to ensure that assets are assigned to the appropriate authority. As the SSA for NMI assets, the DOI will:

- Work with the owners of National Critical NMI assets to identify, prioritize, and coordinate protecting them to prevent, deter, and mitigate the effects of deliberate efforts to destroy, incapacitate, or exploit them;
- Collaborate with relevant federal departments and agencies;
- Conduct vulnerability assessments of DOI-owned assets and facilitate or support similar assessments of non–DOI-owned assets; and
- Encourage adoption of risk management strategies to protect against and mitigate the effects of attacks against CI/KR.

National Monuments and Icons Sector-Specific Plan Goals

The NMI SSP establishes ten overarching goals:

Goal 1: Establish clear criteria to define nationally critical versus state or locally critical assets. To comprehensively implement protective programs, the SSA will work with security partners at all levels of government and the private sector to distinguish National Critical assets from National Significant, Regional Critical, and Local Significant assets and to identify NMI assets whose primary protective responsibility falls within the scope of another sector.

Goal 2: Clearly delineate and define roles and responsibilities for all sector security partners. The NMI Sector will work with security partners to clarify the roles and responsibilities in providing security in the sector to allocate resources effectively, integrate protection plans, and coordinate a response in the event of an emergency.

Goal 3: Perform risk assessments on critical assets. The NMI Sector will conduct or facilitate risk assessments on a priority basis for National Critical monuments and icons.

Goal 4: Enable rapid and robust communications among intelligence and law enforcement agencies and federal, state, local, and private security partners. To adapt security measures to emerging threats, the sector will develop secure information-sharing channels between DHS and state and local law enforcement agencies and the individuals operationally responsible for protecting the sector's assets.

Goal 5: Ensure seamless coordination among federal, state, and local agencies as well as any private sector entities that own or operate sector assets. Effective implementation of sector security programs will require coordination among a wide range of security partners, including DOI, municipal governments, site-specific owners and operators, private sector owners, foundations, or nonprofit stewards of sites and symbols.

Goal 6: Implement cross-sector coordination with regard to NMI assets whose primary protective responsibility resides in another sector. The sector will work with other CI/KR sectors to ensure that protective programs reflect the multi-use nature of certain critical NMI assets. Such cross-sector coordination would include dams, transportation services, government facilities, and commercial facilities.

Goal 7: Integrate robust security technology and practices while preserving the appearance and accessibility of NMI sites. Monuments and icons are important symbols of our nation's heritage and identity. It is imperative to the sector and to the Nation that these assets remain open and accessible to the public. NMI security measures will thus limit, to the extent possible, restrictions on public access or degradation in the scenic appeal of sector assets.

Goal 8: Develop flexible security programs to adjust to seasonal and event-specific security challenges. Many NMI assets experience dramatic seasonal or holiday-specific fluctuations in visitor volume (e.g., Fourth of July celebration on the National Mall), while a special event might increase the public attention given to a monument or icon. These variables can increase the threat, vulnerability, and/or consequences associated with an attack on the asset. Sector security measures must be flexible enough to enable appropriate responses to seasonal and event-driven increases in risk.

Goal 9: Protect against insider threats. NMI security partners will work together to develop guidelines for protecting against insider threats, such as vetting and credentialing security personnel, enhancing surveillance capabilities, and conducting employee background checks as appropriate.

Goal 10: Develop contingency response programs. NMI security partners will create contingency response programs to ensure the safety and control of visitors at critical sites in the event of a terrorist attack or all-hazards incident.[9]

NMI Security Partners

Federal Security Partners

Department of the Interior

The Department of the Interior (DOI) was created by an act of Congress in 1849 to manage public lands. The DOI has long been involved in the protection of NMI assets, such as the Washington Monument and the Statue of Liberty. The DOI manages the third largest federal law enforcement force, with approximately 4,400 commissioned law enforcement personnel spread among the Bureau of Indian Affairs (BIA), Bureau of Land Management (BLM), Bureau of Reclamation (BOR), Fish and Wildlife Service (FWS), and the National Park Service (NPS). In addition, approximately 1,300 tribal and contract law enforcement personnel serve on Indian country lands. DOI is responsible for the safety and security of 70,000 employees and 200,000 volunteers, 1.3 million daily visitors, and more than 507 million acres of public lands, which include historic or nationally significant sites as well as dams and reservoirs.

Smithsonian Institution

The Smithsonian Institution's (SI) Office of Protection Services (OPS) provides security services and operates programs for security management and criminal investigations at SI facilities on and near the National Mall in Washington, DC, in New York City, and in Panama. OPS provides technical assistance and advisory services to SI bureaus, offices, and facilities. It serves SI employees and volunteers and more than 25 million visitors each year. The United States Code (40 U.S.C. 6301-6307) provided OPS the authority to police the buildings and grounds of the SI.

National Archives and Records Administration

The mission of National Archives and Records Administration (NARA) is to take cost-effective steps to protect the holdings of our archival and records center in an appropriate space, ensure protection and preservation of records, and expand storage capacities to meet growing demands. NARA's authority is codified principally under 44 U.S.C. Chapters 21 to 33. NARA also ensures that the president, congress, the courts, public servants, and citizens continue to have access to the essential evidence that documents the rights of American citizens and the actions of federal officials, promotes civic education, and facilitates a historical understanding of our national experience. NARA sets the minimum structural, environmental, property, and life-safety standards that a records storage facility must meet in order to be used to safeguard and preserve the records of our government and ensure that the people can discover, use, and learn from this documentary heritage.

Federal Bureau of Investigation

The Federal Bureau of Investigation (FBI) is the investigative arm of the U.S. Department of Justice (DOJ). The FBI is the lead federal agency in combating terrorism and investigating acts of terrorism. The FBI's investigative authority is explained in 28 U.S.C. 533 and the USA PATRIOT Act of 2001, which granted the FBI new provisions to address the threat of terrorism.

U.S. Secret Service

When an event is designated as a National Special Security Event (NSSE), the United States Secret Service (USSS) assumes its mandated role as the lead agency for the design and implementation of the operational security plan. An NSSE venue may be located at an NMI asset. The USSS has significant responsibility for White House security in coordination with the Executive Office of the President.

U.S. Department of Homeland Security

Specifically within the U.S. Department of Homeland Security (DHS), the Office of Infrastructure Protection (OIP) provides oversight of the NMI SSP with the support of the Science and Technology Directorate (S&T) within the DHS. The DHS will assist the DOI in establishing relationships with the private sector to ensure maximum information exchange within and outside the federal government. The mutual collaboration and agreement between the DOI and DHS is critical regarding overlaps and interdependencies where the type and character of the NMI asset falls primarily into a CI/KR sector for which DHS is the SSA. The DOI will confer with DHS and the other SSAs to clearly identify these overlaps and interdependencies and will reach consensus on responsibilities for these NMI assets within the respective sectors. For example, there will be overlaps between the DOI's NMI and the DHS's CI/KR sectors with respect to the following:

- DHS's Transportation Systems Sector, with respect to bridges, locks, dams, and canals (e.g., the Golden Gate Bridge);
- DHS's Dams key resource category (e.g., Hoover Dam);
- DHS's Government Facilities key resource category (e.g., the U.S. Capitol); and
- DHS's Commercial Facilities key resource category (e.g., the Empire State Building).

The DOI confers with the DHS to clearly delineate lead and support roles and responsibilities. In its support role, the DOI assists the DHS with respect to the overall protection of these assets.

Department of Defense

The Department of Defense (DOD) is responsible for defending the Nation. DOD owns buildings, structures, and systems that could be categorized as NMI assets (e.g., the Pentagon).

U.S. Army Corps of Engineers

The U.S. Army Corps of Engineers (USACE) is responsible for maintaining the Nation's commercial waterways and operates the dams and locks on our Nation's inland waterways. These examples would fall within the Government Facilities and Dams sectors, respectively, and DHS would be the lead SSA. As previously stated, the DOI works with the DHS and the DOD to delineate lead and support roles and responsibilities.

U.S. Office of Science and Technology Policy

The U.S. Office of Science and Technology Policy (OSTP) has a broad mandate to advise the President and others within the Executive Office of the

President on the effects of science and technology on domestic and international affairs. The office also is authorized to lead an interagency effort to develop and implement sound science and technology policies and budgets and to work with the private sector, state and local governments, the science and higher education communities, and other nations toward this end. The OSTP supports the DOI in developing the NMI SSP and is included, as appropriate, in policy development, protective program plans, and related technology development, operational discussions, and coordination meetings.

Other Federal Security Agencies

Although not listed in the DHS guidance document, other federal agencies own or are responsible for buildings, structures, and systems that could be categorized as NMI assets. The assets under the responsibility of these federal agencies would be included as CI/KR under Government Facilities or Transportation Systems sectors, and DHS would be the lead SSA.

State, Local, and Tribal Security Partners

State Offices of Homeland Security

States have designated homeland security advisors that work with the DHS to coordinate law enforcement operations, domestic security, emergency response and recovery, policy development, and implementation of programs to better align resources to protect public and private ventures and to secure the homeland. The DOI works with these advisors through the DHS to develop a list of assets that may be categorized within this sector.

State and Local Law Enforcement

State police agencies are responsible for public safety and domestic security, providing law enforcement and investigative services in cooperation with county and municipal agencies. These state-level agencies link federal government and local agencies by providing statewide jurisdictional administration for law enforcement, domestic security, and antiterrorism issues.

State, Local, and Tribal Authorities

These authorities typically own or regulate regional and local NMI assets. The DOI works closely with DHS in establishing relationships with State Offices of Homeland Security to ensure maximum information exchange within and outside the federal government. These State offices, in conjunction with DHS, develop close working relationships with other state and local agencies responsible for NMI assets as a major part of outreach efforts.

Private Sector Security Partners

Private sector firms function as an adjunct to, but not a replacement for, public law enforcement by helping to reduce and prevent crime. They protect individuals, property, and proprietary information, and provide protection for banks, hospitals, research and development (R&D) centers, manufacturing facilities, defense and aerospace contractors, high-technology businesses, nuclear power plants, chemical companies, oil and gas refineries, airports, communication facilities and operations, office complexes, schools, private universities, residential properties, apartment complexes, gated communities, museums, sporting events, and theme parks. Private sector security and law enforcement entities derive their authority from state, regional, and local laws in effect for their jurisdictions or areas of responsibility. Many assets within the NMI Sector utilize private security guards under contract, both armed and unarmed, as their sole security force or to supplement their law enforcement and security staffs.

Summary

In conclusion, this chapter has outlined the scope, significance, and planning efforts of the national monuments and facilities sectors in the United States. While more work is needed to further develop plans and strategies for the protection of these sectors, the NIPP has injected these communities with the requirement to continue discussions on the safeguarding of life and property. The NIPP coordination has forced entities who previously had not communicated on these issues to collaborate and think critically about the required elements of CI/KR protection. These planning efforts, which continue today, will add to the current body of knowledge on planning, responding, and recovering in the certain, but unfortunate, event of an act of terrorism, natural disaster, or other attack against the United States.

9

....

Environmental: Agriculture and Food, Chemical, and Water Infrastructure

Agriculture and Food Infrastructure

Among the Homeland Security Presidential Directives (HSPDs), HSPD-9: Defense of United States Agriculture and Food, was issued to establish a national policy to defend the Nation's agriculture and food systems against terrorist attacks, major disasters, and other emergencies. The directive recognizes DHS' role as "responsible for coordinating the overall national effort to enhance the protection of the critical infrastructure and key resources of the United States".[1]

....

Mission of the Food and Agriculture Sector

Prevent the contamination of the food supply that would pose a serious threat to public health, safety, and welfare. Provide the central focus for a steadily evolving and complex industry/sector, with particular emphasis on the protection and strengthening of the Nation's capacity to supply safe, nutritious, and affordable food.

....

The U.S. Food and Agriculture Sector, which is predominantly made up of privately owned assets, complex production, processing, and delivery systems, has the capacity to feed not only this Nation, but many other international countries as well. The sector comprises more than two million farms, approximately 900,000 firms, and 1.1 million facilities. The sector accounts for roughly one-fifth of the Nation's economic activity.

The U.S. Department of Agriculture (USDA) has Sector-Specific Agency (SSA) responsibility for production agriculture and shares responsibilities for food safety and defense with the Department of Health and Human Services (HHS) Food and Drug Administration (FDA). Specifically, the FDA is responsible for the safety of 80% of all food consumed in the United States, including the entire domestic and imported food supply; however, meat, poultry, and frozen, dried, and liquid eggs are under the authority of USDA.

There are two primary missions of the Food and Agriculture Sector:

1. Protect against any attack on the food supply, including production agriculture, which would pose a serious threat to public health, safety, welfare, or the national economy; and
2. Strengthen the Nation's capacity to supply safe, nutritious, and affordable food.

Securing the sector presents unique challenges because U.S. agriculture and food systems are extensive; there are more than two million farms covering more than 1 billion acres of land in the Nation. In addition to privately held farms, the USDA Forest Service allows for livestock grazing on portions of National Forest lands. These open, interconnected, diverse, and complex structures provide attractive potential targets for terrorist attacks. Attacks on the sector, such as introducing animal or plant disease or food contamination, could result in severe animal, plant, or public health and economic consequences because food products rapidly move in commerce to consumers without leaving enough time to detect and identify a causative agent.[2]

Another challenge in securing the Food and Agriculture Sector is the fact that it operates in a global context, and the United States plays a significant role in the international market. The U.S. share of the global market for agricultural products is a slightly less than 20%. Therefore, U.S. farms tend to produce more than our domestic needs call for, therefore maintaining a competitive agricultural system is essential to ensuring the economic vitality of U.S. agriculture.[3]

••

The complex and vulnerable **Food and Agriculture** Sector comprises:

- More than two million farms covering more than one billion acres,
- 1.1 million facilities,
- 900,000 firms,
- One-fifth of the Nation's economic activity; and
- One-fifth of the world's global market for agriculture products.

••

Food Products

With more than 26 billion pounds of beef, 22 billion pounds of pork, 40 billion pounds of poultry meat, and 73 billion eggs sold annually, the United States is the largest producer of meat, poultry, and egg products in the world.

This portion of the sector is also almost entirely privately held. The processing facilities are privately owned; however, the government supplies the onsite federal or state inspectors and owns the federal and state laboratories that provide food safety and defense diagnostic services. Imported meat, poultry, and egg products are also an important consideration in sector security because they are distributed with domestic products. It is estimated that there are approximately 21 million trucks transporting products, including a majority of food and agricultural commodities, across the United States every day.

Regulatory oversight for this portion of the sector rests with the Food Safety and Inspection Service (FSIS) of the USDA. This sector provides continuous inspection of all meat, poultry, and egg products prepared for distribution in commerce and are also responsible for re-inspecting imported products to ensure that they meet U.S. food safety standards. In 2002, FSIS established the Office of Food Defense and Emergency Response, which develops, maintains, and coordinates all FSIS activities to prevent, prepare for, respond to, and recover from emergencies resulting from non-intentional contamination or deliberate acts of terrorism affecting meat, poultry, and egg products. FSIS works closely with the FDA because of the similarities in regulatory authority, and with the DHS Customs and Border Patrol for defense of imported products.[4]

In addition, the Public Health Security and Bioterrorism Preparedness and Response Act was enacted in 2002 to address agro-terrorism preparedness and response vulnerabilities identified after September 11, 2001. Agriculture-specific provisions included expanding the FDA's authority over food manufacturing and imports, tightening the control of biological agents and toxins under rules by the Animal and Plant Health Inspection Service (APHIS) and Centers for Disease Control and Prevention (CDC), expanding the agricultural security activities and security upgrades at USDA facilities, and increasing the criminal penalties for terrorism against animal enterprises and violation of the select agent rules. Concurrently, DHS became responsible for coordinating the overall national efforts to enhance the protection of the critical infrastructure and key resources of the United States.[5]

Threats to the Agricultural Sector

The potential for terrorist attacks against agricultural targets, termed agro-terrorism, is increasingly recognized as a national security threat, especially following the events during and after September 11, 2001. Agro-terrorism is a subset of bioterrorism, and is defined as the deliberate introduction of an animal or plant disease with the goal of generating fear, causing economic losses, and/or undermining social stability. The goal of agro-terrorism is simply not to kill cows or plants, but is a means to the end of causing economic damage, social unrest, and loss of confidence in government. Human health could be at risk if contaminated food reaches the table or if an animal pathogen is transmissible to humans.

The agricultural sector has several characteristics that inherently present unique vulnerabilities. Farms are geographically dispersed in typically remote environments. Livestock are frequently concentrated in confined locations and transported or commingled with other herds. Many agricultural disease agents can be easily obtained, handled, and distributed as they may be readily found in many areas outside the United States and do not pose a safety risk to the aspiring agro-terrorist. Because of the relative success of our domestic agricultural disease prevention activities, our herds are free from more than forty internationally significant diseases such as foot and mouth disease (FMD), classical swine fever (formerly known as hog cholera), and African swine fever. This success leads to great vulnerability, however, as international trade in food products is often tied to disease-free status, which could be jeopardized by an attack. Since our herds have been free of these diseases for generations and vaccines do not yet exist for many of them, our animals are highly susceptible to natural or intentional introduction. Moreover, most U.S. veterinarians lack experience with foreign animal diseases that have been eradicated domestically, but remain endemic in foreign countries. In the past five years, agriculture and food production have received a certain degree of increased attention from the counterterrorism community and response capacities have been significantly upgraded.

The risk of an attack on the Nation's livestock is defined by the likelihood of a terrorist attempting to use a biologic agent to infect livestock populations, the vulnerability of those livestock populations to infection with the agent utilized, and the economic or other consequence from the attack. The overall economic impact of a natural or intentional reintroduction of FMD would include the direct supply shortages to livestock-dependent industries such as the meat and milk industries. The feed industry would have an instant overabundance of feedstuffs previously consumed by production animals that could not be sold, and employees of these industries would be adversely impacted. Additionally, and perhaps most significantly, major trade issues would result as many other nations would likely ban the import of all U.S. livestock products such as meat, milk, leather products, and feed. These direct effects on the national economy and potential impacts from quarantines and third and fourth order effects would reach into the transportation, tourism, and defense sectors of our economy.

Computerized risk assessment scenarios conducted by the DHS reveal that a single point introduction of FMD could spread very rapidly and affect millions of animals and cause billions of dollars in economic damage. These risk assessments and impact analyses of an attack with this biologic agent identify the vulnerability of our livestock populations and the potentially devastating consequences of only one livestock disease. The DHS brings a great sense of urgency to develop countermeasures and diagnostics to combat a wide variety of these livestock bioterrorism threats. A major threat in the food and agriculture sectors is a crisis of confidence, where a poorly prevented or recognized event causes people to question the safety of food regionally or nationally. Therefore, a swift confidence-building response is a critical objective of planning and exercising efforts. Another critical element is to continue to provide online training tools for regulators, inspectors, farmers, food producers, and food cooperatives.[6]

Chemical Infrastructure

The DHS has established a significant federal role in the chemical sector by creating ongoing cooperative relationships with chemical facility owners and operators and their related associations. The DHS has completed assessments and made recommendations to all of the chemical facilities that have the potential to affect more than a half-million of surrounding population. The facility owners and operators as well as the DHS have made investments to enhance physical security at each facility by adopting numerous homeland security recommendations, which include strengthening buffer zones, improving access control, implementing detection technologies, and increasing response preparedness capabilities.

Vulnerability assessments are underway for the nearly 300 sites that could potentially affect more than 50,000 of surrounding populations. To date, DHS officials have engaged these sites on more than 110 occasions by conducting a variety of assessments. The DHS continues to visit these facilities on a priority basis in coordination with the state homeland security advisors, state and local law enforcement, and sites owners and operators.

The DHS has adapted the Environmental Protection Agency's (EPA) Risk Management Program (RMP) database from a preparedness and safety approach to one that focuses on the impacts of terrorist attacks. This enables the prioritization of vulnerability identification efforts and protective actions. The DHS has also conducted a risk analysis across the chemical sector to identify the most hazardous or highest-consequence sites. This analysis included:

- Reviewing the amount and toxicity of RMP materials stored at sites;
- Reviewing the population density in the vicinity of large amounts of toxic chemicals;
- Evaluating possible impacts of intentional attack instead of the accidental release model used in safety programs; and
- Conducting plume modeling for more detailed effects prediction.

While the DHS continues to work with state, local, and industry partners to refine the list of chemical sites, there are roughly 3,000 facilities that could impact more than 1,000 people and nearly 300 facilities that could impact 50,000 or more people. To date, DHS officials have visited more than 160 of the more than 300 chemical, petrochemical, and related sites of immediate concern. Further, the DHS continues to inspect these facilities on a priority basis.

Security Programs and Target Hardening Techniques

Protective programs that will more systematically identify and develop best practices across the entire chemical sector and beyond the fence line of a specific plant continue to be an aggressive effort to integrate community assets into the overall security posture of the chemical infrastructure. This effort includes programs such as the Buffer Zone Protection Program (BZPP), which contributes to reducing specific vulnerabilities by developing protective measures that extend from the critical infrastructure site to the surrounding community to deny terrorists an operational environment. The DHS works in collaboration with state, local, and tribal entities by providing training workshops, seminars, technical assistance, and a common template to standardize the BZP development process. To date, 113 plans developed for chemical facilities have been submitted to the DHS via state homeland security advisors.

Sector Collaboration

The DHS works in close coordination with such organizations as the American Chemistry Council to develop security-oriented screening tools, assessment tools, best practices, and other processes to improve understanding both of risk and vulnerability, and to improve security on a site-by-site and infrastructure-wide basis. All 2,040 member companies of the American Chemistry Council, as well as the entire membership of the Synthetic Organic Chemical Manufacturer's Association, and several other chemical industry trade associations, were required to implement strict voluntary security measures by the end of 2004. Outreach programs, information sharing, best practices, and site assistance visits have all encouraged owner/operators to reinforce employee screening.

Water Infrastructure

HSPD-7: Critical Infrastructure Identification, Prioritization, and Protection designates the EPA as the federal lead for the Water Sector's critical infrastructure protection activities. All activities are carried out in consultation with DHS and the EPA's Water Sector partners. HSPD-9: Defense of United States Agriculture and Food establishes a national policy to defend the water, agriculture, and food system against terrorist attacks, major disasters, and other emergencies. It calls on EPA and other federal agencies to:

- Build upon and expand current monitoring and surveillance programs for public health and water quality that provide early detection and awareness of disease, pest, or poisonous agents;
- Develop nationwide laboratory networks for water quality that integrate existing federal and state laboratory resources;
- Develop and enhance intelligence capabilities to include collection and analysis of information concerning threats, delivery systems, and methods that could be directed against the Water Sector; and
- Accelerate and expand countermeasure research and development of detection methods, prevention technologies, agent characterization, and dose–response relationships for high-consequence agents.

There are approximately 160,000 public drinking water utilities, which produce more than 51 billion gallons of drinking water per day, and there are more than 16,000 wastewater utilities in the United States. About 84% of the

U.S. population receives its potable water from these drinking water utilities, and more than 75% have their sanitary sewage treated by these wastewater utilities. Another approximately 27,000 commercial and industrial facilities rely on the drinking water and wastewater utilities. This system relies on approximately 2.3 million miles of distribution pipes and another 77,000 dams and reservoirs in the United States to meet the daily needs of consumers.

A slight majority of water systems are owned by public entities. There is also an inverse relationship to size of community and type of ownership. For example, as the size or population of a community increases so does public ownership of the water system. Approximately 39% of privately owned systems, or 20% of all systems, are ancillary systems (that is, their primary business is not water supply, but they provide water as an integral part of their business). These systems tend to serve small populations, produce smaller quantities of water, and often do not bill customers separately for water. Most systems that rely mainly on surface or purchased water are publicly owned.

The Water Sector, which comprises drinking water and wastewater assets, has a long history of implementing programs to provide clean and safe water, thereby protecting public health and the environment across the Nation. For more than thirty years, utilities have been conducting routine daily, weekly, and monthly water quality monitoring under guidance of the Safe Drinking Water Act (SDWA) and the Clean Water Act (CWA). Researchers also continue to explore ways to improve water quality testing

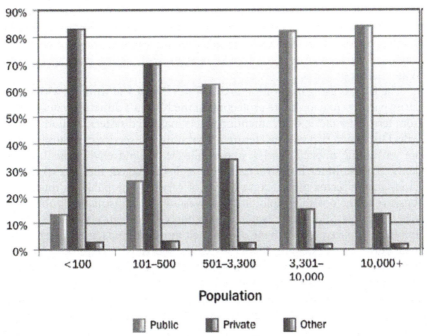

Figure 9.1 Ownership of Public Water Systems[7]

methods. All of the sector's public health, environmental, and security-related efforts rely on a multi-barrier approach. For example, drinking water utilities typically employ a variety of protective programs that include source water protection, treatment and treatment redundancy, monitoring using certified laboratories, appropriately certified operators, and mechanisms to educate members of the public about water quality and inform them of any violations.

The Water Sector is vulnerable to a variety of attacks, including contamination with deadly agents and physical and cyber attacks. If these attacks were to occur, the result could be large numbers of illnesses or casualties or denial of service that would also affect public health and economic vitality. Critical services such as firefighting and healthcare (hospitals), and other dependent and interdependent sectors such as energy, transportation, and food and agriculture, would suffer negative impacts from a denial of Water Sector service.

Because drinking water is consumed directly, health effects associated with contamination have long been major concerns. In addition, interruption or cessation of the drinking water supply can disrupt society, by effecting human health and critical activities such as fire protection that can have significant consequences to the national or regional economies. The public correctly perceives drinking water as central to the life of an individual and of society. Consumers are highly sensitive to the threat of contamination or disruption. The federal and state governments have long been active in addressing these risks and threats through regulations, technical assistance, research, and outreach programs. As a result, an extensive system of regulations governing maximum contaminants levels, of ninety contaminants, construction and operating standards (implemented mostly by the states), monitoring, emergency response planning, training, research, and education have been developed to better protect the Nation's drinking water supply and receiving waters. This regulatory system was created with active participation by Water Sector partners.

The EPA is using its position in the Water Sector and working with its security partners to coordinate protection of the Nation's drinking water supply from terrorist attacks, other intentional acts, natural disasters, and other hazards. Disruption of a wastewater treatment utility or service can cause loss of life, economic impacts, and severe public health and environmental incidents. If wastewater infrastructure were to be damaged, the lack of redundancy in the sector might cause denial of service. The public is much less sensitive to the possible exploitation of wastewater infrastructure vulnerabilities compared to drinking water vulnerabilities. Regulations, research, and outreach, while extensive, have been aimed mostly at impacts to the environment due to service denials. With the exception of requirements in the Bioterrorism Act, implementation and maintenance of protective programs in the Water Sector is voluntary and generally occurs at the local utility (asset) level. EPA has encouraged implementation of protective programs by working with its security partners to develop useful tools, training, technical assistance, guidance, and outreach and communication mechanisms that provide assistance to Water Sector assets to enhance their security posture.

The majority of asset owner/operators in the Water Sector have protective programs in place. Each program is unique depending on local conditions and the risks to a particular asset. The EPA, in collaboration with the Water Sector, is engaged with the DHS and other federal agencies in implementation of protective programs for Water and the other CI/KR sectors.

Furthermore, as Water and other critical infrastructure sectors continue to identify dependencies and interdependencies, SSAs are working together to implement protective actions that help mitigate vulnerable dependencies/interdependencies and better prepare assets to prevent, detect, respond to, and recover from terrorist attacks, other intentional acts, natural disasters, and other hazards. Most drinking water and wastewater programs are delegated to the states. Therefore, the EPA depends heavily on state drinking water primacy agencies and the wastewater-permitting authorities to provide the necessary protection measures.

Threats and Countermeasures

The potential for terrorism is not new. In 1941, Federal Bureau of Investigation (FBI) Director J. Edgar Hoover wrote, "It has long been recognized that among public utilities, water supply facilities offer a particularly vulnerable point of attack to the foreign agent, due to the strategic position they occupy in keeping the wheels of industry turning and in preserving the health and morale of the American populace."[8] Water infrastructure systems also are highly linked with other infrastructure systems, especially electric power and transportation, as well as the chemical industry which supplies treatment chemicals, making security of all of them an issue of concern. These types of vulnerable interconnections were evident, for example, during the August 2003 electricity blackout in the Northeast United States: wastewater treatment plants in Cleveland, Detroit, New York, and other locations that lacked backup generation systems lost power and discharged millions of gallons of untreated sewage during the emergency and power failures at drinking water plants, which led to boil water advisories in many communities. Likewise, natural disasters such as the recent Gulf Coast hurricanes (Karina, Rita, and Ike) and the 2008 Midwest floods caused extensive and costly damage to multiple infrastructure systems—transportation, water, electric power, and telecommunications.

A fairly small number of large drinking water and wastewater utilities located primarily in urban areas (about 15% of the systems) provide water services to more than 75% of the U.S. population. Arguably, these systems represent the greatest targets of opportunity for terrorist attacks, while the large number of small systems that each serve fewer than 10,000 persons are less likely to be perceived as key targets by terrorists who might seek to disrupt water infrastructure systems. However, the more numerous smaller systems also tend to be less protected and, thus, are potentially more vulnerable to attack, whether by vandals or terrorists. A successful attack on even a small system could cause widespread panic, economic impacts, and a loss of public confidence in water supply systems. Attacks resulting in physical destruction to any of these systems could include disruption of operating or distribution system components, power or telecommunications systems, electronic control systems, and actual damage to reservoirs and pumping stations. A loss of flow and pressure would cause problems for customers and would hinder firefighting efforts. Further, destruction of a large dam could result in catastrophic flooding and loss of life. Bioterrorism or chemical attacks could deliver widespread contamination with small amounts of microbiological agents or toxic chemicals, and could endanger the public health of thousands. While some experts believe that risks to water systems are actually small, because it would be difficult to introduce sufficient quantities of agents to cause widespread harm, concern and heightened awareness of potential problems are apparent.

Less attention has been focused on protecting wastewater treatment facilities than drinking water systems, perhaps because destruction of them represents more of an environmental threat (i.e., by release of untreated sewage), than a direct threat to life or public welfare. Vulnerabilities do exist, however. Large underground collector sewers could be accessed by terrorist groups for purposes of placing destructive devices beneath buildings or city streets. Pipelines can be made into weapons via the introduction of a highly flammable substance such as gasoline through a manhole or inlet. Explosions in the sewers can cause collapse of roads, sidewalks, and adjacent structures that could injure and kill people nearby. Damage to a wastewater facility prevents water from being treated and can impact downriver water intakes. Destruction of containers that hold large amounts of chemicals at treatment plants could result in release of toxic chemical agents, such as chlorine gas, which can be deadly to humans if inhaled and, at lower doses, can burn eyes and skin and inflame the lungs. Since the 2001 terrorist attacks, many water and wastewater utilities have switched from using chlorine gas for disinfection to alternatives which are believed to be safer, such as sodium hypochlorite or ultraviolet light. However, some consumer groups remain concerned that many wastewater utilities, including facilities that serve heavily populated areas, continue to use chlorine gas. To prepare for potential accidental releases of hazardous chemicals from their facilities, more than 2,800 wastewater and drinking water utilities, water supply systems, and irrigation systems already are subject to risk management planning requirements under the Clean Air Act. Still, some observers advocate requiring federal standards to ensure that facilities using dangerous chemicals, such as wastewater treatment plants, use the best possible industry practices (practices that are referred to as Inherently Safer Technologies, or ISTs) to reduce hazards.[9,10]

In March 2006, the Government Accountability Office (GAO) reported on a survey of security measures at 200 of the Nation's largest wastewater utilities. The GAO study found that many have made security improvements since the 2001 terrorist attacks. Most utilities said they have completed, or intend to complete, a plan to conduct some type of security assessment. More than half of responding facilities indicated they did not use potentially dangerous gaseous chlorine as a wastewater disinfectant. However, the report noted that these utilities have made little effort to address collection system vulnerabilities, due to the technical complexity and expense of securing collection systems that cover large areas and have many access points. Some told GAO investigators that taking other measures, such as converting from gaseous chlorine, took priority over collection system protections. In a 2007 the GAO reported that actual and projected capital costs to convert from chlorine gas to alternative disinfection methods range from about $650,000 to just over $13 million.[11] Factors affecting conversion costs included the type of alternative method, the size of the facility, and labor, building, and supply costs, which varied considerably.

Evidence suggests that the integrity of the Nation's drinking water and wastewater infrastructure is at risk without a concerted effort to improve the management of key assets—pipelines, treatment plants, and other facilities—and a significant investment in maintaining, rehabilitating, and replacing these assets. According to recent studies by the EPA and other organizations, drinking water and wastewater utilities will need to invest hundreds of billions of dollars in their capital infrastructure over the next two decades.

If utilities maintain current spending levels, however, financing-needed investments could be problematic. Based on a survey of several thousand drinking water and wastewater utilities, the GAO reported in August 2002 that a significant percentage of the utilities—29% of the drinking water utilities and 41% of the wastewater utilities—were not generating enough revenue from user rates and other local sources to cover their full cost of service.[12] Furthermore, roughly one-third of the utilities had deferred maintenance because of insufficient funding, had 20% or more of their pipelines nearing the end of their useful life, and lacked basic plans for managing their capital assets.[13]

Needed Improvements in Infrastructure

Drinking water and wastewater utilities are facing potentially significant investments over the next twenty years to:

- Upgrade an aging and deteriorated infrastructure, including underground pipelines, treatment, and storage facilities;
- Meet new regulatory requirements;
- Serve a growing population; and
- Improve security.

Adding to the problem is that many utilities have not been generating enough revenues from user charges and other local sources to cover their full cost of service. As a result, utilities have deferred maintenance and postponed needed capital improvements. To address these problems and help ensure that utilities can manage their needs cost-effectively, some water industry and government officials advocate the use of comprehensive asset management. Asset management is a systematic approach to managing capital assets in order to minimize costs over the useful life of the assets while maintaining adequate service to customers. While the approach is relatively new to the U.S. water industry, it has been used by water utilities in other countries for as long as ten years. Each year, the federal government makes available

••••••••••••••••••••••••••••••••••••

Asset management is a systematic approach to managing capital assets in order to minimize costs over the useful life of the assets while maintaining adequate service to customers.

••••••••••••••••••••••••••••••••••••

billions of dollars to help local communities finance drinking water and wastewater infrastructure projects. Concerns about the condition of existing infrastructure have prompted calls to increase financial assistance and, at the same time, ensure that the federal government's investment is protected. In recent years congress has been considering a number of proposals that would promote the use of comprehensive asset management by requiring utilities to develop and implement plans for maintaining, rehabilitating, and replacing capital assets, often as assets, often as a condition of obtaining loans or other financial assistance.

Drinking water and wastewater utilities will need to invest hundreds of billions of dollars in their capital infrastructure over the next two decades, according to the EPA, the Congressional Budget Office, and the Water Infrastructure Network, a consortium of industry, municipal, state, and nonprofit associations. The Nation's largest utilities—those serving populations of at least 10,000 people—account for most of the projected infrastructure needs. For example, according to the EPA data, large drinking water systems represent about 7% of the total number of community water systems and account for about 65% of the estimated infrastructure needs.[14] Similarly, about 29% of the wastewater treatment and collection systems are estimated to serve populations of 10,000 or more, and such systems account for approximately 89% of projected infrastructure needs for wastewater utilities.[15] Most of the U.S. population is served by large drinking water and wastewater utilities. For example, systems serving at least 10,000 people provide drinking water to more than 80% of the population. Pipeline rehabilitation and replacement represents a significant portion of the projected infrastructure needs. According to the American Society of Civil Engineers (ASCE), U.S. drinking water and wastewater utilities are responsible for an estimated 800,000 miles of water delivery pipelines and between 600,000 and 800,000 miles of sewer pipelines, respectively.

10

....

Electronic Transmissions

Introduction

More than 20% of the United States' gross domestic product (GDP) is a product of the sectors represented in this chapter. These three sectors (Communications, Information Technology, and Banking/Finance) support our daily activities, thus increasing their need to be reliable and resilient to continue providing us with the essential services we depend on. This chapter will overview the Sector Specific Plans (SSP) for each of these sectors. For more information on SSPs, visit: http://www.dhs.gov/xnews/gc_1179776352521.shtm.

Communications Sector[1]

The communications infrastructure is a complex network of systems that incorporates multiple technologies and services with diverse ownership. The infrastructure includes wireline, wireless, satellite, cable, and broadcasting, and provides the transport networks that support the Internet and other key information systems. Focused risk management and infrastructure protection are integral to the sector's business continuity planning and network design processes. These network level protective strategies and individual owner/operator protective measures are tested, implemented, and used daily to rapidly restore outages caused not only by those with malicious intent (e.g., cyber attacks), but also by accidental or natural incidents such as flooding, earthquake, hurricanes, or tornados. The resiliency built into the communications infrastructure increases the availability of service to its customers and reduces the impact of outages.

Communications Sector owners and operators focus on ensuring overall reliability of the networks, maintaining "always on" capabilities for certain critical customers, and quickly restoring capabilities following a disruption. The sector mitigates cascading effects of incidents by designing and building resilient and redundant communications systems and networks to ensure disruptions remain largely localized and do not affect the national communications backbone. While the sector focuses on ensuring network level systems are resilient and secure, customers must ensure their own critical systems and operations are supported by diverse primary and backup communications capabilities. Recent tragic events have highlighted the importance of communications to our Nation. These disasters, although catastrophic, proved the overall resiliency of the national communications network. Despite the sheer size of the events that occurred, the network backbone remained intact.

Two key policy events helped shape the modern-day communications industry. The first event was the 1984 court-ordered breakup of AT&T, which controlled the majority of the local and long distance markets. The second event was the passage of the Telecommunications Act of 1999, which aims to provide for a pro-competitive, deregulatory national policy framework designed to rapidly accelerate private sector deployment of advanced telecommunications and information technologies and services to all Americans by opening all telecommunications markets to competition. As a result, instead of one company controlling and protecting the entire communications network, hundreds of wireline and wireless companies, including cellular and satellite, provide communications services today.

Scope of the Communications Sector

Driven by 21st century technology transformation and convergence, the Communications and the Information Technology (IT) sectors will become more closely aligned over time. The Communications Sector includes not only physical properties such as wireline, wireless, satellite, cable, and broadcasting, but also services such as the Internet, information services, and cable television networks. In addition, publicly and privately owned cyber/logical assets are inextricably linked with these physical communications structures. Below are brief descriptions of each component.

- **Wireline:** The wireline component consists primarily of the public switched telephone network (PSTN), but also includes cable networks and enterprise networks. The wireline component also includes the Internet and submarine cable infrastructure.
- **Wireless:** The wireless component consists primarily of cellular telephone, paging, personal communications services, high frequency radio, unlicensed wireless, and other commercial and private radio services—including numerous law enforcement, public safety, and land mobile radio systems.
- **Satellite:** Satellite communications systems use a combination of terrestrial and space components to deliver various communications, Internet data, and video

services. Three different types of satellite services exist: fixed, broadcast, and mobile.

- **Cable:** Cable television (CATV) networks are wireline networks offering television, Internet, and voice services that interconnect with the PSTN through end offices.
- **Broadcasting:** Broadcasting elements consist of all parts of a radio or television station transmission system.

While the private sector owns more than 80% of critical infrastructure, government and public safety agencies own and operate communications systems that support their critical missions, including defense, law enforcement, and public safety.

∙∙∙

Telecommunications is defined as: '(1) Any transmission, emission, or reception of signs, signals, writing, images, and sounds or intelligence of any nature by wire, radio, optical, or other electromagnetic systems; or (2) any transmission emission, or reception of signs, signals, writings, images, sounds, or information of any nature by wire, radio, visual, or other electromagnetic systems.'[2]

∙∙∙

Communications Sector Partners

Because of the interconnectivity and interoperability aspects of networks, sector partners have broad requirements to collaborate in numerous areas, such as network interconnection, collocation, equipment and software standards, and response planning. Below, a few of the many partnerships in this sector are identified.

- **Industry–Government**: Industry and government have worked closely together on communications issues since the breakup of AT&T and the Bell System in the early 1980s. Today, various industry partnerships and forums advise government on communications issues, share information about vulnerabilities and threats, and develop best practices for securing the infrastructure.
- **Federal**: The National Communications System (NCS) has a long history of coordinating National Security/Emergency Preparedness (NS/EP) communications with agencies throughout the federal government. As the critical infrastructure protection lead for the Communications Sector within the federal government, the NCS is responsible for coordinating activities with numerous U.S. Department of Homeland Security (DHS) offices, as well as other departments and agencies with Communications Sector responsibilities. The NCS coordinates many of its critical infrastructure protection efforts with other offices within the department, including the National Cyber Security Division (NCSD) on cyber security issues and the Office of Infrastructure Protection (OIP) on cross-sector critical infrastructure and risk management issues.
- **State and Local**: Relationships with state and local agencies in the Communications Sector focus primarily on regulatory issues with State Public Utility Commissions (SPUC), state and local emergency operation centers (EOC), and

emergency response activities with first responders and 911 emergency centers. Since 2001, federal entities have been coordinating homeland security initiatives by establishing information-sharing relationships within the federal government and with states and cities, and conducting vulnerability assessments of their communications networks.

- **International**: Communications networks are global in scope; hence, it is important that infrastructure protection activities for the sector extend beyond U.S. borders. Industry and government are actively involved in international organizations and multilateral/bilateral relationships to share lessons learned, discuss best practices, and set standards.

Communications Sector Specific Plan (CSSP)

This Communications Sector Specific Plan (CSSP) resulted from a close collaboration among the NCS, the Communications Sector Coordinating Council, and the Communications Sector Government Coordinating Council (GCC). It provides a framework for industry and government partners to develop a coordinated protection strategy. Private sector companies have existing protection efforts, which are aimed at limiting risk to the business and maintaining operational capabilities. Business leaders have a board-level responsibility to direct these efforts and ensure they are implemented effectively. The federal government has a responsibility to develop and execute a national plan, which protects the overall security of the Nation.

The vision developed within the CSSP utilizes both public and private resources to establish a single strategic framework for protecting the Nation's critical communications infrastructure. This framework builds upon already strong corporate capabilities, unique government resources, and coordination capabilities beyond what business can provide. This combined capacity will help to maximize Communications Sector efforts to protect critical assets against natural and man-made threats.

The desired security posture will be achieved through the application of the following principles:

- Protective programs will principally focus on response and recovery strategies;
- Communications Sector industry partners are responsible for employing prevention and protection strategies, except when industry may request government assistance for protection of critical communications facilities during extraordinary events, such as Hurricane Katrina and 9/11;
- Customers are responsible for protecting their own assets and access points, and providing for diverse and assured communications that support their specific essential functions;
- Government programs will support the availability of communications services for NS/EP users and protection of government communications assets;
- Communications Sector industry partners will continue to work with government through the NCS on NS/EP, threat dissemination, subject matter expertise, analytic support, information sharing, and contingency planning and response; and
- The Communications Sector recognizes that other critical infrastructures are highly dependent upon communications for basic operations.

Vision Statement for the Communications Sector

The Communications Sector acknowledges the Nation's critical reliance on assured communications. The Communications Sector will strive to ensure that the Nation's communications networks and systems are secure, resilient, and rapidly restored after a natural or man-made disaster.[3]

Sector Goals and Objectives

Goal 1: Protect the overall health of the national communications backbone. The Communications Sector recognizes that other critical infrastructures are highly dependent on its services for basic operations. The overall architecture of the Communications Sector incorporates various technologies and services and has diverse ownership. Interconnection, interoperability, and security are achieved through technology standards, regulation, carrier agreements, and intercarrier cooperation, enabling the communications infrastructure to operate effectively and rapidly restore networks after a disaster. Resiliency is achieved through the technology, redundancy, and diversity employed in the network design and by customers who plan for and employ diverse and resilient primary and backup communications capabilities.

Goal 2: Rapidly reconstitute critical communications services after national and regional emergencies. Industry and government will continue to improve processes and procedures to respond rapidly to all crises to restore critical communications services. The NCS, as lead for Emergency Support Function (ESF) #2 (Communications), will support industry's response and recovery effort in collaboration with states to assist with obtaining necessary resources (e.g., fuel, security), getting access to disaster areas, and setting restoration priorities. The NCS will support the restoration and recovery process.

Goal 3: Plan for emergencies and crises through participation in exercises, and update response and continuity of operations plans. To achieve this goal, the NCS will employ the most likely threat scenarios provided by the Intelligence Community or natural disaster scenarios to evaluate existing contingency and reliability plans. Based on these threat scenarios, federal and state governments and the private sector will jointly plan and participate in emergency response training and exercises that address a spectrum of threats and hazards. The NCS also will support federal government continuity planning efforts to put measures in place to ensure service continuity and availability for National Essential Functions and associated Priority Mission Essential Functions requiring communications within identified Maximum Allowable Outage (MAO) periods.

Goal 4: Develop protocols to manage the exponential surge in utilization during an emergency situation, and ensure the integrity of sector networks during and after an emergency event. To achieve this goal, the NCS and Communications Sector industry partners will coordinate with the international community in the development of protocol standards and technologies to better manage the exponential surge in calls that can occur during emergency situations. The NCS, in collaboration with the Federal Communications Commission (FCC) and the National Association of Regulatory Utility Commissioners (NARUC), also will continue to conduct outreach at conferences and trade shows on priority service programs (e.g., Telecommunications Service Priority [TSP], Wireless Priority Service [WPS], and Government Emergency Telecommunications Service [GETS]) to ensure necessary users and facilities are appropriately registered. The NCS will coordinate with the DHS Science and Technology Directorate (S&T) to promote research and development (R&D) to improve priority service programs and to explore ways of preserving the integrity of sector networks during and after an incident.

Goal 5: Educate stakeholders on communications infrastructure resiliency and risk management practices in the Communications Sector. Awareness and education on communications infrastructure resiliency and risk management practices are critical for stakeholders to maintain their critical operations. The NCS, in partnership with industry, will seek to develop education mechanisms to work with public and private critical infrastructure users to coordinate protection and response strategies to assist customers in employing existing methods and capabilities more effectively. The NCS and industry will partner with other government agencies to analyze and prioritize the full spectrum of critical government and private sector functions that depend on the Communications Sector. Finally, in partnership with NCSD, the NCS and industry will identify and assess critical operational cyber/logical functions for potential impact if a communications infrastructure element is lost.

Goal 6: Ensure timely, relevant, and accurate threat information sharing between the law enforcement and intelligence communities and key decision makers in the sector. Information sharing is an important component of improving awareness and preventing an event or minimizing its impact. To achieve this goal, it is important that information sharing be mutual (two-way) and provide specific and actionable information. The sector will work to obtain the necessary security clearances to receive actionable information and to assist in intelligence and threat analysis as appropriate. The NCS will serve as the focal point for sharing information to and from relevant state and local authorities for the sector, and implement industry–government information-sharing processes to ensure that consistent and accurate information is provided from a centralized source. Industry and government will need to increase threat and vulnerability information sharing to implement the appropriate threat-based security measures and risk management programs.

Goal 7: Establish effective cross-sector coordination mechanisms to address critical interdependencies, including incident situational awareness and cross-sector incident management. To fully understand and determine an acceptable level of risk, all sectors must understand their dependency on and interdependency with the communications infrastructure. The NCS will work with industry and all levels of government to identify cross-sector critical dependencies by leveraging existing industry and government cross-sector groups, task forces, and other mechanisms. NCS will continue to work with existing sector coordination groups (e.g., Information Sharing and Analysis Centers [ISACs], Sector Coordinating

Councils [SCCs]) on procedures for cross-sector incident management and sharing situational awareness information during incidents. The NCS will also coordinate with other Sector Specific Agencies (SSAs) to conduct diversity assessments for high-risk critical infrastructure and NS/EP user facilities.

For more information on the Communications Sector, see the Communications Sector Specific Plan at: http://www.dhs.gov/xlibrary/assets/nipp-ssp-communications.pdf.

Information Technology[4]

Information technology (IT) is central to our Nation's security, economy, public health, and safety. The IT Sector accounts for about 7% of the U.S. GDP. On a daily basis, more than $3 trillion worth of economic activity (e.g., securities sales settlements, check clearances, and interbank transfers) passes over secure federal financial networks. IT systems enable this economic activity, which is essential to maintaining homeland and national security. Critical infrastructure and key resources (CI/KR) sectors rely on the IT Sector for products and services, including the reliable operation of networks and systems and the movement and storage of critical data.

....

Information Technology (IT) Sector Critical Functions

- Provide IT products and services
- Provide incident management capabilities
- Provide domain name resolution services
- Provide identity management and associated trust support services
- Provide internet based content, information, and communications services
- Provide internet routing, access, and connection services[5]

....

Individual IT Sector entities proactively manage risk to their own operations and those of their customers, through constant monitoring and mitigation activities designed to prevent daily incidents from becoming significant disruptions to national security, the economy, and public health and safety. Although the IT infrastructure has a certain level of inherent resilience, its interdependent and interconnected structure presents challenges and opportunities for coordinating public and private sector preparedness activities.

The IT Sector's market-based environment enables rapid innovation and drives investments in security to meet customers' changing needs and promote the resilience of the IT Sector. Prevention and protection through risk management, situational awareness, and response, recovery, and reconstitution efforts are most effective when full participation of public and private sector security partners exists; such efforts suffer without the full participation of either partner.

● ●

Information Technology (IT) Sector Entities

Information Technology (IT) Sector entities include the following:

- Domain Name System (DNS) root and Generic Top-Level Domain operators;
- Internet service providers (ISPs);
- Internet backbone providers;
- Internet portal and e-mail providers;
- Networking hardware companies (e.g., fiber-optics makers and line acceleration hardware manufacturers) and other hardware manufacturers (e.g., personal computer [PC] and server manufacturers and information storage);
- Software companies;
- Security services vendors;
- Communications companies that characterize themselves as having an IT role;
- Edge and core service providers;
- IT system integrators; and
- IT security associations.

In addition, federal, state, and local governments are a component of the IT Sector as providers of government IT services that are designed to meet the needs of citizens, businesses, and employees. The IT Sector includes public and private sector entities.[6]

● ●

Security Partners

As set forth in the National Infrastructure Protection Plan (NIPP), the sector partnership model encourages the public and private sectors to collaborate on their respective CI/KR protection activities. This collaboration is accomplished through Sector Coordinating Councils (SCCs) and Government Coordinating Councils (GCCs), which form a national framework for coordinating CI/KR protection within and across sectors. The IT SCC (composed of IT industry members) and the IT GCC (composed of government representatives) are the primary bodies for communicating their respective public and private perspectives and for developing collaborative policies, strategies, and security efforts to advance CI/KR protection. SCC and GCC representatives share experiences, ideas, best practices, and innovative approaches related to CI/KR protection and risk management for their respective sectors.

● ●

The term **'security partners'** refers to the stakeholders in the National Infrastructure Protection Plan (NIPP) planning process. These stakeholders include all government levels (federal, state, territorial, regional, local, and tribal), regional organizations, international partners, and private sector owners and operators.[7]

● ●

In March 2006, the DHS established the Critical Infrastructure Partnership Advisory Council (CIPAC) to facilitate coordination and dialogue between the SCCs and GCCs. The various SCCs address cross-sector issues and interdependencies through their participation in the Partnership for Critical Infrastructure Security (PCIS). The IT SCC will coordinate with other sectors on cross-sector issues, such as cyber security, through forums such as the PCIS. To achieve an integrated national plan, the DHS must coordinate with all security partners that have equities or interests in CI/KR protection. Public and private sector security partners are crucial not only to the implementation of the IT SSP plan, but also to the broader policy and operational relationships that enhance the IT Sector's overall security posture.

Information Technology Sector Specific Plan

The IT SSP provides a framework for identifying and managing risk during steady-state (i.e., routine day-to-day) business operations to prevent, protect against, mitigate, and prepare for nationally significant events, technological emergencies, or presidentially declared disasters that threaten, disrupt, or cripple IT Sector infrastructure. Specifically, the IT SSP is concerned with all hazard events with cyber or physical consequences that:

- Cause, or are likely to cause, harm to mission-critical functions across the public and private sectors by impairing the confidentiality, integrity, or availability of electronic information, information systems, services, or networks; and/or
- Threaten public health or safety, undermine public confidence, have a negative effect on the national economy, or diminish the security posture of the Nation.

Such nationally significant events likely would affect communications and/or IT services in at least one region and possibly several regions of the country, including at least one major metropolitan area. Events would involve multiple communications service providers and/or IT products and services, resulting in a significant degradation of other essential infrastructures. Such an event would have an impact on the availability and integrity of communications and IT services for at least a significant portion of a business day or longer.

IT SSP Goals and Objectives

Public and private sector security partners collaborated to identify overarching Sector goals that support efforts to prevent, prepare for, protect against, mitigate, respond to, and recover from nationally significant events. These goals create a mutually beneficial framework to develop risk management and protective strategies that will enhance sector security.

Goal 1: Prevention and Protection through Risk Management. Identify, assess, and manage risks to the IT Sector's infrastructure and its international dependencies.

- **Objective 1.1:** Identify and annually review critical IT Sector functions that support the Nation's security, economy, public health, and safety.

....

Vision Statement for the Information Technology (IT) Sector

Public and private Information Technology (IT) Sector security partners will continue building infrastructure resilience to support:

- The Federal Government's performance of essential national security missions and
  preservation of general public health and safety;
- State and local governments' abilities to maintain order and to deliver minimum
  essential public services; and
- The orderly functioning of the economy.

The IT Sector will continue to coordinate with other CI/KR sectors and work to ensure
that any disruptions or manipulations of critical IT Sector functions are brief, infrequent,
manageable, geographically isolated, and minimally detrimental to the welfare of the
United States.[8]

....

- **Objective 1.2:** Assess and prioritize risks to critical IT Sector functions,
  including evaluating emerging threats, vulnerabilities, and technology, and
  mapping them against the infrastructure to prioritize protective efforts.
- **Objective 1.3:** Tailor protective measures, which mitigate associated consequences, vulnerabilities, and threats, to accommodate the diversity of the IT
  Sector and develop and share IT security best practices and protective measures with security partners.
- **Objective 1.4:** Encourage IT Sector entities to exchange information about
  risk management strategies and foster a better understanding of how they
  improve the overall posture of the sector.

Goal 2: Situational Awareness. Improve situational awareness during normal
operations, potential or realized threats and disruptions, intentional or
unintentional incidents, crippling attacks (cyber or physical) against IT Sector
infrastructure, technological emergencies and/or failures, or presidentially declared
disasters.

- **Objective 2.1:** Collaborate, develop, and share appropriate threat and vulnerability information among public and private sector security partners,
  including development of indications and warnings.
- **Objective 2.2:** Expand strategic analytical capabilities that facilitate public
  and private sector security partner collaboration to identify potential
  incidents.

Goal 3: Response, Recovery, and Reconstitution. Enhance the capabilities of public
and private sector security partners to respond to and recover from realized threats
and disruptions, intentional or unintentional incidents, crippling attacks (cyber or
physical) against IT Sector infrastructure, technological emergencies and/or
failures, or presidentially declared disasters, and develop mechanisms for
reconstitution.

- **Objective 3.1:** Develop and maintain communications, including establishing mechanisms and processes for communicating with other sectors during contingencies, and conduct annual tests of the resulting communication plans and programs.
- **Objective 3.2:** Develop and maintain incident response and coordination plans and procedures, and exercise them annually to ensure readiness and resilience.
- **Objective 3.3:** Develop plans, protocols, and procedures to ensure that critical IT Sector functions can be reconstituted rapidly after an incident.
- **Objective 3.4:** Collaborate with law enforcement to identify and mitigate criminal activities that have the potential to harm the sector's infrastructure.

For more information on the Information Technology Sector, see the Information Technology Sector Specific Plan at: http://www.dhs.gov/ xlibrary/assets/nipp-ssp-information-tech.pdf.

Banking and Finance[9]

The United States financial services sector is the backbone of the world economy. With assets estimated to be in excess of $48 trillion, this large and diverse sector accounted for more than $900 billion in 2005, or 8.1% of the United States GDP. Descriptions of the sector's profile and goals necessarily include the diversity of its institutions and the services they provide. Most important to this profile is the understanding that the financial services sector is primarily owned and operated by the private sector, whose institutions are extensively regulated by federal and, in many cases, state government. In addition to these public sector entities, self-regulatory organizations (SROs), such as the Municipal Securities Rulemaking Board (MSRB), National Association of Securities Dealers (NASD), National Futures Association (NFA), designated futures exchanges, and exchanges such as the Chicago Mercantile Exchange (CME) and the New York Stock Exchange (NYSE), also play an important role in industry oversight.

The financial services sector is complex and diverse. From the largest institutions with assets greater than one trillion dollars to the smallest community banks and credit unions, this diversity provides the ability for the sector as a whole to meet the needs of its large and diverse customer base. Whether it is an individual savings account, financial derivatives, credit extended to a large corporation, or investments made by a foreign country, financial institutions provide a broad array of products. These products:

- Allow customers to deposit funds and make payments to other parties (more than $12 trillion in assets);
- Provide credit and liquidity to customers (more than $14 trillion in assets);
- Allow customers to invest funds for both long and short periods (more than $18 trillion in assets); and
- Transfer financial risks between customers (more than $6 trillion in assets).

Despite this diversity, a unifying mission of the U.S. financial sector is to ensure the continued efficiency in and continuity of the sector and its institutions. Through the extensive regulatory regime and formalized information-sharing organizations detailed in the Banking and Finance SSP, the sector has wide-ranging transparency and accountability, which ensures an orderly and efficient financial system that serves a broad range of needs for both investors and consumers. In turn, these factors create a sense of confidence that enables customers to entrust their assets to the care of financial institutions and to avail themselves of credit and liquidity.

As the Banking and Finance SSP details, today's U.S. financial regulatory regime consists of both federal and state agencies, whose oversight assists in ensuring the integrity of individual institutions and the overall U.S. financial system. Working together, the public and private sectors encourage a highly competitive market where identifying and managing a myriad of financial and non-financial risks is essential to success.

Security Partners

As the SSA for the Banking and Finance Sector, the U.S. Department of Treasury recognizes the vital role of both the financial regulators and the private sector. These regulators and the private sector are committed to the Banking and Finance Sector's security partnership. Working collaboratively, this partnership achieves its security goals and addresses the evolving nature of the sector and its potential risks.

Furthermore, the Treasury Department works closely with the DHS to meet the sector's security objectives. As a member of various key working groups, the Treasury Department apprises the DHS of situational priorities and remains fully engaged with the DHS. Some of these working groups include the Information Technology Government Coordinating Council, the Emergency Support Function Leader Group, the Homeland Security Integrated Intelligence Board Task Force, the Infosec Research Council, the National Cyber Response Coordination Group, the Strategic Homeland Infrastructure Risk Assessment, and the Cyber Security and Information Assurance.

In addition to the above working groups, the Treasury Department sponsors the Financial and Banking Information Infrastructure Committee (FBIIC). The FBIIC's role is to coordinate the efforts of federal and state financial regulators with respect to critical infrastructure issues, including preparation for and response to cyber or physical attacks against the financial system or indirect attacks or events that may impact the sector. The FBIIC's membership includes experienced regulators from the following agencies and associations:

- Commodity Futures Trading Commission (CFTC)
- Conference of State Bank Supervisors (CSBS)
- Farm Credit Administration (FCA)
- Federal Deposit Insurance Corporation (FDIC)
- Federal Housing Finance Board (FHFB)

- Federal Reserve Bank of New York
- Federal Reserve Board (FRB)
- National Association of Insurance Commissioners (NAIC)
- National Association of State Credit Union Supervisors
- Office of the Comptroller of the Currency (OCC)
- Office of Federal Housing Enterprise Oversight (OFHEO)
- Office of Thrift Supervision (OTS)
- Securities and Exchange Commission (SEC)
- Securities Investor Protection Corporation (SIPC)
- The Homeland Security Council
- U.S. Department of Treasury

Under the auspices of the FBIIC, the Treasury also facilitated the creation of the Financial Services Sector Coordinating Council for Critical Infrastructure Protection and Homeland Security (FSSCC) in June 2002 as the private sector arm of its protection strategy. The Treasury Department designates the Sector Coordinator for the Banking and Finance Sector, who as a matter of practice, is chosen by the FSSCC to be the chair of the FSSCC. The FSSCC, whose membership represents the sector through financial trade associations and organizations, fosters and facilitates the coordination of sector-wide financial services voluntary initiatives to improve critical infrastructure protection and homeland security.

Lastly, the Treasury Department works closely with the Financial Services Information Sharing and Analysis Center (FS-ISAC), which was set up as the financial sector response to the requirements of Presidential Decision Directive 63: Protecting America's Critical Infrastructures in May 1998. The mission of the FS-ISAC, in collaboration with the Treasury Department and the FSSCC, is to enhance the ability of the financial services sector to prepare for and respond to cyber and physical threats, and vulnerabilities and incidents, and to serve as the primary communications channel for the sector.

> **'Phishing'** is a fraudulent scheme where an e-mail directs its recipients to Websites where they are asked to provide confidential personal or financial information. Reports of phishing attacks rose dramatically between 2006 and 2007.[10]

Banking and Finance Sector Goals

The Banking and Finance Sector is strong and resilient, with an infrastructure that is designed to respond quickly and appropriately to detect, deter, prevent, and mitigate physical and cyber-based intrusions, attacks, or other emergencies. This ability ensures the continuity and efficient operation of the sector's institutions, and thereby serves to strengthen public confidence in the U.S. economic system.

The Banking and Finance Sector has three primary goals to achieve this vision statement. As with all endeavors focused primarily on security, the

••

Vision Statement for the Banking and Finance Sector

To continue to improve the resilience and availability of financial services, the Banking and Finance Sector will work through its public–private partnership to address the evolving nature of threats and the risks posed by the sector's dependency upon other critical sectors.[11]

••

goals form a triad of prevention, detection, and correction of harm with the following objectives for the sector:

1. To maintain its strong position of resilience, risk management, and redundant systems in the face of a myriad of intentional, unintentional, manmade, and natural threats;

2. To address and manage the risks posed by the dependence of the sector on the Communications, Information Technology, Energy, and Transportation sectors; and

3. To work with the law enforcement community, the private sector, and international counterparts to increase the amount of available resources dedicated to tracking and catching criminals responsible for crimes against the sector, including cyber attacks and other electronic crimes. The agencies are mindful of the risk that an unanticipated event, such as a terrorist attack, could occur in a manner that has not been seen before and may not be completely prepared for. The financial services industry cannot fully protect against infrastructure disruptions of telecommunications, and it can provide only limited resilience against disruptions in other elements of the critical infrastructure, such as power, transportation, and water.

For more information on the Banking and Finance Sector, see the Banking and Finance Sector Specific Plan at: http://www.dhs.gov/xlibrary/assets/nipp-ssp-banking.pdf.

11

....

Public Safety

Introduction

Agencies that work in the realm of the public safety community work tirelessly every day to protect the critical infrastructure and key resources (CI/KR) of the United States. Their missions involve the prevention of and protection from events that could endanger the safety of the general public from significant danger, injury/harm, or damage, such as crimes or disasters (natural or man-made). This protection is vital to our national security, health and safety, and economic vitality. It also ensures that the essential government missions, services, and economic functions will continue operation in the event of an attack or disaster. The following chapter will outline two of the seventeen critical infrastructure sectors, Public Health/Healthcare and Emergency Services, and discuss the scope of these sectors and what roles they play in critical infrastructure protection.

Public Health and Healthcare

The Public Health and Healthcare Sector constitutes approximately fifteen percent of the Gross National Product (GNP). Operating in all U.S. states, territories, tribal areas, cities, counties, and towns, the Public Health and Healthcare Sector is integral to the U.S. economy and plays a significant role in response and recovery across all other sectors in the event of a natural or man-made disaster. The Department of Health and Human Services (HHS) is the Sector-Specific Agency (SSA) for the Public Health and Healthcare Sector. The Public Health and Healthcare Sector is highly decentralized.

Sector entities work together under varying circumstances (e.g., managing supplies, providing clinical care); however, other than in catastrophic events, healthcare tends to be localized.[1]

The Public Health and Healthcare Sector consists of health departments, hospitals, health clinics, advanced life support (ALS) services, emergency medical services (EMS, including ambulances, ground and airlift), mental health facilities, nursing homes, blood-supply facilities, laboratories, mortuaries, and pharmaceutical stockpiles. A commonly overlooked component of the public healthcare subsector involves the health of animals—veterinary medicine. In addition, the healthcare delivery industry is tied to the diagnostic and therapeutic decisions of healthcare professionals. As technology has advanced, so has the level of integration of cyber technology within individual institutions (i.e., electronic record keeping systems).

Scope of the Public Health and Healthcare Sector
The Public Health and Healthcare Sector consists of an array of decentralized, loosely coupled organizations, most of which are small in size. This sector is a mixture of private and public organizations, but the majority are privately owned and operated. The private healthcare sector includes:

- More than 6,600 hospitals;
- More than 492,000 ambulatory healthcare facilities;
- Nearly 70,000 nursing and residential care facilities;
- Nearly 175,000 individual or group medical practices;
- Nearly 100 health insurance companies;
- More than 40,000 pharmacies;
- Approximately 2,500 pharmaceutical manufacturers;
- A medical devices and supplies industry; and
- More than 500 blood and organ bank establishments.

Though not nearly as large, the public healthcare sector includes:

- Elements of three federal cabinet-level departments (i.e., Health and Human Services, Veterans Affairs, and Defense);
- Fifty-seven state and territorial health departments;
- Thirty-six local and regional tribal health boards; and
- More than 3,000 local health departments and 2,000 public health laboratories.

In sum, there are approximately 4,300,000 professionals with health-related emergency responsibilities at work across the sector.

Health Infrastructure Protection
According to HHS, health infrastructure protection goes beyond the delivery of patient care and safeguarding public health. It includes the development of an emergency-ready health infrastructure to respond to bioterrorism or other public health emergencies. Working with the MITRE Corporation, HHS has forged productive partnerships with federal agencies that have health-related responsibilities, state and local public health organizations, relevant professional associations, and major private sector groups. These partnerships are designed to provide forums for industry leaders and government officials to

discuss issues of common concern including, but not limited to, critical information protection. These partnerships were used to develop the Public Health and Healthcare Sector Specific Plan (SSP), which attempted to provide the most complete picture possible of the major entities in the Public Health and Healthcare sector that should be protected from attacks. The plan encompassed such topics as:

- Protection of fixed public and private healthcare facilities;
- Emergency capabilities shared by the entire sector;
- The growing role of information technology in the sector, including strengths and vulnerabilities;
- The threat against fixed facilities posed by conventional explosives (e.g., truck bombs);
- Vulnerabilities of the sector that result from its dependence on other sectors (e.g., power, water, ground transportation);
- A preliminary assessment of the sector's critical information protection requirements;
- Recent initiatives to strengthen critical infrastructure protection (CIP) within the sector (e.g., creation of Coordination Groups and Information Sharing and Analysis Centers);
- Initial plans for prioritizing critical infrastructures and key resources and for developing protective strategies and plans; and
- Preliminary metrics for the measurement and communication of results.[2]

The vision statement for this sector includes the following points:

- The Public Health and Healthcare Sector will achieve overall resiliency against all threats—natural and man-made;
- Prevent or minimize damage to, or destruction of, the Nation's healthcare and public health infrastructure;
- Preserve its ability to mount timely and effective responses to both routine and emergency situations; and
- Strive to protect its critical workforce from harm resulting from terrorist or criminal activities, from natural disasters, and from serious infectious disease outbreaks, including those originating outside the United States.[3]

In short, the protection of the Public Health and Healthcare Sector's infrastructure has assumed increasing urgency since September 11, 2001. There are many reasons for this urgency. First, every event involving risks to human life must include a health sector response. These events may include some that are not traditionally perceived as a medical related emergency; therefore, response training and planning must be amplified. Next, elements of the sector itself face increasing threats to facilities, information systems, and workforces. These reasons necessitate an increased emphasis on critical infrastructure protection and the emerging threats that may not yet be realized.

Emergency Services

The Emergency Services Sector (ESS) is a system of response and recovery elements that forms the Nation's first line of defense and prevention and reduction of consequences from any terrorist attack. It is a sector of trained and tested personnel, plans, redundant systems, agreements, and pacts that provide life safety and security services across the Nation via the first responder community comprising federal, state, local, tribal, and private partners. This sector serves as the primary "protector" for other CI/KR sectors with its primary missions including saving lives, protecting property and the environment, assisting communities impacted by disasters, and assisting with recovery efforts.

ESS Disciplines

Law Enforcement
Law enforcement comprises federal, state, local, or tribal officials whose duties are primarily the prevention, investigation, apprehension, or detention of individuals suspected or convicted of offenses against the criminal laws. Law enforcement agencies, depending on size and type of jurisdiction served, can contain various specialized units to fulfill its mission. According to the National Law Enforcement Memorial, there are more than 900,000 sworn law enforcement officers now serving in the United States, which is the highest figure ever in recorded history. About twelve percent of those are female.[4]

Bomb Explosive Ordinance Disposal (EOD)
EOD units, whether at the federal, state, or local levels, are responsible for the search and subsequent rendering safe process to hazardous explosive devices. Technicians are usually members of a law enforcement, fire, or emergency management agency.

Special Weapons and Tactics / Tactical Operations
A tactical law enforcement unit that is trained to perform high-risk operations that fall outside of the abilities of regular patrol officers, including serving high-risk arrest warrants, hostage rescue, counterterrorism, and engaging heavily-armed criminals. These teams are often equipped with specialized firearms including assault rifles, submachine guns, shotguns, riot control agents, stun grenades, and high-powered rifles. They have specialized equipment including, but not limited to, heavy body armor, entry tools, armored vehicles, and advanced night vision optics.

Fire Service
Firefighters are rescuers, both paid and volunteer, extensively trained primarily to extinguish hazardous fires that threaten civilian populations and property and to rescue people from car accidents, collapsed and burning buildings, and other such situations. The increasing complexity of modern industrialized life with an increase in the scale of hazards has stimulated both advances in firefighting technology and a broadening of the firefighter-rescuer's remit. Traditionally, these agencies are from the public sector, but there are several private sector departments throughout the United States.

According to the National Volunteer Firefighter Council, volunteers constitute 72% of firefighters in the United States; of the estimated 1,136,650 firefighters across the country, 823,350 are volunteer.[5]

Emergency Medical Services (EMS)
EMS personnel are dedicated to providing out-of-hospital acute medical care
and/or transport to definitive care to patients with illnesses and injuries. The
goal of most emergency medical services is to either provide treatment to
those in need of urgent medical care, with the goal of satisfactorily treating
the malady, or arranging for timely removal of the patient to the next point of
definitive care. This is most likely an emergency department at a hospital or
another place where physicians are available.

Search and Rescue (SAR)
SAR personnel search for and provide aid to people who are in distress or imminent danger. This disciplines priority is to minimize loss of life, injury, and
property damage through the provision of aid. SAR consists of several spe-
cialty areas to include: mountain rescue, urban search and rescue, as well as
air sea rescue. Mountain Rescue, sometimes referred to as Wilderness Search
and Rescue, relates to search and rescue operations specifically in rugged terrain such as mountains, desert, and forests. Next, Urban Search and Rescue
(USAR), also known as Suburban Search and Rescue, operations are conducted in a city setting, usually related to structural collapses or other technical rescue operations. Finally, Air Sea Rescue specifically refers to the use of
aircraft to both search for and locate or recover individuals lost at sea.

Emergency Management
Emergency management is the managerial function charged with creating
the framework within which communities reduce vulnerability to hazards
and cope with disasters. Emergency management protects communities by
coordinating and integrating all activities necessary to build, sustain, and
improve the capability to mitigate against, prepare for, respond to, and
recover from threatened or actual natural disasters, acts of terrorism, or other
man-made disasters.[6]

Hazardous Materials (HAZMAT)
HAZMAT personnel are responsible for the detection and removal of dangerous goods that can harm people, other living organisms, property, or the
environment. Mitigating the risks associated with hazardous materials may
require the application of safety precautions during their transport, use, storage, and disposal. Most countries regulate hazardous materials by law, and
they are subject to several international treaties as well. Oftentimes, HAZ-
MAT units are housed within a fire department, but may consist of members
from other emergency services sector agencies.

Security Partners

The U.S. Department of Homeland Security (DHS) is the Sector-Specific Agency (SSA) for the ESS. Specifically, responsibilities within DHS have been assigned to the Office of Infrastructure Protection (OIP). One of the primary responsibilities for the SSA is the collaboration with security partners. The following section will identify examples of ESS security partners in the federal, state, local, tribal, and professional organizations.

Federal Partners

Department of Homeland Security (DHS)   The overriding and urgent mission of the DHS is to lead the unified national effort to secure the country and preserve our freedoms. While the DHS was created to secure the United States against those who seek to disrupt the American way of life, the DHS charter also includes preparation for and response to all hazards and disasters. The citizens of the United States must have the utmost confidence that the DHS can execute both missions.[7]

Department of Health and Human Services (HHS)   Through leadership in the medical sciences and public health and human service programs, HHS seeks to improve the health and well-being of people in this country and throughout the world. The broad goals of public health promotion and protection, disease prevention, emergency preparedness, human services, and scientific research and development represent the mission of HHS and encompass its central functions.[8]

Department of Transportation (DOT)   The national objectives of general welfare, economic growth and stability, and the security of the United States require the development of transportation policies and programs that contribute to providing fast, safe, efficient, and convenient transportation at the lowest cost consistent with those and other national objectives, including the efficient use and conservation of the resources of the United States. The DOT is dedicated to improving transportation by making it safer, less congested, better connected, environmentally friendly, and fully operational in all conditions.[9]

Environmental Protection Agency (EPA)   The EPA leads the Nation's environmental science, research, education and assessment efforts. The mission of the EPA is to protect human health and the environment. Since 1970, the EPA has been working for a cleaner, healthier environment for the American people.[10]

Federal Bureau of Investigation (FBI)   The mission of the FBI is to protect and defend the United States against terrorist and foreign intelligence threats, to uphold and enforce the criminal laws of the United States, and to provide leadership and criminal justice services to federal, state, municipal, and international agencies and partners. In order to fulfill this mission, the bureau will produce and use intelligence to protect the Nation from threats and to bring to justice those who violate the law.[11]

National Guard   Administered by the National Guard Bureau (a joint bureau of the departments of the Army and Air Force), the National Guard has both a federal and state mission. The dual mission, a provision of the U.S. Constitution and the U.S. Code of laws, results in each soldier holding membership in both the National Guard of his or her state and in the U.S. Army or the U.S. Air Force. The National Guard's federal mission is to maintain well-trained, well-equipped units available for prompt mobilization during war and provide assistance during national emergencies (such as natural disasters or civil disturbances). When National Guard units are not under federal control, the governor is the commander-in-chief of his or her respective state, territory (Guam, Virgin Islands), or commonwealth (Puerto Rico).[12]

American Red Cross   The American Red Cross, a humanitarian organization led by volunteers guided by its Congressional Charter and the Fundamental Principles of the International Red Cross Movement, provides relief to victims of disasters and helps people prevent, prepare for, and respond to emergencies. The American Red Cross functions independently of the government but works closely with government agencies, such as the Federal Emergency Management Agency (FEMA), during times of major crises. It is responsible for giving aid to members of the U.S. Armed Forces and to disaster victims at home and abroad.[13]

State, Local, and Tribal Governments

State, local, and tribal governments are responsible for implementing the homeland security mission, protecting public safety and welfare, and ensuring the provision of essential services to communities and industries within their jurisdictions. They also play a very important and direct role in enabling the protection of the Nation's CI/KR, including CI/KR under their control, as well as CI/KR owned and operated by other National Infrastructure Protection Plan (NIPP) security partners within their jurisdictions. The efforts of these public entities are critical to the effective implementation. They are equally critical in terms of enabling time-sensitive, post-event CI/KR response, restoration, and recovery activities. CI/KR protection programs form an essential component of state, local, and tribal homeland security strategies, particularly with regard to establishing funding priorities and informing security investment decisions.[14]

With regard to the ESS, state emergency managers oftentimes serve as the central point of contact during a disaster situation. However, all events occur locally, and state managers are only necessary when the event overwhelms the capabilities of local authorities. Local governments may staff these functions by either paid or volunteer personnel. Additionally, many communities have citizen groups who may assist with the planning, response, and recovery from a critical incident. These groups may include the Local Emergency Planning Committees (LEPC) and the DHS sponsored

Citizen Corps. The mission of Citizen Corps is to harness the power of every individual through education, training, and volunteer service to make communities safer, stronger, and better prepared to respond to the threats of terrorism, crime, public health issues, and disasters of all kinds.[15]

Finally, tribal governments are sovereign entities; therefore, they provide their own emergency services. Federal agencies such as the DHS and the Bureau of Indian Affairs assist these governments to ensure that components available comply with mandated requirements.

Professional Associations

Many of the disciplines listed previously in this chapter maintain a professional association, whereby some disciplines maintain several. Below, examples of the associations participating in the ESS plan are presented.

International Association of Chiefs of Police (IACP)   Founded in 1893, the goals of the IACP are to advance the science and art of police services; to develop and disseminate improved administrative, technical, and operational practices and promote their use in police work; to foster police cooperation and the exchange of information and experience among police administrators throughout the world; to bring about recruitment and training in the police profession of qualified persons; and to encourage adherence of all police officers to high professional standards of performance and conduct.[16]

International Association of Fire Chiefs (IAFC)   The IAFC represents the leadership of more than 1.2 million firefighters and emergency responders. IAFC members are the world's leading experts in firefighting, emergency medical services, terrorism response, hazardous materials spills, natural disasters, search and rescue, and public safety legislation. Since 1873, the IAFC has provided a forum for its members to exchange ideas and uncover the latest products and services available to first responders.[17]

International Association of Emergency Managers (IAEM)   The IAEM is a non-profit educational organization dedicated to promoting the goals of saving lives and protecting property during emergencies and disasters. The mission of the IAEM is to serve its members by providing information, networking, and professional opportunities and to advance the emergency management profession.[18]

National Association of State EMS Directors (NASEMSD)   The NASEMSD supports its members in developing EMS policy and oversight, as well as in providing vision, leadership, and resources in the development and improvement of state, regional, and local EMS and emergency care systems. The NASEMSD achieves its mission by the participation of all the states and territories, by being a strong national voice for EMS, an acknowledged key resource for EMS information and policy, and a leader in developing and disseminating evidence-based decisions and policy.[19]

Summary

In conclusion, the ESS sector is critical to the Nation's ability to detect, prevent, respond to, and recover from a disaster or terrorist attack. This capability, vital to the security of residents, is also required for maintaining the Nation's quality of life and continuing economic development. During the events of 9/11, first responders amply demonstrated the importance of their role in saving lives and protecting people. Understandably, enhanced emergency response has been a first priority for homeland security investment, initially in the form of equipment procurement and specialized training. Parallel to upgrading emergency response capability has been the recognition of vulnerability for critical infrastructure service delivery systems, including emergency services.

12

....

Weapons of Mass Destruction

Today, in addition to hostile nation-states, we are focusing on terrorist groups, proliferation networks, alienated communities, charismatic individuals, narco-traffickers, and microscopic influenza.

–John D. Negroponte, Director of National Intelligence, February 2, 2006

Defining Weapons of Mass Destruction (WMD)

A weapon of mass destruction, or WMD, can be characterized as:

- Any weapon or device that is intended, or has the capability, to cause death or serious bodily injury to a significant number of people through the release, dissemination, or impact of toxic or poisonous chemicals or their precursors; a disease organism; or radiation or radioactivity;
- Any explosive, incendiary, or poison gas, bomb, grenade, rocket having a propellant charge of more than four ounces, or a missile having an explosive or incendiary charge of more than one quarter ounce, or mine or device similar to the above; poison gas; any weapon involving a disease organism; or any weapon that is designed to release radiation or radioactivity at a level dangerous to human life.[1]

The Federal Emergency Management Agency (FEMA) cites the differences between WMD incidents and other incidents with the following distinctive characteristics of a WMD event:

- Situation may not be recognizable until there are multiple casualties;
- There may be multiple events;

- Responders are placed at higher risk of becoming casualties;
- Location of the incident will be treated as a crime scene;
- Contamination of critical facilities and large geographic areas may result;
- Scope of the incident may expand geometrically and may affect mutual aid jurisdictions;
- There will be a stronger reaction from the public than with other types of incidents;
- Time is working against responding elements;
- Support facilities are at risk as targets; and
- Specialized state and local response capabilities may be overwhelmed.[2]

Chemical, Biological, Radiological, Nuclear, and Explosive (CBRNE)

CBRNE is the term used in the emergency preparedness and response communities offering shorthand for the spectrum of WMD threats ranging from Chemical, Biological, Radiological, Nuclear, or conventional Explosive agents. Table 12.1 provides high-level profiles of the contemporary CBRNE threats. A brief explanation of each of these types of WMD threats is provided in the sections that follow.

Chemical, biological, and radiological material as well as industrial agents can be dispersed in the air we breathe, the water we drink, or on surfaces we physically contact. Dispersion methods may be as simple as placing a container in a heavily used area, opening a container, or using conventional garden/commercial spray devices, or methods may be as elaborate as detonating an improvised explosive device (IED). Chemical incidents are characterized by the rapid onset of medical symptoms (within minutes to hours) and easily observed signatures (colored residue, dead foliage, pungent odor, and dead insect and animal life).

With respect to a biological incident, the onset of symptoms requires days to weeks and there typically will be no characteristic signatures. Because of the delayed onset of symptoms in a biological incident, the area affected may be greater due to the migration of infected individuals.

Regarding a radiological incident, the onset of symptoms requires days to weeks and there typically will be no characteristic signatures. Radiological materials are not recognizable by the senses and are colorless and odorless. Specialized equipment is required to determine the size of the affected area and whether the level of radioactivity presents an immediate or long-term health hazard. Because of the delayed onset of symptoms in a radiological incident, the affected area may be greater due to the migration of contaminated individuals.

Chemical
Chemical WMD threats are characterized within two classes: chemical agents and industrial toxins.

Table 12.1 Contemporary CBRNE Threat Profiles[3]

Hazard	Application Mode	Hazard Duration	Extent of Effects	Mitigating and Exacerbating Conditions
Chemical Agent	Liquid/aerosol contaminants can be dispersed using sprayers or other aerosol generators; liquids vaporizing from puddles/containers; or munitions.	Chemical agents may pose viable threats for hours to weeks depending on the agent and the conditions in which it exists.	Contamination can be carried out of the initial target area by persons, vehicles, water, and wind. Chemicals may be corrosive or otherwise damaging over time if not remediated.	Air temperature can affect evaporation of aerosols. Ground temperature affects evaporation of liquids. Humidity can enlarge aerosol particles, reducing inhalation hazard. Precipitation can dilute and disperse agents and thereby spread contamination. Wind can disperse vapors but also cause target area to be dynamic. The micro-meteorological effects of buildings and terrain can alter travel and duration of agents. Shielding in the form of sheltering-in-place can protect population.
Biological Agent	Liquid or solid contaminants can be dispersed using sprayers/aerosols generators or by point or line sources.	May pose viable threats for hours to years depending on the agent and environmental conditions.	Depending on the agent used and the effectiveness with which it is deployed, contamination can be spread via wind and water. Infection can be spread via human or animal vectors.	Altitude of release above ground can affect dispersion. Sunlight is destructive to many bacteria and viruses.
Radiological Agent	Radioactive contaminants can be dispersed using sprayers/aerosol generators, or by point or line sources such as munitions, covert deposits, or moving sprayers.	Contaminants may remain hazardous for seconds to years depending on material used.	Initial effects will be localized to site of attack. Depending on meteorological conditions, subsequent behavior of radioactive contaminants may be dynamic.	Duration of exposure, distance from source of radiation, and the amount of shielding between source and target determine exposure to radiation.

(Continued)

Table 12.1 (*Continued*)

HAZARD	APPLICATION MODE	HAZARD DURATION	EXTENT OF EFFECTS	MITIGATING AND EXACERBATING CONDITIONS
Nuclear Weapon	Detonation of nuclear device underground, at the surface, in the air, or at high altitude.	Light/heat flash and blast/shock wave last for seconds; nuclear radiation and fallout hazards can persist for years. Electromagnetic pulse (EMP) from a high-altitude detonation lasts for seconds and affects unprotected electronic systems.	Initial light, heat, and blast effects of a subsurface, ground, or air burst are static and are determined by the device's characteristics and employment.	Harmful effects of radiation can be reduced by minimizing the time of exposure. Light, heat, and blast energy decrease logarithmically as a function of distance from source of blast. Terrain, forestation, and structures in the built environment provide shielding by absorbing or deflecting radiation and radioactive contaminants.
Explosive Devices	Detonation of explosive device on or near a target. Delivery via Vehicle Borne Improvised Explosive Device (VBIED), by person, or by projectile.	Instantaneous. "Secondary devices" may be used to impact emergency responders.	Extent or damage is determined by type and quantity of explosive. Effects generally static other than cascading consequences, incremental structural failure, etc.	Overpressure at a given standoff is inversely proportional to the cube of the distance from the blast.

Chemical Agents
Major categories of Chemical agents are:

- Nerve agents (e.g., sarin, soman, cyclosarin, tabun, VX);
- Vesicating or blistering agents (e.g., mustards, lewisite);
- Choking agents or lung toxicants (e.g., phosgene, diphosgene);
- Blood agent (e.g., hydrogen cyanide, arsine);
- Incapacitating agents (e.g., anti-cholinergic compounds);
- Lacrimating or riot control agents (e.g., pepper gas, cyanide, CS); and
- Vomiting agents (e.g., adamsite).

Industrial Toxins
Industrial toxins can also be used as weapons by terrorists. There are a wide range of toxic industrial chemicals that, although not as toxic as cyanide, mustard, or nerve agents, can be used in much larger quantities to compensate for their lower toxicity. Chlorine and phosgene are industrial chemicals that are transported in multi-ton shipments by road and rail. Rupturing the container can easily disseminate these gases. The effects of chlorine and phosgene are similar to those of mustard agent. Organophosphate pesticides such as parathion are in the same chemical class as nerve agents. Although these pesticides are much less toxic, their effects and medical treatments are the same as for military-grade nerve agents.[4]

···

Chemical Weapons Specifics
Advantages:
- Readily available.
- Easy to employ.
- Low cost.
- No technical requirements.

Disadvantages:
- Unreliable results.
- Extensive planning required.

Likelihood:
Medium. Use of industrial toxins has been planned typically as a secondary effect following explosion. Offers mass casualty potential with minimal resource requirement.

Consequences:
Medium. Limited to surrounding area of employment depending upon weather. Casualty levels may overwhelm emergency responder and medical resources of smaller communities.

···

Chemical Weapons Convention (CWC)
The Convention on the Prohibition of the Development, Production, Stock-piling, and Use of Chemical Weapons and on Their Destruction (commonly

Table 12.2 Characteristics of Chemical Agents[5]

NAME	PHYSICAL CHARACTERISTICS	PERSISTENCY	COMMERCIAL USES OF CHEMICALS OR PRECURSOR CHEMICALS
Blister Agents - Cause blisters on skin and damage the respiratory tract, mucous membranes, and eyes.			
Sulfur Mustard (HD)	Colorless to amber, oily liquid with odor of garlic	Persistent	Paper and rubber manufacturing, pharmaceuticals, insecticides, plastics, detergents, cosmetics, lubricants
Lewisite	Light amber liquid with odor of geraniums	Semi-persistent	Ceramics, insecticides, pharmaceuticals
Nitrogen Mustard (HN-3)	Amber, odorless liquid	Persistent	Toiletries, insecticides, waxes, polishes, lubricants, cosmetics
Mustard-Lewisite (HL)	Liquid with garlic odor	Semi-persistent	Paper and rubber manufacturing, pharmaceuticals, insecticides, plastics, detergents, cosmetics, ceramics, lubricants
Phosgene oxime (CX)	Colorless liquid or crystalline solid with a disagreeable odor	Relatively non-persistent	
Nerve Agents - Lethal substances that disable enzymes responsible for the transmission of nerve impulses.			
Tabun (GA)	Brownish to colorless liquid with odor ranging from none to fruity	Persistent	Insecticides, gasoline additives, detergents, missile fuel, plastics, dyes, and pigments
Sarin (GB)	Colorless liquid with almost no odor	Non-persistent	Fire retardants, insecticides, disinfectants, paint solvents, ceramics, optical brighteners
Soman (GD)	Colorless liquid with fruity to camphor like odor	Semi-persistent	Fire retardants, paint solvents, ceramics, disinfectants, textile softeners
VX	Amber liquid with no odor	Persistent	Insecticides, pyrotechnics, textile softeners, pharmaceuticals
Novichok agents	Unknown	Unknown	Fertilizers, pesticides

(Continued)

Table 12.2 (*Continued*)

Name	Physical Characteristics	Persistency	Commercial Uses of Chemicals or Precursor Chemicals
Choking Agents - Substances that damage respiratory tract, causing extensive fluid build-up in the lungs.			
Chlorine	Colorless to slightly yellow with sharp, irritating odor	Non-persistent	Disinfectants, plastics, pesticides, solvents, chemical synthesis
Phosgene (CG)	Colorless gas with odor of corn or freshly mown hay	Non-persistent	Plastics, pesticides, dyes, herbicides
Diphosgene (DP)	Colorless liquid with odor of corn or freshly mown hay	Non-persistent	Plastics, pesticides, dyes, herbicides
Chloropicrin (PS)	Oily, colorless liquid with pungent odor	Non-persistent	Disinfectant, chemical synthesis
Blood Agents - Agents that interfere with the absorption of oxygen into the bloodstream.			
Hydrogen Cyanide (AC)	Colorless gas with odor of bitter almonds	Non-persistent	Pesticides, fumigating, electroplating, gold and silver extraction
Cyanogen Chloride (CK)	Colorless liquid with sharp, pungent odor	Non-persistent	Dyes and pigments, nylon production
Riot Control (Incapacitating) Agents - Substances that rapidly produce temporary disabling effects.			
Tear Agent 2 (CN)	Colorless, gray solid with sharp, irritating, floral odor	Non-persistent	Commercially available as mace
Tear Agent O (CS)	White crystalline substance with pepper-like odor	Non-persistent	
Psychedelic Agent 3 (BZ)	White crystalline solid with no odor	Non-persistent	Pharmaceuticals, tranquilizers

Note: Riot control agents listed are a partial representation of existing incapacitating agents. Other agents currently stockpiled around the world for law enforcement purposes can cause vomiting and irritation of the skin, among other symptoms.

known as the Chemical Weapons Convention, or CWC) defines chemical weapons as toxic chemicals and their precursors. The CWC is a global treaty that bans the development, production, stockpiling, and use of chemical weapons. Parties to the treaty are obligated to destroy their chemical weapons and production facilities within a specified period of time. They also must not assist other states in the production of chemical weapons. The United States has been destroying its stockpile of chemical weapons at a cost of many billions of dollars.

CWC negotiations began in 1980 as part of the United Nations (UN) Conference on Disarmament. The CWC went into effect on April 29, 1997, four days after the United States signed it. The CWC places controls on toxic chemicals and their precursors, which are listed on three schedules according to their toxicity, military and commercial utility, and risk. Schedule 1 lists military agents with no or low commercial use, such as nerve agents and mustards as well as their direct precursors. Schedule 2 lists high-risk precursors and toxic chemicals that are not produced in large quantities for commercial use. Schedule 3 lists dual-use chemicals, some of which have been used as weapons or precursors, but which are produced in large quantities for purposes not prohibited by the CWC.

Biological

A bioterrorism attack is the deliberate release of viruses, bacteria, or other germs (agents) used to cause illness or death in people, animals, or plants. These agents are naturally occurring, but it is feasible that they could be changed to increase their ability to cause disease, make them resistant to current medicines, or to increase their ability to be spread into the environment. Biological agents can be spread through the air, through water, or as food-borne agents. Terrorists may use biological agents because they can be extremely difficult to detect and do not cause illness for several hours to several days. Some bioterrorism agents can be spread from person to person, and others, such as anthrax, cannot.

Bioterrorism agents can be separated into three categories, depending on how easily they can be spread and the severity of illness or death they cause. Category A agents are considered the highest risk, and Category C agents are those that are considered emerging threats for disease. The categories are detailed below with examples provided in Table 12.3.

Category A: These high-priority agents include organisms or toxins that pose the highest risk to the public because:

- They can be easily spread or transmitted from person to person;
- They result in high death rates and have the potential for major health impact;
- They might cause public panic and social disruption; and
- They require special action for public health preparedness.

Category B: These agents are the second highest priority because:

- They are moderately easy to spread;
- They result in moderate illness rates and low death rates; and

- They require specific enhancements of the Centers for Disease Control and Prevention's (CDC) laboratory capacity and enhanced disease monitoring.

Category C: These third highest priority agents include emerging pathogens that could be engineered for mass spread in the future because:

- They are easily available,
- They are easily produced and spread, and
- They have potential for high morbidity and mortality rates and major health impact.

••

Biological Weapons Specifics
Advantages:
- Delay in initial effects offers distance from action.
- Far reaching psychological effects.
- Secondary infections.
- Shock value.

Disadvantages:
- Difficult to obtain.
- Difficult to store.
- Danger to perpetrators.
- High cost.
- Unpredictable results.

Likelihood:
Low. Use has been both planned and executed.

Consequences:
High. Effects may occur well beyond initial area of employment. Treatment of large quantities of victims may overwhelm smaller medical communities. Identification, tracking, and containment of the utilized disease may cause severe problems. Use would bring about intense pursuit by law enforcement.

••

The Select Agent Registration Program was established by the U.S. Department of Health and Human Services (HHS) to enhance the security of specific biological pathogens and toxins. Under the Public Health Security and Bioterrorism Preparedness and Response Act of 2002, the Attorney General has the responsibility to query criminal, immigration, national security, and other electronic databases to determine whether an individual applying for select agent status is a restricted person. Further, the Animal Plant Health Inspection Service (APHIS) and CDC Select Agent Program personnel have the responsibility of determining whether a facility and/or an individual is properly trained and has the appropriate skills to handle the listed select agents and toxins and has proper laboratory facilities to contain and dispose

Table 12.3 Categorized Bioterrorism Agents[6]

AGENT	CATEGORY
Anthrax (Bacillus anthracis)	A
Arenaviruses	A
Bacillus anthracis (anthrax)	A
Botulism (Clostridium botulinum toxin)	A
Brucella species (brucellosis)	B
Brucellosis (Brucella species)	B
Burkholderia mallei (glanders)	B
Burkholderia pseudomallei (melioidosis)	B
Chlamydia psittaci (psittacosis)	B
Cholera (Vibrio cholerae)	B
Clostridium botulinum toxin (botulism)	B
Clostridium perfringens (Epsilon toxin)	B
Coxiella burnetii (Q fever)	B
Ebola virus hemorrhagic fever	A
E. coli O157:H7 (Escherichia coli)	B
Emerging infectious diseases such as Nipah virus and hantavirus	C
Epsilon toxin of Clostridium perfringens	B
Escherichia coli O157:H7 (E. coli)	B
Food safety threats (e.g., Salmonella species, Escherichia coli O157:H7, Shigella)	B
Francisella tularensis (tularemia)	A
Glanders (Burkholderia mallei)	B
Lassa fever	A
Marburg virus hemorrhagic fever	A
Melioidosis (Burkholderia pseudomallei)	B
Plague (Yersinia pestis)	A
Psittacosis (Chlamydia psittaci)	B
Q fever (Coxiella burnetii)	B
Ricin toxin from Ricinus communis (castor beans)	B
Rickettsia prowazekii (typhus fever)	B
Salmonella species (salmonellosis)	B
Salmonella Typhi (typhoid fever)	B
Salmonellosis (Salmonella species)	B
Shigella (shigellosis)	B
Shigellosis (Shigella)	B
Smallpox (variola major)	A
Staphylococcal enterotoxin B	B
Tularemia (Francisella tularensis)	A
Typhoid fever (Salmonella Typhi)	B
Typhus fever (Rickettsia prowazekii)	B
Variola major (smallpox)	A
Vibrio cholerae (cholera)	B
Viral encephalitis (alphaviruses [e.g., Venezuelan equine encephalitis, Eastern equine encephalitis, Western equine encephalitis])	B
Viral hemorrhagic fevers (filoviruses [e.g., Ebola, Marburg] and arenaviruses [e.g., Lassa, Machupo])	A
Water safety threats (e.g., Vibrio cholerae, Cryptosporidium parvum)	B
Yersinia pestis (plague)	A

of listed agents and toxins, including provisions to ensure that facilities and individuals seeking to register have a legitimate purpose to receive, possess, or transfer such agents and toxins. Lastly, the Federal Bureau of Investigation (FBI) Criminal Justice Information Services Division (CJIS) has been designated to conduct the Security Risk Assessments (background checks) mandated under the Bioterrorism Act. CJIS processes the background checks on the facility owner/operator, the Responsible Official, and all facility employees requesting access to listed biological agents and toxins.

Radiological

Radiological Dispersal Devices (RDD)

In nuclear weapons, fission and fusion of certain slightly radioactive materials release energy in a huge explosion. Radiological Dispersal Devices (RDD) simply scatter radioactive material, and their main physical effect is contaminating an area. A terrorist group could create an RDD much more easily than a nuclear weapon. The radiological threat is related to the nuclear threat, since the type of material used to devise a weapon is the same and many health effects are related. The radiological threat is covered in some detail in different fact sheets, including the Radiological Attack, Dirty Bombs, and Other Devices by the National Academies of Engineering (NAE) and the U.S. Department of Homeland Security (DHS). Excerpts from this fact sheet are provided below, which describe the nature of possible attacks, based mostly on conjecture.

A radiological attack is the spreading of radioactive material with the intent to do harm. Radioactive materials are used every day in laboratories, medical centers, food irradiation plants, and for industrial uses. If stolen or otherwise acquired, many of these materials could be used in a 'radiological dispersal device' (RDD).

The term dirty bomb and RDD are often used interchangeably in technical literature. However, RDDs could also include other means of dispersal, such as placing a container of radioactive material in a public place, or using an airplane to disperse powdered or aerosolized forms of radioactive material.[7]

It is very difficult to design an RDD that would deliver radiation doses high enough to cause immediate health effects or fatalities in a large number of people. Therefore, experts generally agree that an RDD would most likely be used to contaminate facilities or places where people live and work, disrupting lives and livelihoods; and to cause anxiety in those who think they are being, or have been, exposed. However, terrorists could try to achieve several goals with RDDs, among these are:

- **Deaths and injuries** - Initial casualties would most likely come only from the explosion of a dirty bomb; many experts believe these would be few in numbers.
- **Panic** - Small amounts of radioactive material might cause as much panic as larger amounts.
- **Recruitment** - The worldwide media coverage of an RDD attack would be a powerful advertisement for a terrorist group claiming responsibility.
- **Asset denial** - Public concern over the presence of radioactive material might lead people to abandon a subway system, building, or university for months to years.

- **Economic disruption** - If a port or the central area of a city were contaminated with radioactive material, commerce there might be suspended.
- **Long-term casualties** - Inhalation of radioactive material or exposure to gamma sources could lead to such casualties, probably in small numbers.[8]

RDDs are a combination of conventional explosives and radioactive material designed to scatter dangerous and sub-lethal amounts of radioactive material over a general area. Terrorist use of RDDs is considered far more likely than use of a nuclear device because they require very little technical knowledge to build and deploy compared to that of a nuclear device. RDDs also appeal to terrorists because certain radiological materials are used widely in medicine, agriculture, industry, and research and are much more readily available compared to weapons-grade uranium or plutonium. The possible use of RDDs appears to have more of an impact psychologically than in terms of physical harm. Further, a RDD's effectiveness depends on many factors, including:

- Some isotopes do more harm than others, and some elements (including their radioisotopes), such as cesium, bond strongly to concrete and asphalt;
- Smaller particles disperse more easily and are more readily inhaled, but may be harder to make;
- Using more material increases physical effects;
- More explosive would disperse the material more widely; and
- Weather would play a large role.

···

Radiological Dispersion Device (RDD) Specifics
Advantages:
- Far reaching psychological effects.
- Radiological source is available in medical/industrial communities.
- Shock value.

Disadvantages:
- Limited mass casualty/damage potential.
- Possible radiation exposure.
- Difficult to store
- Expertise required.

Likelihood:
Low. 'Dirty bomb' use has been discussed, but historically there has been limited employment of simple exposure device.

Consequences:
Medium. Limited to surrounding area depending upon weather and dissemination means. Radiation treatment and decontamination may hinder medical communities. Use would bring about intense pursuit by law enforcement.

···

Table 12.4 Effects of Blast from Nuclear Explosion (1-megaton burst at 6,000 feet)[9]

Pressure	Effects Detail	Effect Radius
20 psi	Multi-story reinforced concrete buildings demolished; winds, 500 miles per hour.	1.8 mi
10 psi	Most factories and commercial buildings collapsed; small wood and brick residences destroyed; winds, 300 miles per hour.	2.7 mi
5 psi	Unreinforced brick and wood houses destroyed; heavier construction, severely damaged; winds, 160 miles per hour.	4 mi
2 psi	Moderate damage to houses (wall frames cracked, severe damage to roofs, interior walls knocked down); people injured by flying glass and debris; winds, about 60 miles per hour.	7 to 8 mi

Radiation monitoring equipment would be needed to determine whether an explosion has led to a radiological release, so the correct response would be very difficult to discern for almost all people in the short term. If emergency responders have radiation detection equipment, determination and notification of radiological contamination could begin.

Nuclear Weapons and Improvised Nuclear Devices (IND)

Table 12.4 gives some idea of a nuclear weapon blast effects from a 1-megaton blast at 6,000 feet. However, many smaller devices cause more damage. The U.S. nuclear weapons arsenal typically consists of final delivered devices much smaller than 1-megaton, although with multiple warheads, one missile might have a greater destructive capacity. The Russian warhead arsenals are similar although sometimes larger, in the 0.6-megaton range per device. China apparently has some older 3- and 5-megaton warhead missiles.

The National Research Council (NRC) report *Making the Nation Safer*, in evaluating potential threats from terrorists, identifies the state-owned nuclear weapons of Pakistan and India as medium risk due to potential political instabilities and those of Russia as medium risk due to large numbers of weapons and poor inventory controls. All other nuclear powers are identified as low risk relative to state-owned arsenals. This NRC effort, however, did not consider North Korea or Iran, both of which have made headlines since then, so the nuclear threat continues to evolve.[10]

An Improvised Nuclear Device (IND) is intended to cause a yield-producing nuclear explosion. An IND could consist of diverted nuclear weapon components, a modified nuclear weapon, or indigenous-designed device. INDs can be categorized into two types: implosion and gun assembled. Unlike RDDs that can be made with almost any radioactive material, INDs require fissile material—highly enriched uranium or plutonium—to produce nuclear yield.[11] Homeland Security Presidential Directive (HSPD)-14: Domestic

Nuclear Detection directs the implementation of policy to enhance detection of and response to the use of a nuclear explosive device, fissile material, or radiological material in the United States. The directive also establishes the Domestic Nuclear Detection Office (DNDO), which is described in greater detail later in this chapter.

....

Nuclear Weapons and Improvised Nuclear Devices (IND) Specifics

Advantages:

- Large potential for mass casualties and destruction.
- Far reaching psychological effects.
- Secondary radiation effects.
- Shock value.

Disadvantages:

- Difficult to obtain.
- Possible radiation exposure.
- Difficult to store.
- Danger to perpetrators.

Likelihood:

Very Low. Has been discussed, but never used.

Consequences:

High. Effects will reach well beyond initial area of employment. Treating contaminated victims may cause problems. Treatment of large quantities of victims may hinder medical resources in smaller communities. Radiation treatment and decontamination will hinder most communities. Use would bring about intense pursuit by law enforcement.

....

Conventional Explosives

From the standpoint of structural design, the vehicle bomb is the most important consideration in addressing conventional explosives use by terrorists. Vehicle bombs are able to deliver a sufficiently large quantity of explosives to cause potentially devastating structural damage.

For a vehicle bomb, the critical location is taken to be at the closest point that a vehicle can approach, assuming that all security measures are in place. This may be a parking area directly beneath the occupied building, the loading dock, the curb directly outside the facility, or at a vehicle-access control gate where inspection takes place, depending on the level of protection incorporated into the design. Another explosive attack threat is the small bomb that is hand delivered. Small weapons can cause the greatest damage when brought into vulnerable, unsecured areas of the building interior, such as the building lobby, mail room, and retail spaces.

Recent events around the world make it clear that there is an increased likelihood that bombs will be delivered by persons who are willing to sacrifice their own lives—the homicide or suicide bomber. Hand carried explosives are typically on the order of five to ten pounds of Trinitrotoluene (TNT) equivalent. However, larger charge weights, in the fifty- to 100-pounds TNT equivalent range, can be readily carried in rolling cases. Mail bombs are typically less than ten pounds of TNT equivalent.

The Bureau of Alcohol, Tobacco, Firearms, and Explosives (ATF) has developed and disseminated to the response community the ATF Vehicle Bomb Explosion Hazard and Evacuation Distance Table, as shown in Figure 12.1. This guide consists of six different sized vehicles and the estimated maximum potential destruction that could be caused by that sized vehicle packed with explosives. Further, the guide includes information for the multiple categories of different sized vehicles and provides standoff distances based on the following criteria: maximum explosives capacity, lethal air blast range, minimum evacuation distance, and falling glass hazard. The distances are provided in both feet and meters, and the estimated explosives capacity is provided in both pounds and kilograms. The ATF provides the information with the following notations:

- Minimum evacuation distance is the range at which a life-threatening injury from blast or fragment hazards is unlikely. However, non-life-threatening injury or temporary hearing loss may occur.
- Hazard ranges are based on open, level terrain.
- Minimum evacuation distance may be less when explosion is confined within a structure.
- Falling glass hazard range is dependent on line-of-sight from the explosion source to windows. Hazard is from falling shards of broken glass.
- Metric equivalent values are mathematically calculated.
- Explosion confined within a structure may cause structural collapse or building debris hazards.
- Additional hazards include vehicle debris.

Some of the common attributes, characteristics, and indicators of potential vehicle-based improvised explosive devices (VBIED) include the following:

- License plates inconsistent with vehicle registration;
- Vehicle obviously carrying a heavy load;
- Modification of truck or van with heavy duty springs to handle heavier loads;
- Rentals of vans with false papers for dry runs;
- Rental of self-storage space for the purpose of storing chemicals or mixing apparatus;
- Delivery of chemicals directly from the manufacturer to a self-storage facility or unusual deliveries of chemicals to residential or rural addresses;
- Theft of explosives, blasting caps, fuses, or certain chemicals used in the manufacture of explosives;

ATF	VEHICLE DESCRIPTION	MAXIMUM EXPLOSIVES CAPACITY	LETHAL AIR BLAST RANGE	MINIMUM EVACUATION DISTANCE	FALLING GLASS HAZARD
	COMPACT SEDAN	500 Pounds 227 Kilos (In Trunk)	100 Feet 30 Meters	1,500 Feet 457 Meters	1,250 Feet 381 Meters
	FULL SIZE SEDAN	1,000 Pounds 455 Kilos (In Trunk)	125 Feet 38 Meters	1,750 Feet 534 Meters	1,750 Feet 534 Meters
	PASSENGER VAN OR CARGO VAN	4,000 Pounds 1,818 Kilos	200 Feet 61 Meters	2,750 Feet 838 Meters	2,750 Feet 838 Meters
	SMALL BOX VAN (14 FT BOX)	10,000 Pounds 4,545 Kilos	300 Feet 91 Meters	3,750 Feet 1,143 Meters	3,750 Feet 1,143 Meters
	BOX VAN OR WATER/FUEL TRUCK	30,000 Pounds 13,636 Kilos	450 Feet 137 Meters	6,500 Feet 1,982 Meters	6,500 Feet 1,982 Meters
	SEMI-TRAILER	60,000 Pounds 27,273 Kilos	600 Feet 183 Meters	7,000 Feet 2,134 Meters	7,000 Feet 2,134 Meters

Figure 12.1 ATF Vehicle Bomb Explosion Hazard and Evacuation Distance Table (Image Courtesy: U.S. Department of Justice, Bureau of Alcohol, Tobacco, Firearms, and Explosives)

- Chemical fires, toxic odors, brightly colored stains, or rusted metal fixtures in apartments, hotel/motel rooms, or self-storage units due to chemical activity;
- Small test explosions in rural wooded areas;
- Treatment of chemical burns or treatment for missing hands/fingers; and/or
- Untreated chemical burns or missing hands/fingers.[12]

....

Conventional Explosives Specifics

Advantages:
- Easy to obtain.
- Easy to store.
- Easy to employ.
- Low cost.
- Reliable results.

Disadvantages:
- Technical expertise required.

Likelihood:
High. Use has been both planned and conducted.

Consequences:
Medium. Effects are limited to area of employment in conventional explosions. Treatment of large quantities of victims may temporarily hinder smaller medical communities.

....

Electromagnetic Pulse (EMP) and Radio Frequency (RF) Weapons

Electromagnetic Pulse (EMP) Weapons

Electromagnetic Pulse (EMP) is defined by the U.S. Department of Defense (DOD) as the electromagnetic radiation from a strong electronic pulse, most commonly caused by a nuclear explosion that may couple with electrical or electronic systems to produce damaging current and voltage surges. The electromagnetic radiation from a nuclear explosion is caused by Compton-recoil electrons and photoelectrons from photons scattered in the materials of the nuclear device or in a surrounding medium. The resulting electric and magnetic fields may couple with electrical/electronic systems to produce damaging current and voltage surges. EMP effects may also be caused by non-nuclear means. The EMP effect was first observed during the early testing of high-altitude airburst nuclear weapons. The effect is characterized by the production of a very short (hundreds of nanoseconds) but intense EMP, which propagates away from its source with ever diminishing intensity governed by the theory of electromagnetism.

The EMP is in effect an electromagnetic shock wave. This pulse of energy produces a powerful electromagnetic field, particularly within the vicinity of the weapon burst. The field can be sufficiently strong to produce short-lived transient voltages of thousands of Volts (i.e., kiloVolts) on exposed electrical conductors, such as wires or conductive tracks on printed circuit boards where exposed. It is this aspect of the EMP effect which is of military significance, as it can result in irreversible damage to a wide range of electrical and electronic equipment, particularly computers and radio or radar receivers. The damage inflicted is not unlike that experienced through exposure to close proximity lightning strikes, and may require complete replacement of the equipment, or at least substantial portions thereof.

Commercial computer equipment is particularly vulnerable to EMP effects, as it is largely built up of high-density Metal Oxide Semiconductor (MOS) devices, which are very sensitive to exposure to high-voltage transients. What is significant about MOS devices is that very little energy is required to permanently damage or destroy them; any voltage typically in excess of tens of Volts can produce an effect termed gate breakdown, which effectively destroys the device. If the pulse is not powerful enough to produce thermal damage, the power supply in the equipment will readily supply enough energy to complete the destructive process. Computers used in data processing systems, communications systems, displays, industrial control applications, including road and rail signaling, and those embedded in military equipment, such as signal processors, electronic flight controls, and digital engine control systems, are all potentially vulnerable to the EMP effect.

Other electronic devices and electrical equipment may also be destroyed by the EMP effect. Telecommunications equipment can be highly vulnerable, due to the presence of lengthy copper cables between devices. Receivers of all types are sensitive to EMP. The highly sensitive miniaturized high-frequency components in such equipment are easily destroyed by exposure to high-voltage electrical transients. Therefore, radar and electronic warfare equipment, satellite, microwave, UHF, VHF, HF, and low-band communications equipment and television equipment are all potentially vulnerable to the EMP effect.

Radio Frequency (RF) Weapons

State-of-the-art semiconductors are vulnerable to the effects of radio frequency energy, particularly as semiconductor features become smaller and smaller. Commercial microelectronics make heavy use of MOS devices, which fail when subjected to voltages that exceed the dielectric strength of the component or when the device melts as a result of heating from currents induced by the RF pulse.[13]

An RF weapon is one that uses intense pulses of RF energy to destroy ("burnout") or degrade ("upset") the electronics in a target. These weapons can be used on a narrow beam over a long distance to a point target. They are also able to cover broad targets. They are categorized as high-power microwave (HPM) weapons and ultra-wide band (UWB) weapons.

The phrase non-nuclear electromagnetic pulse is sometimes used, because these weapons, which are indeed non-nuclear, project the same type of pulse we first learned of in conjunction with nuclear weapons. As a practical matter, a piece of electronic gear on the ground or in a vehicle, ship, or plane does not really care whether it is hit by a nuclear magnetic pulse or a non-nuclear one.

In congressional testimony, military experts have identified a class of RF weapons referred to as RF munitions. These small munitions contain high explosives that produce radio frequency energy as their primary kill mechanism. Generally, they produce a short but very intense pulse. Open source literature provides information on at least nine RF munitions:

1. Magnetohydrodynamic Generator Frequency
2. Explosive Magnetic Generator of Frequency
3. Implosive Magnetic Generator of Frequency
4. Cylindrical Shock Wave Source
5. Spherical Shock Wave Source
6. Ferromagnetic Generator of Frequency
7. Superconductive Former of Magnetic Field Shock Wave
8. Piezoelectric Generator of Frequency
9. Superconducting Ring Burst Generator.[14]

Some of these weapons are said by the Russians to be now available as a hand grenade, a briefcase-like object, a mortar, or artillery round. Applications or potential targets (like those of the larger HPM weapons) would include all military computers, circuit boards, or chips, of any description, and include the key components of our military and national infrastructure. They would have equal impact on civilian targets with the advantage that less power would be required. Further, the critical infrastructure and key resources (CI/KR) elements that can be targeted with these types of weapons can include:

- National telecommunications systems;
- National power grid;
- National transportation system (ranging from the Federal Aviation Administration [FAA] to simple things as our traffic signaling for roadway and rail systems);
- Oil and gas control and refining and the Supervisory Control And Data Acquisition (SCADA) systems that support them;
- Manufacturing processing, inventory control, shipment, and tracking;
- Public works;
- Emergency response systems and services;
- Healthcare infrastructure (including medical diagnostic and life support systems); and
- Finance and banking systems (to include ATM services and networks).

Senior military leadership members have reported to the US Congress that the United States is doubly vulnerable because we are, and will remain, in an era of dual use of military and civilian systems. For example, 90% of our military communications now passes over public networks.[15]

Cyber Threats

The U.S. economy and national security are highly dependent upon the global cyber infrastructure. Cyber infrastructure enables all sectors' functions and services, resulting in a highly interconnected and interdependent global network of CI/KR. Key aspects of the cyberterrorism threat are that:

- A spectrum of malicious actors could conduct attacks against the cyber infrastructure using cyber attack tools. Because of the interconnected nature of the cyber infrastructure, these attacks could spread quickly and have a debilitating impact.
- The use of innovative technology and interconnected networks in operations improves productivity and efficiency, but also increases the Nation's risk to cyber threats if cyber security is not addressed and integrated appropriately.
- The interconnected and interdependent nature of the Nation's CI/KR makes it problematic to address the protection of physical and cyber assets independently.
- The National Infrastructure Protection Plan (NIPP) developed by the U.S. Department of Homeland Security (DHS) in 2006 addresses reducing cyber risk and enhancing cyber security in two ways: (1) as a cross-sector cyber element that involves DHS, Sector-Specific Agencies (SSAs), and private sector owners and operators; and (2) as a major component of the Information Technology (IT) Sector's responsibility in partnership with the Telecommunications Sector.

Threat Assessments

A threat assessment can be defined as a methodology to identify and evaluate the threat level of each potential threat element (PTE). Here a PTE is any group or individual in which there are allegations or information indicating a possibility of the unlawful use of force or violence, specifically the utilization of a WMD, against persons or property to intimidate or coerce a government, the civilian population, or any segment thereof, in furtherance of a specific motivation or goal, possibly political or social in nature. The DHS defines threat assessment as a systematic effort to identify and evaluate existing or potential terrorist threats to a jurisdiction and its target assets. These assessments consider the full spectrum of threats, such as natural disasters, criminal activity, and major accidents, as well as terrorist activity. Conversely, threat levels are based on the degree to which combinations of the following factors are present:

- **Existence:** A terrorist group is present, or is able to gain access to a given locality.
- **Capability:** The capability of a terrorist group to carry out an attack has been assessed or demonstrated.
- **Intent:** Evidence of terrorist group activity, including stated or assessed intent to conduct terrorist activity.
- **History:** Demonstrated terrorist activity in the past.
- **Targeting:** Current credible information or activity exists that indicate preparations for a specific terrorist operations—intelligence collections by a suspect group, preparation of destructive devices, other actions.
- **Security Environment:** Indicates whether and how the political and security posture of the threatened jurisdiction affects the capability of the terrorist elements to carry out their intentions. This addresses whether the jurisdiction is concerned with terrorism and whether it has taken strong proactive countermeasures to deal with such at threat.[16]

Table 12.5 provides a threat matrix that identifies likely means and weapons used by terrorists, the difficulty of preparation, and the history of use.

DHS Homeland Infrastructure Threat and Risk Analysis Center (HITRAC)

The DHS Homeland Infrastructure Threat and Risk Analysis Center (HITRAC) conducts integrated threat analysis for all critical infrastructure/ key resources (CI/KR) sectors. As specified in Section 201 of the Homeland Security Act of 2002, HITRAC brings together intelligence and infrastructure specialists to ensure a complete and sophisticated understanding of the risks to U.S. CI/KR. HITRAC works in partnership with the U.S. Intelligence Community and the national law enforcement agencies to integrate and analyze intelligence and law enforcement information on the threat. It also works in partnership with the Sector Specific Agencies (SSAs) and owners and operators to ensure that their expertise on infrastructure operations is integrated into threat analysis. This HITRAC-SSA coordination is carried out through a number of mechanisms including: the use of liaison personnel from the private sector, use of on-call subject matter experts (SME), and coordination with existing government–industry organizations such as National Coordinating Center for Telecommunications (NCCT) and the Sector Coordinating Councils (SCC) or Information Sharing and Analysis Centers (ISACs).[17]

Table 12.5 Threat Matrix

Activity	Means and Weapons	Delivery Medium	Required Personnel	Risk	Difficulty with Preparation — Facilities	Technical Skill	Material	Probability	History
Assassination (including decapitation)	Explosive								
	conventional	Ground (Gnd)	Few/single	Med	Lo	Lo	Lo	Hi	Yes
	nuclear	Gnd/air	Many	Hi	Hi	Hi	Hi	Lo	No
	unconventional	Gnd/air/water	Few/single	Med	Lo	Lo	Lo	Hi	Yes
	CW agent	Gnd/air	Many	Hi	Hi	Hi	Hi	Lo	No
	Common toxin	Gnd/air	Few/single	Hi	Lo	Med	Lo	Lo	No
	BW agent	Gnd/air	Few/single	Hi	Med	Hi	Med	Lo	No
	Poision	Gnd/air/water	Few/single	Med	NA	Lo	Med	Lo	Yes
	Fire	Gnd/air	Few/single	Med	NA	Lo	Lo	Lo	No
	Small arms	Ground	Few/single	Hi	NA	Lo	Lo	Hi	Yes
Physical Destruction (less mass casualties)	Explosive								
	conventional	Gnd/air	Few/single	Med	Lo	Lo	Lo	Hi	Yes
	nuclear	Ground	Many	Hi	Hi	Hi	Hi	Lo	No
	unconventional	Gnd/air/water	Few/single	Med	Lo	Lo	Lo	Hi	Yes
	Fire	Gnd/air	Few/single	Med	NA	Lo	Lo	Hi	Yes
Contamination (including environmental degradation)	Radioligical	Gnd/air/water	Many	Med	Hi	Hi	Hi	Lo	No
	CW agent	Gnd/air	Many	Hi	Hi	Hi	Hi	Lo	No
	Common toxin	Gnd/air	Few/single	Hi	Lo	Med	Lo	Hi	No
	BW agent	Gnd/air/water	Few/single	Hi	Med	Hi	Hi	Lo	No

(Continued)

Table 12.5 (*Continued*)

Activity	Means and Weapons	Delivery Medium	Required Personnel	Risk	Difficulty with Preparation			Probability	History
					Facilities	Technical Skill	Material		
Mass Causalities (including livestock)	Explosive								
	conventional	Gnd/air	Few/single	Med	Lo	Lo	Lo	Hi	Yes
	nuclear	Gnd/air	Many	Hi	Hi	Hi	Hi	Lo	No
	unconventional	Gnd/air/water	Few/single	Med	Lo	Lo	Lo	Hi	Yes
	CW agent	Gnd/air	Many	Hi	Hi	Hi	Hi	Lo	Yes
	Common toxin	Gnd/air	Few/single	Hi	Lo	Med	Lo	Hi	Yes
	BW agent	Gnd/air	Few/single	Hi	Med	Hi	Hi	Med	Yes
	Poision	Gnd/water	Few/single	Med	NA	Lo	Med	Lo	Yes
	Fire	Gnd/air	Few/single	Med	NA	Lo	Lo	Hi	No
	Small arms	Gnd/air/water	Many	Hi	NA	Lo	Lo	Lo	Yes
Hostage-taking (minor relevance for emergency responders)	Explosive (conv)	Gnd/air	Few/single	Hi	Na	Lo	Lo	Hi	Yes
	Small arms	Gnd/air	Few/single	Hi	NA	Lo	Lo	Hi	Yes

HITRAC develops analytical products by combining intelligence expertise based on all-source information, threat assessments, and trend analysis with practical business and CI/KR operational expertise informed by current infrastructure status and operations information. This comprehensive analysis provides an understanding of the threat, CI/KR vulnerabilities, the potential consequences of attacks, and the effects of risk mitigation actions on not only the threat, but also on business and operations. This combination of intelligence and practical knowledge allows HITRAC to provide CI/KR risk assessment products that contain strategically relevant and actionable information. It also allows HITRAC to identify intelligence collection requirements in conjunction with owners and operators so that the intelligence community can provide the type of information necessary to support the CI/KR protection mission. HITRAC coordinates closely with security partners outside the federal government through the private sector and state coordinators and ISACs to ensure that its analytic products are relevant to security partner needs, and that they are accessible to the partners who need them.

The HITRAC utilizes the Federal Bureau of Investigation (FBI) four-level threat assessment schema. The four levels are described as:

Level Four (Minimal Threat) – Received threats do not warrant actions beyond normal liaison notifications or placing assets or resources on a heightened alert.

Level Three (Potential Threat) – Intelligence or an articulated threat indicates the potential for a terrorist incident; however, this threat has not yet been assessed as credible.

Level Two (Credible Threat) – A threat assessment indicates that a potential threat is credible and confirms the involvement of WMD in a developing terrorist incident. The threat increases in significance when the presence of an explosive device or WMD capable of causing a significant destructive event, prior or actual injury or loss is confirmed or when intelligence and circumstances indicate a high probability that a device exists.

Level One (WMD Incident) – A WMD terrorism incident has occurred resulting in mass casualties that requires immediate federal planning and preparation to provide support to state and local authorities. The federal response is primarily directed toward the safety and welfare of the public and the preservation of human life.

Domestic Nuclear Detection Office (DNDO)

As part of the national effort to protect the Nation from radiological and nuclear threats, the Domestic Nuclear Detection Office (DNDO) has been established as a national office staffed by representatives from several federal departments and state and local agencies. The office resides within the DHS, and the DNDO director reports to the Secretary of Homeland Security.

The DNDO provides a single accountable organization with dedicated responsibilities to develop the global nuclear detection architecture and to acquire and support the deployment of the domestic detection system to detect

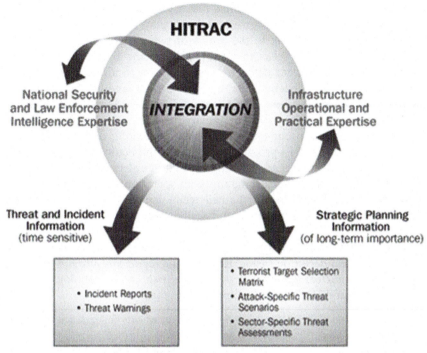

Figure 12.2 Threat Analysis Tools and Information (Courtesy: U.S. Department of Homeland Security)

and report attempts to import or transport a nuclear device or fissile or radio-logical material intended for illicit use.[18]

The mission of the office addresses a broad spectrum of radiological and nuclear protective measures, but is focused directly on nuclear detection. This includes establishing strong linkages across multiple Departments and levels of government for:

- The development of the global nuclear detection architecture;
- The acquisition and support to the deployment of the domestic detection system;
- The enhancement of effective sharing and use of nuclear detection-related information and intelligence;
- The coordination of nuclear detection research and development to continually improve detection capability; and
- The establishment of procedures and training for the end users of equipment developed and deployed through the new office.

The DNDO is an essential part of a multi-layered defense strategy to protect the Nation from a terrorist nuclear or radiological attack. While no single layer is capable of providing one hundred percent effectiveness in detecting and interdicting nuclear materials intended for illicit use, the overseas components of this strategy are aimed first at securing nuclear materials and detecting their movements overseas and will play a vital role in providing layers of protection closest to the points of potential origination of threat materials. The DNDO seeks to integrate these crucial overseas programs with the domestic nuclear detection system and with all nuclear detection efforts undertaken by federal, state, territorial, tribal, and local governments and the private sector.

The DNDO conducts both evolutionary (near-term, requirements-driven) and transformational (long-term, high-payoff) research, development, test, and evaluation (RDT&E) programs to improve the Nation's capabilities for detection, identification, and reporting of radiological and nuclear materials. By integrating these RDT&E programs with operational support responsibilities, the DNDO will ensure that all technologies will be appropriately deployed with training materials and well-developed operational response protocols.

The DNDO will develop, acquire, and support the deployment of a domestic nuclear detection system to detect and report any attempt to import or transport a nuclear explosive device, fissile material, or radiological material intended for illicit use. To accomplish this, the DNDO will:

- Develop the global detection architecture and ensure linkages across federal, state, territorial, tribal, and local agencies;
- Enhance the effective sharing and use of nuclear detection-related information and intelligence;
- Maintain continuous awareness by analyzing information from all mission-related detection systems;
- Conduct aggressive evolutionary and transformational research and development programs to improve probability of detection by integrating and deploying current technologies and improving those capabilities over time;
- Enhance the nuclear detection efforts of federal, state, territorial, tribal, and local governments, and the private sector to ensure a coordinated response; and
- Establish standards, response protocols, and training across the federal, state, territorial, tribal, and local levels to ensure that detection leads to timely response actions.

The DNDO organization comprises the following functional elements:

Office of the Director: Responsible for the execution of all DNDO mission areas. The Director will ensure the development of an integrated global and domestic nuclear detection architecture, ensure the acquisition and support to deployment of the domestic nuclear detection system, lead research and development (R&D) coordination, and ensure protocols are developed to seamlessly progress from detection through alarm resolution to search and response.

Office of System Engineering: This office is responsible for the development of an integrated global detection architecture and a comprehensive system engineering master plan.

Office of Systems Development and Acquisition: This office provides the central focus for operationally-driven systems research, development, and, ultimately, acquisition and transition of systems to deployment.

Office of Assessments: This office is responsible for establishing an operational test and evaluation (OTE) program to ensure that required technical performance is achieved, and that operational protocols and procedures are effective.

Office of Transformational Research and Development: This office will identify technology opportunities and execute programs designed to dramatically improve the detection capability and overall system performance.

Office of Operations Support: This office will establish and operate a real-time situational awareness and support capability by monitoring the status of, and collecting information from, both overseas and domestic detection systems. Operational support services will include the development of protocols and standards as well as a technical support infrastructure or reach back to ensure appropriate expertise is in place to support prompt resolution of alarms.[19]

Although the DNDO is principally focused on domestic detection, its coordinating work extends overseas through the design of a global nuclear detection architecture. Equally, while detection technologies developed by DNDO will be directed primarily by operational requirements for domestic application, many technologies developed will have direct application to overseas detection programs, such as cargo screening and non-intrusive inspection technologies validated by the DNDO for implementation at port terminals throughout the worldwide maritime cargo supply chain.[20]

13

....

Natural Disasters

Calamity is the perfect glass wherein we truly see and know ourselves.
—Sir William D'Avenant

Introduction

A disaster is a situation or event, which overwhelms local capacity, necessitating a request to national or international level for external assistance. It is an unforeseen and often sudden event that causes great damage, destruction, and human suffering. A natural disaster can be defined as a disaster caused by natural forces based on natural hazards. A natural hazard is a threatening event or probability of occurrence of a potentially damaging phenomenon within a given time period and area.[1] Hazards evoke natural disasters when an extreme event in nature adversely impacts human life, property, or activity. No human settlements are free from the risk of natural hazards. Therefore, it is vital that researchers and decision-makers have access to all available hazards information.

Munich Reinsurance (Munich Re) reports that 2005 was the most expensive natural catastrophe year in insurance history and for the world's economies as a whole. The hurricane losses in North and Middle America and in the Caribbean alone caused roughly 80% of the overall economic losses and 88% of the insured losses.[2] Further, 2005 was marked by weather-related natural catastrophes. Roughly half of all the loss events recorded were windstorms, with costs to be borne by the world's economies exceeding U.S. $185 billion.[3] The most severe human catastrophe was triggered by an earthquake

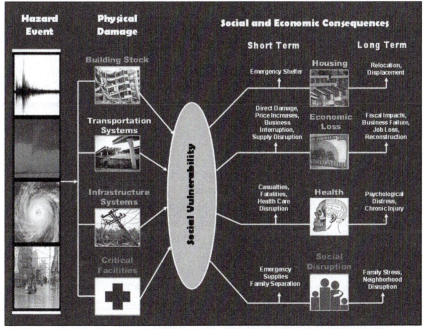

Figure 13.1 Social and Economic Consequences of Natural Disasters[4] (Image Courtesy: Federal Emergency Management Agency)

that occurred in October in the border area between Pakistan and India and, with a death toll of 88,000, was one of the five most destructive quakes of the last 100 years.

Overall, 2005 was marked by 100,995 fatalities and 648 loss events. Such a large number of fatalities has been recorded only twice in the last 25 years: in 1991 following a storm surge in Bangladesh, and in 2004 following the tsunami in South Asia. Consequently, it is not surprising that insured losses also reached unprecedented dimensions. The year's overall balance for the insurance industry was U.S. $94 billion, doubling the previous record set in 2004.

As Figure 13.1 illustrates, events originating from natural disasters can cause physical damage to critical infrastructure and key resources, creating a social vulnerability. The effects here are both short-term and long-term in duration.

In the short-term, populations may require emergency shelter as part of mass care, along with water, food, and medical supplies when dislocated from their communities. Damage to residential housing stock and commercial properties could contribute to supply disruptions. Business interruption adds to the logistical impediments hindering distribution of commodities needed for recovery and reconstitution. The healthcare and public health systems may be overwhelmed with casualties and fatalities. Long-term implications of natural disasters include population displacement and relocation, economic impacts of business failure, business interruption, job loss, and costly reconstruction. In terms of social disruption, particularly the medical and public health dimensions, chronic injuries and illnesses and the psycho-logical effects of critical incident stress can produce secondary casualties from a disaster. Among the meteorological hazards that present the most frequent and consequential impacts on society are drought, flooding, hurricane/tropical cyclone, severe storms, snow and ice (blizzards and ice storms), tornado, and wildfires. These hazards are discussed in detail in the sections that follow.

Drought

Drought is a normal, recurrent feature of climate. It occurs almost every-where, although its features vary from region to region. Defining drought is therefore difficult; it depends on differences in regions, needs, and discipli-nary perspectives. Generally, drought originates from a deficiency of precipi-tation over an extended period of time, resulting in a water shortage for some activity, group, or environmental sector.[5]

Drought is a temporary aberration; it is distinguished from aridity, which is restricted to low rainfall regions and is a permanent feature of climate. Three operational definitions of drought are important to understand:

- **Meteorological drought** is typically defined on the basis of the degree of dryness (in comparison to some normal or average amount) and the duration of the dry period.
- **Agricultural drought** links various characteristics of meteorological (or hydro-logical) drought to agricultural impacts, focusing on precipitation shortages, dif-ferences between actual and potential evapotranspiration, soil water deficits, reduced ground water or reservoir levels, and so forth.
- **Hydrological drought** is associated with the effects of periods of precipitation (including snowfall) shortfalls on surface or subsurface water supply (i.e., streamflow, reservoir and lake levels, ground water).

Drought should be considered relative to some long-term average or nor-mal condition of balance between precipitation and evapotranspiration (i.e., evaporation + transpiration) in a particular area. It is also related to the tim-ing (i.e., principal season of occurrence, delays in the start of the rainy sea-son, occurrence of rains in relation to principal crop growth stages) and the effectiveness (i.e., rainfall intensity, number of rainfall events) of the rains. Other climatic factors such as high temperature, high wind, and low relative humidity are often associated with drought in many regions of the world and can significantly aggravate its severity.

Drought should not be viewed as merely a physical phenomenon or natu-ral event. Its impacts on society result from the interaction between a natural event and the demand human activity places upon the water supply.

Palmer Drought Severity Index
In 1965, Wayne Palmer developed the Palmer Drought Severity Index (PDSI) to measure the departure of the moisture supply. Palmer based his

index on the supply-and-demand concept of the water balance equation, taking into account more than merely the precipitation deficit at specific locations. The objective of the PDSI is to provide measurements of moisture conditions that are standardized so that comparisons using the index could be made between locations and between months.[6]

The PDSI is a meteorological drought index, and it responds to weather conditions that have been abnormally dry or abnormally wet. The PDSI is calculated based on precipitation and temperature data, as well as the local available water content of the soil. From the inputs, all the basic terms of the water balance equation can be determined, including evapotranspiration, soil recharge, runoff, and moisture loss from the surface layer. Human impacts on the water balance, such as irrigation, are not considered.

The PDSI soil moisture algorithm can be calibrated for relatively homogeneous regions. Many U.S. government agencies and states rely on the PDSI to trigger drought relief programs. The PDSI is characterized as the first comprehensive drought index developed in the United States.

It is noteworthy that experience has shown PDSI values may lag emerging droughts by several months, and, therefore, it is less suited for mountainous land or areas of frequent climatic extremes.

Preparedness and Prediction
The National Drought Mitigation Center (NDMC) helps develop and implement measures to reduce societal vulnerability to drought, stressing preparedness and risk management rather than crisis management. The NDMC, established in 1995, is based in the School of Natural Resources at the University of Nebraska–Lincoln. NDMC's services are directed to state, federal, regional, and tribal governments that are involved in drought and water supply planning. The NDMC's activities include maintaining an information clearinghouse and drought portal and drought monitoring, including participation in the preparation of the U.S. Drought Monitor and maintenance of a

Table 13.1 PDSI Classifications[7]

CLASSIFICATION	DESCRIPTION
4.0 or More	Extremely Wet
3.0 to 3.99	Very Wet
2.0 to 2.99	Moderately Wet
1.0 to 1.99	Slightly Wet
0.5 to 0.99	Incipient Wet Spell
0.49 to −0.49	Near Normal
−0.5 to −0.99	Incipient Dry Spell
−1.0 to −1.99	Mild Drought
−2.0 to −2.99	Moderate Drought
−3.0 to −3.99	Severe Drought
−4.0 or Less	Extreme Drought

publicly-accessible Website (http://www.drought.unl.edu). The NDMC also supports:

- Mitigation planning and research;
- Drought policy;
- Advising of policy makers;
- Collaborative research;
- K–12 outreach;
- Workshops for federal, state, and foreign governments and international organizations;
- Organizing and conducting seminars, workshops, and conferences; and
- Providing data to and answering questions for the media and the general public.

Floods

During the 20th century, floods were the number one natural disaster in the United States in terms of number of lives lost and property damage. They can occur at any time of the year, in any part of the country, and at any time of the day or night. Most lives are lost when people are swept away by flood currents, whereas most property damage results from inundation by sediment-laden water. Flood currents also possess tremendous destructive power, as lateral forces can demolish buildings and erosion can undermine bridge foundations and footings leading to the collapse of structures.

••

The **U.S. Geological Survey** (USGS) reports that most flood-related deaths are due to flash floods; 50% of all flash-flood fatalities are vehicle related, and 90% of those who die in hurricanes drown.[8]

••

Floods are the result of a multitude of naturally occurring and human-induced factors. A flood can be defined as the accumulation of too much water in too little time in a specific area.[9] Types of floods include regional floods, flash floods, ice-jam floods, storm-surge floods, dam and levee failure floods, and debris, landslide, and mudflow floods. These type of floods of discussed in detail in the following sections.

Regional Floods

Regional floods can occur seasonally when winter or spring rains, coupled with melting snow, fill river basins with too much water too quickly. The ground may be frozen, reducing infiltration into the soil and thereby increasing runoff. Such was the case for the New England flood of March 1936, in which more than 150 lives were lost and property damage totaled $300 million.

Extended wet periods during any part of the year can create saturated soil conditions, after which any additional rain runs off into streams and rivers until river capacities are exceeded. Regional floods are often associated with slow-moving, low-pressure or frontal storm systems including decaying hurricanes or tropical storms. Persistent wet meteorological patterns are usually responsible for very large regional floods such as the Mississippi River Basin flood of 1993, wherein damages were estimated to exceed $20 billion.

Flash Floods

Flash floods can occur within several seconds to several hours, with little warning. Flash floods can be deadly because they produce rapid rises in water levels and have devastating flow velocities. Several factors can contribute to flash flooding. Among these are rainfall intensity, rainfall duration, surface conditions, and topography and slope of the receiving basin. Urban areas are susceptible to flash floods because a high percentage of the surface area is composed of impervious streets, roofs, and parking lots where runoff occurs very rapidly. Mountainous areas also are susceptible to flash floods as steep topography may funnel runoff into a narrow canyon.

Floodwaters accelerated by steep stream slopes can cause the floodwave to move downstream too fast to allow people to escape, resulting in many deaths. For example, a flash flood caused by 15 inches of rain in five hours from slow-moving thunderstorms killed 237 people in Rapid City, South Dakota, in 1972. Further, floodwaves in excess of thirty feet high have occurred many miles from the rainfall area, catching vulnerable populations without warning. Even desert arroyos are not immune to flash floods, as distant thunderstorms can produce rapid rises in water levels in otherwise dry channels. Early-warning gages upstream save lives by providing advanced notice of potential deadly floodwaves.

Ice-Jam Floods

Ice-jam floods occur on rivers that are totally or partially frozen. A rise in stream stage will break up a totally frozen river and create ice flows that can pile up on channel obstructions such as shallow riffles, log jams, or bridge piers. The jammed ice creates a dam across the channel over which the water and ice mixture continues to flow, allowing for more jamming to occur. Backwater upstream from the ice dam can rise rapidly and overflow the channel banks. Flooding moves downstream when the ice dam fails and the water stored behind the dam is released. At this time the flood takes on the characteristics of a flash flood, with the added danger of ice flows that, when driven by the energy of the floodwave, can inflict serious damage on structures.

Storm-Surge Floods

Storm-surge flood is water that is pushed up onto otherwise dry land by onshore winds. Friction between the water and the moving air creates drag that, depending upon the distance of water and the velocity of the wind, can pile water up to depths greater than twenty feet. Intense, low-pressure systems and hurricanes can create storm-surge flooding. The storm surge is widely considered the most dangerous part of a hurricane, as pounding waves create very hazardous flood currents.

Nine out of ten hurricane fatalities are caused by the storm surge.[10] Concurrence of high tide with a storm surge presents the greatest threat to life and property. Stream flooding is much worse inland during the storm surge because of backwater effects. In September 1900, the hurricane and storm surge at Galveston, Texas killed more than 6,000 people, making it the worst natural disaster in the Nation's history in terms of loss of life.[11] For a stunning exposition on the events of the Galveston hurricane of 1900, the reader is referred to *Isaac's Storm: A Man, a Time, and the Deadliest Hurricane in History* by Erik Larson.

Dam and Levee Failure Floods

Dams and levees are built for flood protection. They usually are engineered to withstand a flood with a computed risk of occurrence. For example, a dam or levee may be designed to contain a flood at a location on a stream that has a certain probability of occurring in any one year. If a larger flood occurs, then that structure will be overtopped. If during the overtopping, the dam or levee fails or is washed out, the water behind it is released to become a flash flood. Failed dams or levees can create floods that are catastrophic to life and property because of the tremendous energy of the released water.

The Federal Emergency Management Agency (FEMA) states that dam owners are responsible for the safety and the liability of the dam and for financing its upkeep, upgrade, and repair. While most infrastructure facilities, such as roads, bridges, and sewer systems, are owned by public entities, the majority of dams in the United States are privately owned. The exception to this is that very large dams are owned and regulated by the federal government. Figure 13.2 characterizes the ownership of dams by entities and individuals within the U.S.

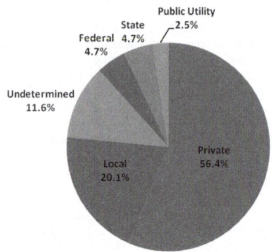

Figure 13.2 Dam Ownership in the United States[12]

History is replete with tragic tales of loss and suffering caused by the failure of dams or levees. Long before the catastrophic failure of the levee system in New Orleans following Hurricane Katrina in 2005, one of the most significant losses of lives in the United States occurred in Conemaugh Valley of Pennsylvania. The story of the Johnstown Flood has elements of a wealthy resort, an intense storm, an unfortunate failure of a dam, the destruction of a working class city, and an inspirational humanitarian relief, response, and recovery effort. More than 2,209 people died in the great flood of 1889 which destroyed Johnstown, Pennsylvania. Thousands more were injured. For a historical perspective on the tragic consequences of this dam failure, refer to the Johnstown Flood National Memorial, under the auspices of the National Park Service: http://www.nps.gov/jofl.

Debris, Landslide, and Mudflow Floods
Debris, landslide, and mudflow floods are created by the accumulation of debris, mud, rocks, and (or) fallen timber/logs in a channel, which form a temporary dam. Flooding occurs upstream as water becomes stored behind the temporary dam and then becomes a flash flood as the dam is breached and rapidly washes away. Landslides can create large waves on lakes or embayments and can be deadly. Mudflow floods can occur when volcanic activity rapidly melts mountain snow and glaciers, and the water mixed with mud and debris moves rapidly downslope. These mudflow events are also called lahars and, after the eruption of Mount St. Helens in 1980, one such lahar caused significant damage downstream along rivers in southwest Washington State.

Prediction and Preparedness
The U.S. Geological Survey (USGS) maintains more than 7,000 stream-gauging stations throughout the United States, Puerto Rico, and the Virgin Islands. These stations monitor streamflow and provide data to various federal, state, and local cooperating agencies as well as the general public. Some of the USGS stream-gauging stations have been in operation since before 1900, providing more than a century of water information. In addition to providing critical information on flood heights and discharges, these stations provide data used in the effective management of water-supply and water-quality needs, protection of aquatic habitat, recreation, and water-resources research.

The building block for a stream-flow data network is the stage-discharge relation that is developed at each gauging-station location. Measurements of the flow (discharge) are related graphically to the respective water depths (stage), which then enables discharge to be determined from stage data. An illustration of the inner workings of a stream-gauging station is depicted in Figure 13.3.

Discharge measurements can either be direct, using a current meter, or indirect, using mathematical flow equations. Both methods require that an elevation of the floodwater surface be determined by a water-depth gage or

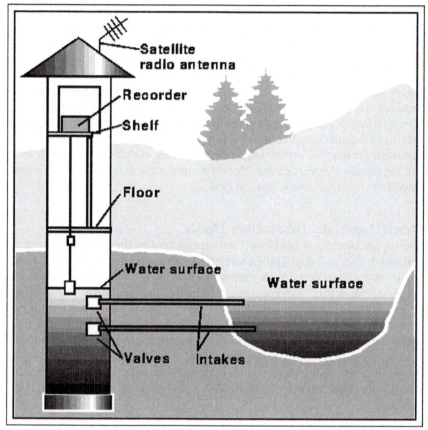

Figure 13.3 Inner Workings of a Stream-Gauging Station (Image Courtesy: U.S. Geological Survey)

by a detailed survey of high-water marks. In safe conditions and with adequate time, USGS hydrographers can conduct direct measurements. During major floods, however, direct measurements are high-risk to personnel safety and require indirect methods for measurement. USGS streamflow data are provided to the National Weather Service (NWS) and are included in forecast data products nationwide.

Flood Mitigation
Flood mitigation has been an important program area in the emergency management practice. The U.S. government consistently reminds the public that most homeowners insurance policies do not cover floodwater damage, and individuals and business owners can protect themselves from property losses by purchasing flood insurance through FEMA's National Flood Insurance Program (NFIP). The Mitigation Division, a component of the FEMA, manages the NFIP, which consists of three components:

1. Flood insurance;
2. Floodplain management; and
3. Flood hazard mapping.

FEMA reports that nearly 20,000 communities across the United States and its territories participate in the NFIP by adopting and enforcing flood-plain management ordinances to reduce future flood damage. In exchange, the NFIP makes federally-backed flood insurance available to homeowners, renters, and business owners in these communities. Community participation in the NFIP is voluntary.

Flood insurance is designed to provide an alternative to disaster assistance to reduce the escalating costs of repairing damage to buildings caused by floods. Flood damage is reduced by nearly $1 billion a year through communities implementing sound floodplain management requirements and property owners purchasing of flood insurance. Additionally, buildings constructed in compliance with NFIP building standards suffer approximately 80% less damage annually than those not built in compliance. FEMA reports that for every $3 paid in flood insurance claims, the U.S. taxpayers save $1 in disaster assistance payments.

In addition to providing flood insurance and reducing flood damages through floodplain management regulations, the NFIP identifies and maps the Nation's floodplains. Mapping flood hazards creates broad-based awareness of the flood hazards and provides the data needed for floodplain management programs and to actuarially rate new construction for flood insurance.[13]

Supplemental information on floods can be found via the following links:

- Dam Safety: http://www.usbr.gov/ssle/dam_safety/
- Flood Safety: http://www.nws.noaa.gov/floodsafety/
- River Forecast Centers: http://www.nwrfc.noaa.gov/misc/rfcs.cgi
- U.S. Army Corps of Engineers: http://www.usace.army.mil
- USGS Streamflow Data: http://waterdata.usgs.gov/nwis/rt

Hurricanes

A hurricane is a tropical cyclone with maximum sustained surface wind of 74 mph or more. The term *hurricane* is used for Northern Hemisphere tropical cyclones east of the International Dateline to the Greenwich Meridian. The term *typhoon* is used for Pacific tropical cyclones north of the Equator west of the International Dateline. The terms

Hurricane is derived from *Hurican*, the Carib god of evil.

hurricane and *typhoon* are regionally specific names for a strong *tropical cyclone*. A *tropical cyclone* is the generic term for a non-frontal synoptic scale low-pressure system over tropical or sub-tropical waters with organized convection (i.e., thunderstorm activity) and definite cyclonic surface wind circulation.[14]

Tropical cyclones with maximum sustained surface winds of less than 39 mph are called *tropical depressions*. Once the tropical cyclone reaches winds of at least 39 mph, they are typically called a *tropical storm* and assigned a name. If winds reach 74 mph, then they are called a:

- **Hurricane** (in the North Atlantic Ocean, the Northeast Pacific Ocean east of the dateline, or the South Pacific Ocean east of 160E);
- **Typhoon** (in the Northwest Pacific Ocean west of the dateline);
- **Severe Tropical Cyclone** (in the Southwest Pacific Ocean west of 160E or Southeast Indian Ocean east of 90E);
- **Severe Cyclonic Storm** (in the North Indian Ocean); or
- **Tropical Cyclone** (in the Southwest Indian Ocean).[15]

Storm surge is the onshore rush of sea or lake water caused by the high winds associated with a landfalling cyclone and secondarily by the low pressure of the storm. *Tidal surge* is often misused to describe storm surge, but storm surge is independent of the usual tidal ebb and flow. In some inlets, such as the Bay of Fundy in Nova Scotia, rapid changes in sea level due to the tides will cause a tidal bore or surge to move in to or out of the inlet. This surge occurs independent of the present weather.

The *Saffir-Simpson Hurricane Scale* is a one to five rating based on the hurricane's present intensity. This is used to give an estimate of the potential property damage and flooding expected along the coast from a hurricane landfall. Wind speed is the determining factor in the scale, as storm surge values are highly dependent on the slope of the continental shelf and the shape of the coastline in the landfall region.[16] The five Safir-Simpson Hurricane Scale categories and their descriptions are provided in Table 13.2.

Only three Category Five Hurricanes have made landfall in the United States since records began: The Labor Day Hurricane of 1935, Hurricane Camille (1969), and Hurricane Andrew (1992). The 1935 Labor Day Hurricane struck the Florida Keys with a minimum pressure of 892 mb—the lowest pressure ever observed in the United States. Hurricane Camille struck the Mississippi Gulf Coast causing a 25-foot storm surge, which inundated Pass Christian, Mississippi. Hurricane Andrew of 1992 made landfall over southern Miami-Dade County, Florida causing $26.5 billion in losses, making it among the costliest hurricanes on record at the time. Conversely, Hurricane Katrina made landfall as a Category Three Hurricane, but killed more than 1,330 people and caused $96 billion in damage.[17] The end result of Hurricane Katrina was the most destructive natural disaster in U.S. history.[18]

Preparedness and Prediction

The Tropical Prediction Center (TPC) is a component of the National Centers for Environmental Prediction (NCEP) located at Florida International

Table 13.2 Safir-Simpson Hurricane Scale Categories and Descriptions[19]

CATEGORY ONE HURRICANE	CATEGORY TWO HURRICANE	CATEGORY THREE HURRICANE	CATEGORY FOUR HURRICANE	CATEGORY FIVE HURRICANE
• Winds 74 to 95 mph (64 to 82 kt or 119 to 153 km/hr).	• Winds 96 to 110 mph (83 to 95 kt or 154 to 177 km/hr).	• Winds 111 to 130 mph (96 to 113 kt or 178 to 209 km/hr).	• Winds 131 to 155 mph (114 to 135 kt or 210 to 249 km/hr).	• Winds greater than 155 mph (135 kt or 249 km/hr).
• Storm surge generally 4 to 5 ft above normal.	• Storm surge generally 6 to 8 ft above normal.	• Storm surge generally 9 to 12 ft above normal.	• Storm surge generally 13 to 18 ft above normal.	• Storm surge generally greater than 18 ft above normal.
• No real damage to building structures.	• Some roofing material, door, and window damage of buildings.	• Some structural damage to small residences and utility buildings, with a minor amount of curtain wall failures.	• More extensive curtain wall failures, with some complete roof structure failures on small residences.	• Complete roof failure on many residences and industrial buildings.
• Damage primarily to unanchored mobile homes, shrubbery, and trees.	• Considerable damage to shrubbery and trees with some trees blown down.	• Damage to shrubbery and trees with foliage blown off trees and large trees blown down.	• Shrubs, trees, and all signs are blown down. Complete destruction of mobile homes.	• Some complete building failures, with small utility buildings blown over or away.
• Some damage to poorly constructed signs.	• Considerable damage to mobile homes, poorly constructed signs, and piers.	• Mobile homes and poorly constructed signs are destroyed.	• Extensive damage to doors and windows.	• All shrubs, trees, and signs blown down.
• Some coastal road flooding and minor pier damage.	• Coastal and low-lying escape routes flood 2 to 4 hours before arrival of the hurricane center.	• Low-lying escape routes are cut by rising water 3 to 5 hours before arrival of the center of the hurricane.	• Low-lying escape routes may be cut by rising water 3 to 5 hours before arrival of the center of the hurricane.	• Complete destruction of mobile homes.

(Continued)

Table 13.2 (*Continued*)

Category One Hurricane	Category Two Hurricane	Category Three Hurricane	Category Four Hurricane	Category Five Hurricane
	• Small craft in unprotected anchorages break moorings.	• Flooding near the coast destroys smaller structures, with larger structures damaged by battering from floating debris. • Terrain continuously lower than 5 ft above mean sea level may be flooded inland 8 miles (13 km) or more. • Evacuation of low-lying residences with several blocks of the shoreline may be required.	• Major damage to lower floors of structures near the shore. • Terrain lower than 10 ft above sea level may be flooded, requiring massive evacuation of residential areas as far inland as 6 miles (10 km).	• Severe and extensive window and door damage. • Low-lying escape routes are cut by rising water 3 to 5 hours before arrival of the center of the hurricane. • Major damage to lower floors of all structures located less than 15 ft above sea level and within 500 yards of the shoreline. • Massive evacuation of residential areas on low ground within 5 to 10 miles (8 to 16 km) of the shoreline may be required.

University in Miami, Florida. The TPC mission is to save lives, mitigate property loss, and improve economic efficiency by issuing the best watches, warnings, forecasts, and analyses of hazardous tropical weather, and by increasing understanding of these hazards.

Through international agreement, the TPC has responsibility within the World Meteorological Organization (WMO) to generate and coordinate tropical cyclone analysis and forecast products for twenty-four countries in the Americas, Caribbean, and for the waters of the North Atlantic Ocean, Caribbean Sea, Gulf of Mexico, and the eastern North Pacific Ocean. TPC products are distributed through a close working relationship with the media and emergency management communities. To meet its mission the TPC is composed of three branches: (1) National Hurricane Center (NHC); (2) Tropical Analysis and Forecast Branch (TAFB); and (3) The Technical Support Branch (TSB).

National Hurricane Center (NHC)

The National Hurricane Center (NHC) maintains a continuous watch on tropical cyclones from May 15th in the eastern Pacific and June 1st in the Atlantic through November 30th. The NHC prepares and issues forecasts, watches, and warnings within text advisories and graphical products. Although many countries issue their own warnings, they generally base them on direct discussions with and guidance from the NHC. During the "off-season," the NHC conducts an extensive outreach and education program and trains U.S. emergency managers and representatives from many other countries affected by tropical cyclones.

The NHC issues advisories based on tracking of tropical cyclones. In the Atlantic Basin, these include the Hurricane Warning and the Hurricane Watch, which are described below.

- A **Hurricane Warning** is a warning that sustained winds of 74 mph or higher associated with a hurricane are expected in a specified coastal area in twenty-four hours or less. A hurricane warning can remain in effect when dangerously high water or a combination of dangerously high water and exceptionally high waves continue, even though winds may be less than hurricane force.
- A **Hurricane Watch** is an announcement for specific coastal areas that hurricane conditions are possible within 36 hours.
- **Landfall** occurs at the intersection of the surface center of a tropical cyclone with a coastline. Because the strongest winds in a tropical cyclone are not located precisely at the center, it is possible for a cyclone's strongest winds to be experienced over land even if landfall does not occur. Similarly, it is possible for a tropical cyclone to make landfall and have its strongest winds remain over the water.

Tropical Analysis and Forecast Branch (TAFB)

The Tropical Analysis and Forecast Branch (TAFB) provides year-round marine weather analysis and forecast products over the tropical and subtropical waters of the eastern North and South Pacific and the North Atlantic basin.

The branch also produces satellite-based weather interpretation and rainfall estimates for the international community.

Technical Support Branch (TBS)

The Technical Support Branch (TSB) provides support for TPC computer and communications systems. The TSB also maintains a small applied research and techniques development unit, which develops tools for hurricane and tropical weather analysis and prediction. TSB also has a storm surge group, which provides information for developing evacuation procedures for coastal areas.

Severe Storms

The need for more accurate, timely, and meaningful weather information has grown as production, transportation, and communication processes become more complex, interdependent, and more weather-sensitive. Aviators, agriculturists, builders, shippers, and insurers are among those who increasingly depend on information concerning the present and forecast occurrences of storm hazards.

Tornado and Severe Winds

According to the American Meteorological Society (AMS), a *tornado* is a "violently rotating column of air, pendant from a cumuliform cloud or underneath a cumuliform cloud, and often (but not always) visible as a funnel cloud."[20] About a thousand tornadoes hit the United States yearly. The actual average is unknown, because tornado spotting and reporting methods have changed so much in the last several decades that the officially recorded tornado climatologies are believed to be incomplete. In the course of recording thousands of tornadoes, errors are likely. Events can be missed or misclassified, and some non-damaging tornadoes in remote areas could still be unreported. On average, U.S. tornadoes kill about sixty people per year, and most are from flying or falling (crushing) debris.

Literally, in order for a vortex to be classified as a tornado, it must be in contact with the ground and the cloud base. Weather scientists have not found it so simple in practice, however, to classify and define tornadoes. For example, the difference is unclear between a strong mesocyclone (parent thunderstorm circulation) on the ground and a large, weak tornado. There is also disagreement as to whether separate touchdowns of the same funnel constitute separate tornadoes. Further, it is well known that a tornado may not have a visible funnel. Also, at what wind speed of the cloud-to-ground vortex does a tornado begin? How close must two or more different tornadic circulations become to qualify as one multiple-vortex tornado, instead of separate tornadoes? There are no firm answers.

How do tornadoes form? The classic answer—warm moist Gulf air meets cold Canadian air and dry air from the Rockies—is an oversimplification.

Many thunderstorms form under those conditions (near warm fronts, cold fronts, and drylines, respectively), which never even come close to producing tornadoes. Even when the large-scale environment is extremely favorable for tornadic thunderstorms, not every thunderstorm spawns a tornado. The most destructive and deadly tornadoes occur from *supercells*, which are rotating thunderstorms with a well-defined radar circulation called a mesocyclone. Supercells can also produce damaging hail, severe non-tornadic winds, unusually frequent lightning, and flash floods.

Tornado formation is believed to be dictated mainly by things which happen on the storm scale, in and around the mesocyclone. Recent research suggests that once a mesocyclone is underway, tornado development is related to the temperature differences across the edge of downdraft air wrapping around the mesocyclone. Mathematical modeling studies of tornado formation also indicate that it can happen without such temperature patterns. In fact, very little temperature variation was observed near some of the most destructive tornadoes in history in Oklahoma on May 3, 1999.

Dr. T. Theodore Fujita developed a damage scale for winds (known as the Fujita-Scale or F-scale) including tornadoes, which was supposed to relate the degree of damage to the intensity of the wind. Researchers offer an important note about F-Scale winds: one should not use F-scale winds literally. These precise wind speed numbers are actually *guesses* and have never been scientifically verified. Different winds may be needed to cause the same damage depending on how well-built a structure is, wind direction, wind duration, battering by flying debris, and a host of other factors. Also, the process of rating the damage itself is largely a judgment call, which is quite inconsistent and arbitrary.[21] Even meteorologists and engineers highly experienced in damage survey techniques often come up with different F-scale ratings for the same damage. Even with all its flaws, the original F-scale was the only widely used tornado rating method for more than three decades. The National Oceanic and Atmospheric Administration (NOAA) recommends that without a thorough engineering analysis of tornado damage in any event, the actual wind speeds needed to cause that damage are unknown.

• •

A **waterspout** is a tornado over water, usually meaning non-supercell tornadoes over water. Waterspouts are common along the southeast U.S. coast—especially off southern Florida and the Keys—and can happen over seas, bays, and lakes worldwide.

Although waterspouts are always tornadoes by definition, they do not officially count in tornado records unless they hit land. They are smaller and weaker than the most intense Great Plains tornadoes, but still can be quite dangerous. Waterspouts can overturn small boats, damage ships, do significant damage when hitting land, and kill people.

The National Weather Service (NWS) will often issue special marine warnings when waterspouts are likely or have been sighted over coastal waters, or tornado warnings when waterspouts can move onshore.

• •

Table 13.3 Fujita Tornado Damage Scale[22]

Scale	Wind Estimate (mph)	Typical Damage
F0	< 73	**Light damage:** Some damage to chimneys; branches broken off trees; shallow-rooted trees pushed over; sign boards damaged.
F1	73 to 112	**Moderate damage:** Peels surface off roofs; mobile homes pushed off foundations or overturned; moving autos blown off roads.
F2	113 to 157	**Considerable damage:** Roofs torn off frame houses; mobile homes demolished; boxcars overturned; large trees snapped or uprooted; light-object missiles generated; cars lifted off ground.
F3	158 to 206	**Severe damage:** Roofs and some walls torn off well-constructed houses; trains overturned; most trees in forest uprooted; heavy cars lifted off the ground and thrown.
F4	207 to 260	**Devastating damage:** Well-constructed houses leveled; structures with weak foundations blown away some distance; cars thrown and large missiles generated.
F5	261 to 318	**Incredible damage:** Strong frame houses leveled off foundations and swept away; automobile-sized missiles fly through the air in excess of 100 meters (109 yds); trees debarked; incredible phenomena will occur.

In February 2007, an Enhanced F-scale was implemented. The Enhanced F-scale still is a set of wind estimates (not measurements) based on damage. Its uses three-second gusts estimated at the point of damage based on a judgment of eight levels of damage to the twenty-eight indicators listed below. These estimates vary with height and exposure.

Preparedness and Prediction

The mission of the National Severe Storms Laboratory (NSSL) is to enhance NOAA's capabilities to provide accurate and timely forecasts and warnings of hazardous weather events (e.g., blizzards, ice storms, flash floods, tornadoes, lightning, etc.). NSSL, located in Norman, Oklahoma, incorporates cutting-edge scientific understanding of severe weather signatures into tools designed to help NWS forecasters make better and faster warning decisions. The latest tool, NSSL's Warning Decision Support System II, includes automated algorithm detection tools for the NEXRAD Doppler radar and other sensors to identify rotation in storms preceding tornadoes, likelihood and size of hail, as well as simply identifying and tracking storms. This information is presented in an easy-to-use display including tables, graphs, and data interrogation tools.

Table 13.4 Enhanced F-Scale for Tornado Damage[23]

	Fujita Scale			Derived EF Scale		Operational EF Scale
F Number	Fastest 1/4-Mile (mph)	3-Second Gust (mph)	EF Number	3-Second Gust (mph)	EF Number	3-Second Gust (mph)
0	40 to 72	45 to 78	0	65 to 85	0	65 to 85
1	73 to 112	79 to 117	1	86 to 109	1	86 to 110
2	113 to 157	118 to 161	2	110 to 137	2	111 to 135
3	158 to 207	162 to 209	3	138 to 167	3	136 to 165
4	208 to 260	210 to 261	4	168 to 199	4	166 to 200
5	261 to 318	262 to 317	5	200 to 234	5	Over 200

NSSL researchers will soon be adapting radar technology currently deployed on U.S. Navy ships for use in spotting severe weather. *Phased array radar* reduces the scan or data collection time from five or six minutes to less than one minute, potentially extending the average lead time for tornado warnings beyond the current average of eleven minutes. When combined with other technology being developed at NSSL, warning lead times could be extended even farther.

Snow and Ice

Heavy snowfall and extreme cold can immobilize an entire region. Even areas that normally experience mild winters can be hit with a major snow-storm or extreme cold. Winter storms can result in flooding, storm surge, closed highways, blocked roads, downed power lines, and hypothermia. Winter storms include blizzards and ice storms, which are described below.

- A **blizzard** occurs when sustained winds or frequent gusts to thirty-five miles per hour or greater accompany considerable amounts of falling or blowing snow (reducing visibility to less than a quarter mile), and when these conditions are expected to prevail for a period of three hours or longer.
- An **ice storm** is when half an inch or more of ice accumulates on structures and the ground. Such an accumulation causes damage to power lines and trees. **Ice Storm Warnings** are issued when there is a high degree of confidence that the entire event is expected to be ice.

In 1998, an ice storm event beset the New York and New England region with devastating impact. Extensive power outages occurred. The National Guard was mobilized in multiple states to assist the continuity of operations of critical infrastructure through use of transportable generators and distribution of essential supplies.

The ice storm was caused by an upper level low system that stalled over the Great Lakes, pumping warm and moist air from the Gulf of Mexico toward the upper St. Lawrence Valley. The upper flow then turned Eastward and brought this air mass down toward the Bay of Fundy. At the same time, a high-pressure center was sitting farther north in Labrador, keeping an easterly flow of very cold air near the surface. For winter, an unusually strong Bermuda High Pressure was anchored over the Atlantic Ocean, which prevented these systems from moving farther to the east, as most winter storms do when they pass over the Great Lakes–St. Lawrence region.

For more than eighty hours, steady freezing rain and drizzle fell over an area of several thousand square miles of Canada, northern New York, and northern New England. The area near St.-Jean-sur-Richelieu, Quebec, east of Montreal, received the most precipitation and was given the nickname of "the triangle of darkness" as the "electric pylons fell like dominos, and it took more than a month to reestablish power to the region."[24] The 1998 ice storm resulted in damages in excess of $5 to 7 billion and took the lives of nearly fifty-six people.

Wildland Fire

A *wildland fire* is any non-structure fire that occurs in the wildland. Three distinct types of wildland fire have been defined and include wildfire, wildland fire use, and prescribed fire.

1. **Wildfire:** An unplanned, unwanted wildland fire, including unauthorized human-caused fires, escaped wildland fire use events, escaped prescribed fire projects, and all other wildland fires where the objective is to put the fire out.
2. **Wildland Fire Use:** The application of the appropriate management response to naturally ignited wildland fires to accomplish specific resource management objectives in predefined designated areas outlined in Fire Management Plans.
3. **Prescribed Fire:** Any fire ignited by management actions to meet specific objectives. A written, approved prescribed fire plan must exist, and National Environmental Policy Act (NEPA) requirements (where applicable) must be met, prior to ignition.[25]

The National Interagency Coordination Center (NICC) is the focal point for coordinating the mobilization of resources for wildland fire and other incidents throughout the United States.

In the United States, wildfire suppression is built on a three-tiered system of support: (1) local area, (2) one of the eleven geographic areas, and (3) national level. When a fire is reported, the local agency and its firefighting partners respond. If the fire continues to grow, the agency can ask for help from within its geographic area. When a geographic area has exhausted all its resources, it can turn to the NICC at the National Interagency Fire Center (NIFC) for help in locating what is needed, from air tankers to radios to firefighting crews to incident management teams.

Located within the National Interagency Fire Center (NIFC) in Boise, Idaho, the NICC also provides intelligence and predictive services–related products designed to be used by the internal wildland fire community for wildland fire and incident management decision-making. Among the primary responsibilities of the NICC are to:

- Provide the general public incident information with daily updates on large fires throughout the United States;
- Provide operational and predictive products;
- Provide operational and administrative logistics and dispatch; and
- Provide the tools, background information, and other administrative components that help make fire and incident operations work.

••

Wildfire Facts

- More land has been affected by wildfires in recent years than at any time since the 1960s. In 2004, wildfires burned more than 8 million acres in forty States.
- The greater Yellowstone National Park fire of 1988 burned more than 1.2 million acres.
- Wildfire severity has increased and fire frequency has decreased during the past 200 years.
- Many species depend on wildfires to improve habitat, recycle nutrients, and maintain diverse communities.
- Land management agencies light 'prescribed fires' under controlled conditions for specific management objectives.[26]

••

Heat

The National Weather Service (NWS) defines a *heat wave* as "a period of abnormally and uncomfortably hot and unusually humid weather lasting two or more days."[27] Heat waves present deadly consequences to human population. For example, a persistent heat event in July 1995 in Chicago, Illinois resulted in approximately 500 deaths recorded within the city over a five-day period.[28] A contributing factor in this heat wave is the so-called *urban heat island*. *Urban heat islands* are caused by the high concentration of buildings, parking lots, and roads in urban areas, which tend to absorb more heat in the day and radiate more heat at night than comparable rural sites. Based on this phenomenon, urban areas usually experience a lot less cooling at night than do rural sites. In addition to the urban heat island, other factors that contributed to the high number of deaths in Chicago included:

- Most of the victims were the elderly in the heart of the urban area;
- Many of the poorer older citizens either had no air conditioning or could not afford to operate the system they had;
- Many older citizens were also hesitant to open windows and doors at night for fear of crime;
- An inadequate local heat wave warning system;

- Power failures;
- Inadequate ambulance service and hospital facilities; and
- The aging of the population in the urban areas.[29]

In after-action review, it was determined that city officials did not release a heat emergency warning until June 15, the last day of the heat wave. Therefore, emergency measures such as the refuge of Chicago's five cooling centers were not fully utilized. The medical system of Chicago was also severely taxed, as thousands were taken to local hospitals with heat-related problems. In some cases, fire trucks were used as substitute ambulances.

For a more detailed treatment of the events of the 1995 heat wave disaster, please refer to *Heat Wave: A Social Autopsy of Disaster in Chicago* by Eric Klinenberg. Within the book, Klinenberg reported that the 1995 Chicago heat wave resulted in the loss of water, widespread power outages, thousands of hospitalizations, and 739 deaths in a devastating week.[30]

Unfortunately, Chicago and other large urban areas will continue to be vulnerable to heat waves because of the urban heat island and the socio-economic makeup of the urban area (i.e., high percentage of lower-income elderly). Emergency and medical planners suggest that the number of deaths from a future event similar to the 1995 heat wave may be reduced by:

- Implementing an early-warning system that takes into account the local conditions;
- Better defining the heat island conditions associated with heat waves to improve forecasts;
- Developing a uniform means for classifying heat-related deaths; and
- Increasing research on the conditions of heat stress and heat waves.

Additional Resources for Natural Disaster and Hazard Learning

The U.S. Geological Survey maintains the Natural Hazards Gateway through its agency Website and provides numerous resources on natural hazards to include earthquakes, floods, hurricanes, landslides, tsunamis, volcanoes, and wildfires. The Natural Hazards Gateway can be accessed at: http://www. usgs.gov/hazards/.

14

....

Geological Hazards

Introduction

Among the dominant geological hazards that have produced disastrous consequences for humankind are:

- Avalanche;
- Earthquake;
- Landslide;
- Tsunami; and
- Volcano.

These hazards and others are detailed in this chapter.

Avalanche

A snow avalanche is a mass of snow, ice, and debris flowing and sliding rapidly down a steep slope. An avalanche has three main parts:

1. Starting zone;
2. Avalanche track; and
3. Runout zone.

The *starting zone* is the most volatile area of a slope, where unstable snow can fracture from the surrounding snow cover and begin to slide. Typical starting zones are higher up on slopes, including the areas beneath cornices and "bowls" on mountainsides. Under the proper conditions, snow can fracture at any point on the slope.

The *avalanche track* is the path or channel that an avalanche follows as it goes downhill. Large vertical swaths of trees missing from a slope or chute-like clearings are often signs that frequent, large avalanches have occurred, creating their own tracks.

The *runout zone* is where the snow and debris finally comes to a stop. Similarly, this is also the location of the deposition zone, where the snow and debris pile the highest. Although terrain variations such as gullies or boulders can create conditions that will bury a person further up the slope during an avalanche, the deposition zone is typically where a victim will most likely be buried.

Several factors may affect the likelihood of an avalanche, including:

- Weather;
- Temperature;
- Slope steepness;
- Slope orientation (whether the slope is facing north or south);
- Wind direction;
- Terrain;
- Vegetation; and
- General snowpack conditions.

Different combinations of these factors can create low, moderate, or extreme avalanche conditions.

Preparedness and Prediction

The National Snow and Ice Data Center (NSIDC) is part of the University of Colorado Cooperative Institute for Research in Environmental Sciences (CIRES), and is affiliated with the National Oceanic and Atmospheric Administration (NOAA) National Geophysical Data Center (NGDC) through a cooperative agreement. NSIDC serves as one of eight Distributed Active Archive Centers (DAAC) funded by the National Aeronautics and Space Administration (NASA) to archive and distribute data from NASA's past and current satellites and field measurement programs. NSIDC also supports the National Science Foundation (NSF) through the Arctic System Science Data Coordination Center (ARCSS) and the Antarctic Glaciological Data Center (AGDC). Established by NOAA as a national information and referral center in support of polar and cryospheric research, NSIDC archives and distributes digital and analog snow and ice data. NSIDC also maintains information about snow cover and avalanches.

Earthquake

According to the U.S. Geological Survey (USGS), 2004 was the deadliest year for earthquakes since the Renaissance, making it the second most fatal in recorded history with more than 275,950 deaths reported from the magnitude 9.0 earthquake and subsequent tsunami that hit the Indian Ocean on December 26. The total death toll for earthquakes in 2004 was 276,856. Less than 1,000 casualties were reported around the world prior to the Indian Ocean tsunami event.[1]

Figure 14.1 San Francisco Earthquake of 1906 (Image Courtesy: The National Archives, Archival Research Catalog)

Earthquakes are the result of forces deep within Earth's interior that continuously affect its surface. The energy from these forces is stored in a variety of ways within the rocks. An earthquake occurs when this energy is released suddenly by shearing movements along faults in the crust of Earth. The area of the fault where the sudden rupture takes place is called the *focus*, or hypocenter, of the earthquake. The point on Earth's surface directly above the focus is called the *epicenter* of the earthquake.[2]

The severity of an earthquake can be expressed in terms of both intensity and magnitude. The two terms are quite different, however, and they are often confused. Intensity is based on the observed effects of ground shaking on people, buildings, and natural features. It varies from place to place within the disturbed region depending on the location of the observer with respect to the earthquake epicenter. Magnitude is related to the amount of seismic energy released at the hypocenter of the earthquake. It is based on the amplitude of the earthquake waves recorded on instruments, which have a common calibration. Magnitude is thus represented by a single, instrumentally determined value. An earthquake is caused by a sudden slip on a fault. The tectonic plates are always moving; however, they get stuck at their edges due to friction. When the stress on the edge overcomes the friction, there is an earthquake that releases energy in waves that travel through the Earth's crust and cause the shaking that is felt.

....

Plate tectonics is the continual slow movement of the tectonic plates, the outermost part of the Earth. This motion is what causes earthquakes and volcanoes and has created most of the spectacular scenery around the world.

....

A *fault* is a fracture or zone of fractures between two blocks of rock. Faults allow the blocks to move relative to each other. This movement may occur rapidly, in the form of an earthquake, or may occur slowly, in the form of creep. Faults may range in length from a few millimeters to thousands of kilometers. Most faults produce repeated displacements over geologic time. During an earthquake, the rock on one side of the fault suddenly slips with respect to the other. The fault surface and the slip direction can be horizontal or vertical or some arbitrary angle in between.

Measuring Earthquakes

The Richter Scale

The magnitude of most earthquakes is measured on the *Richter scale*, invented by Charles F. Richter in 1934. The Richter magnitude is calculated from the amplitude of the largest seismic wave recorded for the earthquake. The Richter magnitudes are based on a logarithmic scale (base ten). This means that for each whole number increment on the Richter scale, the amplitude of the ground motion recorded by a seismograph goes up ten times. Therefore, using this scale, a magnitude 5 earthquake would result in ten times the level of ground shaking as a magnitude 4 earthquake (and thirty-two times as

Table 14.1 Earthquake Magnitude Scale

EARTHQUAKE SEVERITY RICHTER MAGNITUDES	EARTHQUAKE EFFECTS
Less than 3.5	Generally not felt, but recorded.
3.5 to 5.4	Often felt, but rarely causes damage.
5.5 to 6.0	Can cause major damage to poorly constructed buildings over small regions.
6.1 to 6.9	Can be destructive in areas up to about 100 kilometers across where people live.
7.0 to 7.9	Major earthquake. Can cause serious damage over larger areas.
8 or greater	Great earthquake. Can cause serious damage in areas several hundred kilometers across.

much energy would be released). To provide an idea how these numbers can add up, think in terms of the energy released by explosives. A magnitude one seismic wave releases as much energy as blowing up six ounces of trinitrotoluene (TNT). A magnitude eight earthquake releases as much energy as detonating six million tons of TNT. Most of the earthquakes that occur each year are magnitude 2.5 or less, too small to be felt by most people.

Seismologists use a *magnitude* scale to express the seismic energy (ground-shaking intensity) released by each earthquake. Table 14.1 provides the typical effects of earthquakes in various magnitude ranges.

Although Richter originally proposed this way of measuring an earthquake's "size," he only used a certain type of seismograph and measured shallow earthquakes in Southern California. Scientists have now made other "magnitude" scales, all calibrated to Richter's original method, to use a variety of seismographs to measure the depths of earthquakes of all sizes.

The Mercalli Scale

Another way to measure the strength of an earthquake is to use the *Mercalli scale*. Invented by Giuseppe Mercalli in 1902, this scale uses the observations of the people who experienced the earthquake to estimate its intensity, which is the effect of an earthquake on the Earth's surface. The intensity scale consists of a series of certain key responses such as people awakening, movement of furniture, damage to chimneys, and, finally, total destruction.

Modified Mercalli Intensity Scale

Although numerous intensity scales have been developed over the last several hundred years to evaluate the effects of earthquakes, the one currently used in the United States is the Modified Mercalli Intensity Scale, which was developed in 1931 by American seismologists Harry Wood and Frank Neumann. This scale, composed of twelve increasing levels of intensity that range from imperceptible shaking to catastrophic destruction, is designated by

Roman numerals. It does not have a mathematical basis, instead it is an arbitrary ranking based on observed effects. The Modified Mercalli Intensity value assigned to a specific site after an earthquake has a more meaningful measure of severity to the nonscientist than the magnitude because intensity refers to the effects actually experienced at that place. The maximum observed intensity generally occurs near the epicenter. The lower numbers of the intensity scale generally deal with the manner in which the earthquake is felt by people, whereas the higher numbers of the scale are based on observed structural damage. Structural engineers usually contribute information for assigning intensity values of VIII or above. Table 14.2 provides an abbreviated description of the twelve levels of Modified Mercalli Intensity Scale.[3]

Preparedness and Prediction

The National Earthquake Information Center (NEIC), a part of the USGS, is located in Golden, Colorado, ten miles west of Denver. The mission of the NEIC is to rapidly determine the location and size of all destructive earthquakes worldwide and to immediately disseminate this information to concerned national and international agencies, scientists, and the general public. The NEIC in its role as a partner in the World Data Center for Seismology compiles and maintains an extensive, global seismic database on earthquake parameters and their effects, which serves as a solid foundation for basic and applied earth science research. Within the United States, the NEIC is the national data center and archive for earthquake information. The NEIC has three main missions:

1. Determine, as rapidly and as accurately as possible, the location and size of all destructive earthquakes that occur worldwide.
2. Disseminate information immediately to concerned national and international agencies, scientists, and the general public.
3. Collect and provide to scientists and to the public an extensive seismic database that serves as a solid foundation for scientific research, principally through the operation of modern digital national and global seismograph networks and through cooperative international agreements.

The NEIC operates a 24-hour-a-day service, and the information it gathers is communicated to federal and state government agencies who are responsible for emergency response, to government public information channels, to national and international news media, to scientific groups (including groups planning aftershock studies), and to private citizens who request information.

When a damaging earthquake occurs in a foreign country, the earthquake information is passed to the staffs of the American embassies and consulates in the affected countries and to the United Nations (UN) Department of Humanitarian Affairs (DHA). The NEIC issues rapid reports for those earthquakes which register at least 4.5 on the Richter Scale in the United States or

Table 14.2 Modified Mercalli Intensity Scale Intensity Descriptions

INTENSITY LEVEL	INTENSITY DESCRIPTION
I	Not felt except by a very few under especially favorable conditions.
II	Felt only by a few persons at rest, especially on upper floors of buildings.
III	Felt quite noticeably by persons indoors, especially on upper floors of buildings. Many people do not recognize it as an earthquake. Standing motor cars may rock slightly. Vibrations similar to the passing of a truck. Duration estimated.
IV	Felt indoors by many, outdoors by few during the day. At night, some awakened. Dishes, windows, doors disturbed; walls make cracking sound. Sensation like heavy truck striking building. Standing motor cars rocked noticeably.
V	Felt by nearly everyone; many awakened. Some dishes, windows broken. Unstable objects overturned. Pendulum clocks may stop.
VI	Felt by all, many frightened. Some heavy furniture moved; a few instances of fallen plaster. Damage slight.
VII	Damage negligible in buildings of good design and construction; slight to moderate in well-built ordinary structures; considerable damage in poorly built or badly designed structures; some chimneys broken.
VIII	Damage slight in specially designed structures; considerable damage in ordinary substantial buildings with partial collapse. Damage great in poorly built structures. Fall of chimneys, factory stacks, columns, monuments, walls. Heavy furniture overturned.
IX	Damage considerable in specially designed structures; well-designed frame structures thrown out of plumb. Damage great in substantial buildings, with partial collapse. Buildings shifted off foundations.
X	Some well-built wooden structures destroyed; most masonry and frame structures destroyed with foundations. Rails bent.
XI	Few, if any (masonry) structures remain standing. Bridges destroyed. Rails bent greatly.
XII	Damage total. Lines of sight and level are distorted. Objects thrown into the air.

6.5 on the Richter Scale (or are known to have caused damage) anywhere else in the world.

To enable the detection and location of all felt earthquakes with the U.S., the NEIC is currently deploying the U.S. National Seismograph Network (USNSN). When complete, the USNSN will include about sixty field stations consisting of modern broadband seismometers, data processors, and

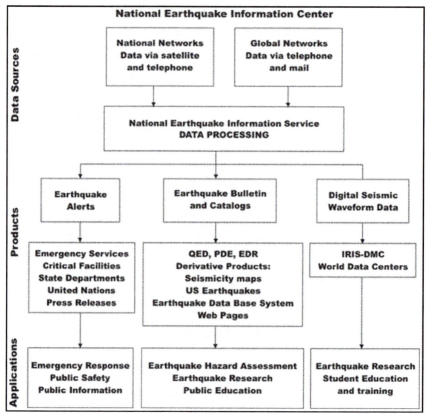

Figure 14.2 NEIC Data, Products, and Applications Process

satellite antennas that transmit the data to a master Earth station at the NEIC. Within the United States, several active research and preparedness initiatives have been underway based upon federal and state sponsorship. Notable among these are the National Earthquake Hazards Research Program (NEHRP) and the Central U.S. Earthquake Consortium (CUSEC).

•••

The **National Earthquake Information Center** (NEIC) staff locates and publishes information on approximately 20,000 earthquakes on a yearly basis. These are the most important of the many million earthquakes which are estimated to occur each year. The NEIC collects its data through the operation of national and global networks and through cooperative agreements. More than 3,000 stations report data to the NEIC. The NEIC also collects non-instrumental reports of the effects of U.S. earthquakes on people and man-made structures and prepares isoseismic maps showing the distribution of intensities in widely felt or damaging shocks.

•••

Supporting the Research – National Earthquake Hazards Reduction Program (NEHRP)

The National Earthquake Hazards Reduction Program (NEHRP) is the U.S. government's program to reduce the risks to life and property from earthquakes. Four agencies work in collaboration to implement the NEHRP:

1. Federal Emergency Management Agency (FEMA);
2. National Institute of Standards and Technology (NIST), the lead agency;
3. National Science Foundation (NSF); and
4. USGS.

The goals of the NEHRP are to:

- Develop effective practices and policies for earthquake loss-reduction and accelerate their implementation;
- Improve techniques to reduce seismic vulnerability of facilities and systems;
- Improve seismic hazards identification and risk-assessment methods and their use; and
- Improve the understanding of earthquakes and their effects.

The NEHRP agencies work in close coordination to improve the Nation's understanding of earthquake hazards and to mitigate their effects as well as to:

- Improve understanding, characterization, and assessment of hazards and vulnerabilities;
- Improve model building codes and land use practices;
- Reduce risks through post-earthquake investigations and education;
- Improve design and construction techniques;
- Improve the capacity of government at all levels and the private sector to reduce and manage earthquake risk; and
- Accelerate the application of research results.

Applying the Research – Central U.S. Earthquake Consortium (CUSEC)

The Central U.S. Earthquake Consortium (CUSEC) is a partnership of the federal government and the eight states most affected by earthquakes in the central United States within the New Madrid Seismic Zone: Alabama, Arkansas, Illinois, Indiana, Kentucky, Mississippi, Missouri, and Tennessee. Established in 1983 with funding support from FEMA, CUSEC's primary mission is "… the reduction of deaths, injuries, property damage, and economic losses resulting from earthquakes in the Central United States."[4] CUSEC serves as a "coordinating hub" for the region, performing the critical role of coordinating the multi-state efforts of the central region.

Landslide

Landslides constitute a major geologic hazard because they are widespread, occur in all fifty states and U.S. territories, and cause $1 to 2 billion in damages and more than twenty-five fatalities on average each year.[5] Land-slides pose serious threats to highways and structures that support fisheries, tourism, timber harvesting, mining, and energy production as well as general transportation. Expansion of urban and recreational developments into hill-side areas results in ever increasing numbers of residential and commercial properties that are threatened by landslides.

Landslides commonly occur in connection with other major natural dis-asters such as earthquakes, volcanoes, wildfires, and floods. Effects of these disasters exacerbate relief and reconstruction efforts. Growth of urban areas and expanded land use elsewhere have increased the incidence of landslide disasters.

Preparedness and Prediction

Within the United States, the USGS National Landslide Hazards Program (NLHP) has operated since the mid-1970s in gathering information, conduct-ing research, responding to emergencies and disasters, and producing scien-tific reports and other products for a broadly based user community. The National Landslide Information Center (NLIC) is the outreach entity for the NLHP. The NLIC is responsible for distributing information about land-slides to the public, researchers, planners, and local, state, and federal agen-cies. The NLIC provides a toll-free number (1-800-654-4966) where anyone can make inquiries about landslides.

Tsunami

A *tsunami* is a sea wave of local or distant origin that results from large-scale seafloor displacements associated with large earthquakes, major submarine slides, or exploding volcanic islands.[6] Stated another way, tsunamis are ocean waves produced by earthquakes or underwater landslides.[7] Tsunamis are often incorrectly referred to as tidal waves, but a tsunami is actually a se-ries of waves that can travel at speeds averaging 450 (and up to 600) miles per hour in the open ocean.

In the open ocean, tsunamis would not be felt by ships because the wave-length would be hundreds of miles long, with an amplitude of only a few feet. This would also make them unnoticeable from the air, further confounding the use of direct observations by seafarers as a real-time warning resource. As the waves approach the coast, their speed decreases and their amplitude increases. Unusual wave heights have been known to be more than 100 feet high. Waves that are ten to twenty feet high, however, can be very destructive and cause many deaths or injuries.

The word **tsunami** is Japanese and means 'har-bor wave,' because of the devastating effects these waves have had on low-lying Japanese coastal communities.

Tsunamis are most often generated by earthquake-induced

movement of the ocean floor. Landslides, volcanic eruptions, and even mete-orites can also generate a tsunami. If a major earthquake is felt, a tsunami could reach the coast within a few minutes, even before a warning is issued. Areas at greatest risk are less than twenty-five feet above sea level and within one mile of the shoreline.

From an initial tsunami-generating source area, waves travel outward in all directions much like the ripples caused by throwing a rock into a pond. As these waves approach coastal areas, the time between successive wave crests varies from five to ninety minutes. The first wave is usually not the largest in the series of waves, nor is it the most significant. Furthermore, one coastal community may experience no damaging waves while another, not that far away, may experience destructive deadly waves. Depending on a number of factors, some low-lying areas could experience severe inundation of water and debris more than 1,000 feet inland.

Most deaths caused by a tsunami are by the way of drowning. Other asso-ciated risks include flooding, contamination of drinking water, fires from rup-tured tanks or gas lines, and the loss of vital community infrastructure (police, fire, medical facilities, wastewater treatment, public works, etc.). The world witnessed the tragic consequences of the tsunami in the December 2004 disaster in South Asia, particularly Banda Aceh. More than 275,000 people perished due to the total devastation wrought by the tsunami across multiple Pacific nations.

Preparedness and Prediction
Tsunami warnings, watches, or advisory warnings issued by the National Oceanic and Atmospheric Administration (NOAA) Tsunami Warning Cen-ters (TWC) are alphanumeric products providing tsunami warning and watch and advisory warning information for potentially damaging tsunamis. The TWC's operational objectives are to:

- Locate and size major earthquakes in the Pacific basin;
- Determine their "tsunamigenic" potential;
- Predict tsunami wave arrival times and, when possible, run-up on the coast; and
- Provide timely and effective tsunami information and warnings to the popula-tion of the Pacific to reduce the hazards of tsunamis, especially to human life.

These bulletins are prepared by each of two NOAA TWC's. The West Coast/Alaska Tsunami Warning Center (WC/ATWC), located at Palmer, Alaska, issues tsunami bulletins to its Area of Responsibility (AOR), which is Alaska, British Columbia, Washington, Oregon, and California. The WC/ATWC also has the primary responsibility for the detection, location, and magnitude determination of magnitude of potentially tsunamigenic earth-quakes occurring in its AOR. The Pacific Tsunami Warning Center (PTWC) is located at Ewa Beach, Oahu, Hawaii. PTWC has the responsibility for issuing tsunami bulletins to its AOR, which includes Hawaii, all other U.S. interests in the Pacific, and most other countries within the Pacific and around its rim. The PTWC has the primary responsibility for the detection, location, and magnitude determination for potentially tsunamigenic earthquakes occurring anywhere in the Pacific Basin outside the WC/ATWC AOR. When major earthquakes occurring in the Pacific Rim have magnitudes large enough to warrant concern, NOAA's PTWC will notify authorities and others through advisory messages.

These NOAA messages are information bulletins, warnings, or watches. In any case, the message will be posted at the PTWC Website. The type of message will depend on the situation as interpreted initially from seismic data and can be one of the following:

- **Tsunami Information Bulletin** – Though a threat exists, there is no evidence that a tsunami is making its way across the Pacific.
- **Tsunami Warning** – The PTWC finds conditions serious enough to issue immediate concern to parts of the Pacific. The message will include approximate arrival times for various parts of the Pacific.
- **Tsunami Watch** – The PTWC has determined the earthquake may very likely have created a tsunami and is advising parties to be alert as the PTWC awaits tide data to support tsunami generation.

Volcano

A volcano is the solid structure created when lava, gases, and hot particles escape to the Earth's surface through *vents*. Volcanoes are usually conical. A volcano is *active* when it is erupting or has erupted recently. Volcanoes that have not erupted recently but are considered likely to erupt in the future are said to be *dormant*. A volcano that has not erupted for a long time and is not expected to erupt in the future is defined as *extinct*.[8] According to the Smithsonian Institution, there are about 1,511 active volcanoes around the world.[9]

The Roman god of fire, Vulcan, lived in Hiera (now known as Vulcan) in the Lipari Islands. The word **volcano** comes from the name for this island.

In addition to damage caused by explosive volcanic eruptions (e.g., Mount St. Helens in 1980), houses, buildings, roads, and fields can become covered with ash from volcanic activity. If the ash fall is particularly concentrated it can impede breathing and presents a serious health threat. Lava flows are almost always too slow to run over people; however, they can overrun houses, roads, and other structures. Lastly, pyroclastic flows are mixtures of hot gas and ash, and they travel very quickly down the slopes of volcanoes (100 to 200 km/hour) and cannot be out-run. Figure 14.3 illustrates the key characteristics of an active volcano.

Lahar

Lahar is an Indonesian term that describes a hot or cold mixture of water and rock fragments flowing down the slopes of a volcano and (or) river valleys.

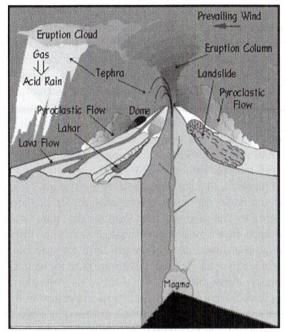

Figure 14.3 Characteristics of an Active Volcano
(Image Courtesy: U.S. Geological Survey)

When moving, a lahar looks like a mass of wet concrete that carries rock debris ranging in size from clay to boulders more than ten meters in diameter. Lahars vary in size and speed. Small lahars less than a few meters wide and several centimeters deep may flow a few meters per second. Large lahars, hundreds of meters wide and tens of meters deep, can flow several tens of meters per second, a velocity much too fast for people to outrun.

As a lahar rushes downstream from a volcano, its size, speed, and the amount of water and rock debris it carries constantly changes. The beginning surge of water and rock debris often erodes rocks and vegetation from the side of a volcano and along the river valley it enters. This initial flow can also incorporate water from melting snow and ice (if present) and the river it overruns. By eroding rock debris and incorporating additional water, lahars can easily grow to more than ten times their initial size. As a lahar moves farther away from a volcano, it will eventually begin to lose its heavy load of sediment and decrease in size.

Preparedness and Prediction
Until recently, most warnings of a lahar rushing down a valley toward a town or city were based on visual sightings either from video cameras or from

observers located along the valley. Maintaining video cameras in remote valleys and in extreme weather conditions is very costly, and the incoming images have to be watched continuously by a person. Relying on many observers in several valleys for extended periods of time is extremely time-consuming, and sometimes the warnings come too late or not at all.

The USGS and local emergency managers are evaluating a new, automated lahar detection system that relies on a series of acoustic-flow monitor (AFM) stations installed downstream from a volcano. Each station consists of a seismometer that senses ground vibrations from an approaching and passing lahar and a microprocessor that analyzes the signal. A radio at the station sends and receives information from a base station, usually a volcano observatory. A battery and solar panel powers the system.

At regular intervals, the microprocessor samples the amplitude of the vibration detected by the seismometer. Periodically, data is sent to the base station in the form of an emergency message sent any time the vibrations exceed a programmed threshold for longer than forty seconds. The microprocessor continues to send alert data every minute for as long as the amplitude stays above the threshold level.

A two-year cooperative pilot project is now underway to develop, deploy, and make operational the aforementioned automated system to detect the occurrence of a lahar in the Puyallup River Valley. The Puyallup River drains the west flank of Mount Rainier in Washington State, and the densely populated Puyallup Valley extends about seventy kilometers diagonally across Pierce County, Washington from Mount Rainier to the Port of Tacoma on Puget Sound. The USGS Volcano Hazards Program (VHP) and the Pierce County Department of Emergency Management are full partners in the pilot project. Upon detection of a lahar in the valley, the system is intended to issue an automatic notice to county emergency management officials that would trigger immediate, preplanned emergency response actions.

In addition to partnerships discussed above, the USGS also operates five geographically distributed volcano observatories, three of which are based within the conterminous U.S. The facilities are located in Alaska, California, Hawaii, Washington, and Wyoming.

The USGS operates the Alaska Volcano Observatory (AVO) in Fairbanks, Alaska. The AVO is a joint program of the USGS, the Geophysical Institute of the University of Alaska–Fairbanks, and the State of Alaska Division of Geological and Geophysical Surveys. AVO was formed in 1988 and uses federal, state, and university resources to monitor and study Alaska's hazardous volcanoes, to predict and record eruptive activity, and to mitigate volcanic hazards to life and property.

The Long Valley Observatory (LVO) is based at Menlo Park, California. The LVO was established to coordinate research and observations on the Long Valley caldera. The Long Valley caldera is a 15-km by 30-km oval-shaped depression located along the east side of the Sierra Nevada in east-central California. This area of eastern California has produced numerous volcanic eruptions over the past 3 million years, including the massive caldera-forming eruption 760,000 years ago.

The Hawaiian Volcano Observatory (HVO) has been in existence since 1912 at facilities on the big island of Hawaii near the Kilauea caldera. The observatory maintains vigil over both the Mauna Loa and Kilauea volcanoes.

The USGS operates the Cascades Volcano Observatory (CVO) in Vancouver, Washington. CVO assesses hazards before they occur by identifying and studying past hazardous events. The observatory provides warnings during volcanic crises by intensively monitoring restless volcanoes and interpreting results in the context of current hazards assessments. CVO investigates and reports on hazardous events after they occur to improve assessment and prediction skills and to help develop new concepts of how volcanoes work.

The fifth USGS observatory is the Yellowstone Volcano Observatory (YVO), which focuses on the sleeping giant which is the Yellowstone caldera in Wyoming. The YVO was created as a partnership among the USGS, Yellowstone National Park, and University of Utah to strengthen the long-term monitoring of volcanic and earthquake unrest in the Yellowstone National Park region.

Solar–Terrestrial Hazards

On an approximately eleven-year cycle, changes in the sun's magnetic field bring an increase in sunspots, solar flares, and events called coronal mass ejections (CME). The result is a barrage of charged particles hurling toward Earth from the sun. The peak in this cycle is called a *solar maximum* or *solar max*. Solar flares, one type of space weather associated with solar maximums, release tremendous amounts of energy, equivalent to a million hundred-megaton nuclear explosions in few moments.

During the last solar maximum in 1989, a power surge triggered by solar energy damaged transformers of the Hydro-Quebec power system, leaving 6 million people in Canada and the northeast United States without power for more than nine hours. The event also knocked satellites out of orbit and disrupted radio communications.[10] Increased reliance on satellites for communication, cellular telephones, pagers, and the Global Positioning System (GPS) presents new and perhaps more profound vulnerabilities. With nearly 2,000 satellites in orbit around the Earth, a future solar max event could have significant impact on services.

Preparedness and Prediction

The Solar and Heliospheric Observatory (SOHO) is stationed 1.5 million kilometers away from the Earth. SOHO constantly watches the sun, returning pictures and data of the storms that rage across its surface. SOHO's studies range from the sun's hot interior, through its visible surface and stormy atmosphere, and out to distant regions where the wind from the sun battles with a breeze of atoms coming from among the stars. The SOHO mission is a joint European Space Agency (ESA)/National Aeronautics and Space

....

SOHO moves around the Sun on the sunward side of the Earth, providing an uninterrupted view of the Sun. This a spot in space where the gravitational fields of the Earth and the Sun cancel each other and keep SOHO in an orbit locked in line with the two bodies.

....

Administration (NASA) project. SOHO also sees explosions, remarkable shock waves, and tornadoes in the sun's atmosphere. SOHO is expected to be in operation until 2045. Thus, SOHO should assist future emergency managers in monitoring solar activity during the next cyclical peak anticipated to occur in 2010.

Global Environmental Change

The U.S. Global Change Research Program (USGCRP) was established by the Global Change Research Act of 1990 to:

- Enhance understanding of natural and human-induced changes in the Earth's global environmental system;
- Monitor, understand, and predict global change; and
- Provide a sound scientific basis for national and international decision making.

Further, the U.S. Climate Change Science Program (CCSP) was established in 2002 to "empower the Nation and the global community with the science-based knowledge to manage risks and opportunities of change in the climate and related environmental systems."[11] CCSP incorporates and integrates the USGCRP with the U.S. Climate Change Research Initiative (CCRI).

According to the CCSP, *climate change* is defined as a statistically significant variation in either the mean state of the climate or in its variability, persisting for an extended period (typically decades or longer).[12] Climate change may be due to natural internal processes or to external forces, including changes in solar radiation and volcanic eruptions or persistent human-induced changes in atmospheric composition or in land use.

The Intergovernmental Panel on Climate Change (IPCC) has been established by the World Meteorological Organization (WMO) and the United Nations Environment Program (UNEP) to assess scientific, technical, and socio-economic information relevant for the understanding of climate change, its potential impacts, and options for adaptation and mitigation. It is open to all members of the UN and of WMO.

According to provisional calculations by the WMO, the mean global temperature in 2005 deviated by +0.47°C from the average of the climate normal period of 1961 to 1990. Thus, it was one of the warmest years since recordings began in 1861 and currently ranks as the second warmest year worldwide. Nothing provides more striking evidence of the continual warming of our planet than the fact that the nine warmest years have all occurred between 1995 and 2005. In fact, 2005 is likely to go down as the warmest year ever recorded in the Northern Hemisphere, with an anomaly of +0.65°C. Further, in September 2005, ocean ice in the north covered less than six million square kilometers for the first time since satellite observations began in the 1970s. September is the month in which it typically reaches its minimum. The sea ice cover registered at the end of that month showed a reduction of 8% in the last twenty-five years. A major part in this development was played by the North Atlantic, where the surface temperature in 2005 currently ranks as the warmest annual mean figure ever registered.

The exceptionally large anomalies in a belt around 50°N latitude along with record values in the Caribbean and the tropical Atlantic were also particularly noticeable. One of the effects of this was the extreme drought in the Amazon region. This was due to the higher level of evaporation and precipitation formation over the warm sea surfaces, while in the neighboring region of North Brazil prevailing conditions were a subsidence of air and cloud dispersion.

Since the late 1980s, the international scientific community has engaged in robust research programs to discern anthropogenic impacts from those of natural variability in effort to predict and perhaps mitigate what the impacts may be to regional and global environmental changes. The body of scientific knowledge and policy debate is substantial, and the suggested readings below will allow for a more thorough exploration of the context and multi-dimensional challenges of environmental change and how these changes could affect the occurrence and severity of natural disasters:

- The U.S. Global Change Research Program: http://www.usgcrp.gov
- The U.S. Climate Change Science Program http://www.climatescience.gov
- The Intergovernmental Panel on Climate Change, United Nations World Meteorological Organization: http://www.ipcc.ch

Subcommittee on Disaster Reduction (SDR)

The Subcommittee on Disaster Reduction (SDR) is an element of the President's National Science and Technology Council and facilitates national strategies for reducing disaster risks and losses that are based on effective use of science and technology. The SDR is made up of representatives from federal government agencies addressing natural hazards from the points of view of assessment, mitigation, and warning. The goal of the SDR is to create a sustainable society, resilient to natural hazards. The SDR provides a senior-level interagency forum to leverage expertise, inform policy-makers, promote technology applications, coordinate activities, and promote excellence in research. The SDR mission encompasses catastrophic and non-catastrophic hazards, whether domestic or foreign, natural or technological in origin. The SDR facilitates U.S. government and private/academic activities to reduce vulnerability to natural and technological hazards through:

- Coordinating national research goals and activities for federal research related to natural and technological hazards and disasters;

- Identifying and coordinating opportunities for the U.S. government to coordinate and collaborate with state, local, and foreign governments, international organizations and private/academic/industry groups;
- Facilitating the identification and assessment of risks;
- Providing information to the president and congress to summarize relevant resources and work within SDR agencies;
- Providing information to the president and congress in response to current disaster situations;
- Serving as liaison to the president, congress, non-governmental organizations (NGOs), and other policy development bodies;
- Promoting disaster reduction practices; and
- Facilitating the exploitation of dual-use systems and fusion of classified and unclassified data streams and research for disaster reduction applications.

Toward Deeper Understanding

An enriched understanding of the phenomenology of natural hazards, the science underlying the prediction of naturally occurring events and natural disasters, and contemporary information sources for research, education, preparedness, and mitigation may be found through the various links provided in this section.

Natural Hazards Research and Applications Information Center
University of Colorado
Boulder, CO
http://www.colorado.edu/hazards

Emergency Management Institute
Federal Emergency Management Agency
Emmitsburg, MD
http://training.fema.gov

Homeland Security Digital Library
Naval Postgraduate School
Monterey, CA
http://www.hsdl.org

NOAA Central Library
1315 East–West Highway, Second Floor
Silver Spring, MD 20910
http://www.lib.noaa.gov

Coastal Services Center (CSC)
2234 South Hobson Avenue
Charleston, SC 29405-2413
http://www.csc.noaa.gov

National Climatic Data Center (NCDC)
151 Patton Avenue
Asheville, NC 28801
http://www.ncdc.noaa.gov

National Environmental Satellite, Data, and Information Service
Building SSMC
1335 East–West Highway
Silver Spring, MD 20910-3284
http://www.nesdis.noaa.gov

National Geophysical Data Center (NGDC)
Code E/GC
325 Broadway
Boulder, CO
http://www.ngdc.noaa.gov

National Severe Storms Laboratory (NSSL)
1313 Halley Avenue,
Norman, OK 73069
http://www.nssl.noaa.gov

Pacific Marine Environmental Laboratory (PMEL), and National Tsunami Hazard Mitigation Program
7600 Sand Point Way N.E.
Seattle, WA 98115-6349
http://netr.pmel.noaa.gov

Earthquake Hazards Program
12201 Sunrise Valley Drive, MS-90 National Center
Reston, VA 20192
http://earthquake.usgs.gov

Earth Resources Observation Systems Data Center
Mundt Federal Building
47914 252nd Street
Sioux Falls, SD 57198
http://edc.usgs.gov

Earth Science Information Center
12201 Sunrise Valley Drive, MS-507
National Center
Reston, VA 20192
http://www.usgs.gov

National Earthquake Information Center
MS-967
P.O. Box 25046
Federal Center
Denver, CO 80225-0046
http://earthquake.usgs.gov/regional/neic

National Landslide Information Center, U.S. Geological Survey
MS-966
P.O. Box 25046
Federal Center
Denver, CO 80225
http://geohazards.cr.usgs.gov

National Water Information Center
12201 Sunrise Valley Drive, MS-427
National Center
Reston, VA 20192
http://water.usgs.gov

Volcano Hazards and Landslide Hazards Programs
12201 Sunrise Valley Drive, MS-904, National Center
Reston, VA 20192
http://volcanoes.usgs.gov

National Snow and Ice Data Center
CIRES, 449 UCB
University of Colorado
Boulder, CO 80309-0449
http://nsidc.org

15

....

Accidents

Technological progress is like an axe in the hands of a pathological criminal.
                                                                    – *Albert Einstein*

Introduction

Technological hazards are an increasing source of risk to human populations and both natural and built environments. Serious accidents have afflicted thousands of people across the globe. One only needs to think of the following tragic incidents as a reminder that technological hazards persist in the environment surrounding us:

- Bhopal, India chemical release (1984);
- Exxon Valdez oil tanker spill in Prince William Sound, Alaska (1989);
- Chernobyl nuclear power plant release (1986);
- Love Canal, New York; or,
- Fires at the Cocoanut Grove Nightclub in Boston (1942) and the MGM Grand Hotel in Las Vegas (1980).

These examples of technological accidents, disasters, and hazards have shaped national policy and the practice of risk

....

Technological hazards can be organized in general classes by hazard type. Among these are:

- Fire;
- Hazardous materials;
- Chemical emergencies;
- Biological emergencies; and
- Nuclear power plant emergencies.

....

management, consequence analysis, and contingency planning for decades following their tragic impact on humankind. Further, the spectrum of technological hazards exists in every aspect of contemporary life. These hazards include:

- Release of chemicals to the atmosphere by explosion or fire;
- Release of chemicals into water (groundwater, rivers, lakes) by tank rupture, pipeline rupture, or chemicals dissolved in water;
- Oil spills in the marine environment;
- Satellite crash (carrying radionuclides);
- Radioactive sources in metallurgical processes;
- Other sources of radionuclides released into the environment;
- Contamination by waste management activities;
- Soil contamination;
- Accidents with groundwater contamination;
- Groundwater contamination by waste dumps (slow moving);
- Aircraft accidents;
- Release and contaminations as a consequence of military operations (unexploded ordnance, depleted uranium); and
- Release as a consequence of industrial use or research (e.g., genetic research on anti-virals) of biological material (e.g., bacteria, fungi, viruses).

....

For more information on the unintended consequences (social and economic impacts) of technological disasters, the following publications are recommended:

- Chiles, J. R. 2001. *Inviting Disaster: Lessons from the Edge of Technology.* New York: HarperCollins Publishing.
- Dorner, D. 1996. *The Logic of Failure: Recognizing and Avoiding Error in Complex Situations.* New York: Metropolitan Books.
- Tenner, E., and Knopf, A. A. 1996. *Why Things Bite Back: Technology and the Revenge of Unintended Consequences.* New York: Vintage Books.

....

Hazard Analysis

Hazard analysis is the basis for both mitigation efforts and the development of effective emergency operations plans (EOP). From an emergency operations planning perspective, hazard analysis helps a planning team decide what hazards merit special attention, what actions must be planned for, and what resources are likely needed. Hazard analysis requires the planning team to:

1. **Identify hazards** to know what kinds of emergencies have occurred or could occur in the jurisdiction.

   - Begin with a list of hazards that concern emergency management in your jurisdiction. Laws, previous plans, and elected officials can help define the universe of hazards which the planning team should address in the all-hazard EOP.

- For each of these potential emergencies, determine whether it has happened or could happen in the jurisdiction. There are three lines of investigation: history (including statistical compilations), expert opinion, and maps—which summarize results of the first two.

2. **Profile hazards** and their potential consequences.

- Deciding that one hazard poses more of a threat than another may require only a qualitative estimate (e.g., high vs. medium), but to plan for health and medical needs the planning team would also need to have an estimate for likely fatalities and injuries.[1]
- Another factor is the availability of information and time. It may be necessary to take a long view of hazard analysis, and have each version build on the preceding one as part of a research agenda for emergency management.
- Develop information on each of the hazards identified for the community. Of particular interest is each hazard's:

  - Frequency of occurrence (both historical and predicted or probable), magnitude, and intensity;
  - Location (if the hazard is associated with a facility or landscape feature);
  - Spatial extent (either around the known location of the hazard) and duration;
  - Seasonal pattern (based on month by month historical occurrence);
  - Speed of onset; and
  - Availability of warning.
  - Develop information on the potential consequences of the hazard. This depends on identifying a vulnerable zone (if the hazard is localized) or relating the estimated spatial extent of the hazard to the jurisdiction (by a simple ratio of the hazard's extent to the jurisdiction's area to obtain gross estimates of lives and property at risk, or by overlaying the estimated spatial extent of the hazard on a portion of the jurisdiction and determining what would be affected).
  - Several kinds of consequences can be investigated, including response planning (concerned with effects on people, e.g., total affected, likely deaths and injuries), critical facilities and community functions, property, and sites of potential secondary hazards (e.g., dams, chemical processing plants).
  - The planning team can use both historical information and modeling to arrive at estimates for planning. In modeling, the general process is to consider what is exposed to a given intensity of the hazard, how susceptible it is to a type of damage or consequence (e.g., death, destruction, days of service loss or repair time for critical facilities), and some measure of loss (e.g., dollars for property damage).
  - Over time, collection of this information can be made easier by sectoring the jurisdiction (optimally, in sectors that will also be used for damage

assessment) and developing a profile of each sector (e.g., rough number of structures falling into different classes of construction, number of different kinds of critical facilities, rough number of people in different age groups or having special needs, etc.).

3. **Compare and prioritize risks** to determine which hazards merit special attention in planning.

   - The planning team must consider frequency of the hazard and the likely or potential severity of its consequences in order to develop a single indicator of the threat. This allows comparison and setting of priorities. While a mathematical approach is possible, it is easier to manipulate qualitative ratings (e.g., high, medium, low) or index numbers (e.g., reducing quantitative information to a 1 to 3, 1 to 5, or 1 to 10 scale based on defined thresholds) for different categories of information used in the ranking scheme.

4. **Utilize scenarios** to assure needed hazard specific planning provisions and estimate hazard-specific resource requirements.

   - While it is important to have a sense of magnitudes involved whether by the single indicator used to rank hazards or the estimated numbers of people affected, it must be remembered that these are static. Planning is concerned with actions that take place in time. For the top-ranked hazards, or hazards that rate above a certain threshold, the planning team should consider scenarios.
   - Using information from the hazard profile, the planning team should think about how the hazard occurrence would develop in the jurisdiction. Starting with a given intensity of the hazard, the team can imagine the hazard's development from initial warning (if available) to its impact on a specific part of the jurisdiction (as identified through analysis) and its generation of specific consequences (e.g., collapsed buildings; loss of critical services and infrastructure; death, injury, or displacement). Through this initial brainstorming, which can be refined in formal tabletop exercises, the team can decide what actions and resources are necessary.

Community-Based Hazard Planning

Local Emergency Planning Committee (LEPC)
The Emergency Planning and Community Right-to-Know Act of 1986 (EPCRA) establishes requirements for federal, state, territorial and local governments, tribes, and industry regarding emergency planning and "Community Right-to-Know" reporting on hazardous and toxic chemicals. The Community Right-to-Know provisions help increase the public's knowledge and access to information on chemicals at individual facilities, their uses, and releases into the environment. States and communities, working with facilities, can use the information to improve chemical safety and protect public health and the environment.

Table 15.1 Technological Hazard Threat Reduction Elements

PREVENTION MEASURES	ALERT AND WARNING	DETECTION AND RESPONSE MEASURES	ORGANIZATIONAL AWARENESS AND ACTION
Preventive measures include: • Qualification of personnel on site; • Training programs; • Information awareness program; • Alarm and alert systems; • Quality assurance (QA) management plan; • Facility design; • Material control; • Process planning; and • Risk analysis.	Establishing an effective alert and warning capability involves: • Consequence analysis/assessment; • Pathway analysis; • Reaction of products under varying conditions of accidental release, including variable weather conditions; and • Mutual aid agreements (MAA) and off-site entities.	Effective detection and effective response capabilities carefully address: • Sensor networks and detection systems; • Weather conditions; • Prediction modeling and simulation; • Communications systems (interoperability, multi-jurisdictional); • Evacuation plans; • Emergency operations and EOPs; and • Response team warning and arrival times.	Effective organizational response and decision-making involves: • Local, regional, and national authorities; • Conventions and statutory obligations; • Emergency public information; and • Incident management protocols (including the National Incident Management System [NIMS]).

EPCRA was passed in response to concerns regarding the environmental and safety hazards posed by the storage and handling of toxic chemicals. These concerns were triggered in 1984 by the disaster in Bhopal, India, in which more than 3,000 people suffered death or serious injury from an accidental release of methyl isocyanate, which is used in the manufacturing of adhesives and rubbers. To reduce the likelihood of such a disaster in the United States, Congress imposed requirements on both states and regulated facilities through the EPCRA. The EPCRA has four major provisions:

1. Emergency planning (Sections 301 to 303);
2. Emergency release notification (Section 304);
3. Hazardous chemical storage reporting requirements (Sections 311 and 312); and,
4. Toxic chemical release inventory (Section 313).

Regulations implementing EPCRA are codified in Code of Federal Regulations (CFR).

....

The **Bhopal, India incident** took place in the early hours of the morning of December 3, 1984, in the heart of the city. A Union Carbide subsidiary pesticide plant released 42 tons of methyl isocyanate gas, exposing at least 520,000 people to the toxic gas. The release resulted in the immediate deaths of more than 3,000 people, according to the Indian Supreme Court. It is also estimated that 8,000 died within two weeks of the incident and that an additional 8,000 have since died from gas related diseases. The Bhopal incident is frequently cited as the world's worst industrial disaster.[2]

....

Emergency Planning

The emergency planning section of the law is designed to help communities prepare for and respond to emergencies involving hazardous substances. Since every community in the United States must be part of a comprehensive plan, the Governor designates a State Emergency Response Commission (SERC) which is responsible for implementing EPCRA provisions within their state. The SERCs in turn have designated about 3,500 local emergency planning districts and appointed a Local Emergency Planning Committees (LEPC) for each district. The SERC supervises and coordinates the activities of the LEPC, establishes procedures for receiving and processing public requests for information collected under EPCRA, and reviews local emergency response plans.

The LEPC membership must include, at a minimum, local officials including police, fire, civil defense, public health, transportation, and environmental professionals, as well as representatives of facilities subject to the emergency planning requirements, community groups, and the media. The LEPCs must develop an emergency response plan, review it at least annually, and provide information about chemicals in the community to citizens.

Under the EPCRA framework, there are required elements for each community emergency response plan. These elements include:

- Identification of facilities and transportation routes of extremely hazardous substances;
- Description of emergency response procedures, both on- and off-site;
- Designation of a community coordinator and facility coordinator(s) to implement the plan;
- An outline of emergency notification procedures;
- Description of how to determine the probable affected area and population by releases;
- Description of local emergency equipment and facilities and the persons responsible for them;
- An outline of evacuation plans;
- Provisions for a training program for emergency responders (including schedules); and
- Provisions of methods and schedules for exercising emergency response plans.

Community Hazards Emergency Response – Capability Assurance Process (CHER-CAP)

The Community Hazards Emergency Response-Capability Assurance Process (CHER-CAP) is offered by the Federal Emergency Management Agency (FEMA) Regional Offices to assist local communities and tribal governments in obtaining a greater understanding of community hazard risks, identifying planning deficiencies, updating of plans, training of first responders, and stimulating and testing the system for strengths and needed improvements. CHER-CAP is offered as an additional tool for state and local governments to use as they develop and enhance preparedness and response capabilities that will address any hazard that communities face throughout the Nation.

As a voluntary program, CHER-CAP uses the skills and resources of federal, state, tribal, and local governments and industry partners to identify community hazard risks and address local jurisdictions' preparedness needs. It also enhances a community's ability to operate within the framework of the National Oil and Hazardous Substances Pollution Contingency Plan, more commonly referred to as the National Contingency Plan (NCP). CHER-CAP's purpose is to:

- Identify opportunities for plan revisions;
- Identify communication needs;
- Identify resource needs;
- Improve coordination;
- Comply with training requirements;
- Clarify roles and responsibilities;
- Improve individual performance;
- Serve as a Train-the-Trainer initiative for additional jurisdictions;
- Test plans and systems in a comprehensive HAZMAT exercise;

- Motivate public and private officials to support emergency programs; and
- Increase general awareness of proficiency and needs.[3]

Community Emergency Response Team (CERT)

The Community Emergency Response Team (CERT) program helps train people to be better prepared to respond to emergency situations in their communities. When emergencies occur, CERT members can give critical support to first responders, provide immediate assistance to victims, and organize spontaneous volunteers at a disaster site. CERT members can also help with non-emergency projects that help improve the safety of the community. The CERT concept was developed and implemented by the Los Angeles City Fire Department in 1985. FEMA made this training available nationally in 1993. Since that time, CERT programs have been established in more than 340 communities in forty-five states.[4]

The CERT training program is a twenty-hour course, typically delivered over a seven-week period. Training sessions cover disaster preparedness, disaster fire suppression, basic disaster medical operations, light search and rescue, and team operations. The training also includes a disaster simulation in which participants practice skills that they learned throughout the course. The CERT course is taught in the community by a trained team of first responders who have completed a CERT Train-the-Trainer course conducted by their state training office for emergency management, or FEMA's Emergency Management Institute (EMI), located in Emmitsburg, Maryland.

Hazards and Governmental Responsibilities

International

The global community of nations has learned through bitter experience that a lack of coordinated, interoperable, and standards-based operational practices, laws and regulations, systems, and networks places lives and property at an unacceptable risk level. Current international programs that are effective are provided below.

- International maritime law provides the Law of the Sea, which guides safe shipping and passage on international shipping lanes while also addressing life safety;
- The International Civil Aviation Organization (ICAO) helps to assure an integrated seamless air traffic control and air transport safety framework worldwide;
- The World Health Organization (WHO) works with United Nations (UN) member nations to enhance global disease surveillance; and
- The World Meteorological Organization (WMO) serves to assure that compatible standards of global weather and climate monitoring contribute to operational and research needs.

These are but a few examples of how international regulatory bodies or international laws serve to enhance life safety and enable global commerce to proceed in a more secure and safe environment.

Federal

In the United States, the federal government has a significant role to assure environmental safety and health, occupational safety and health, food safety and security, and transportation safety. Examples of key agencies or government administrative bodies designed to support these mission areas include:

- Environmental Protection Agency (EPA);
- Food and Drug Administration (FDA);
- National Institute for Occupational Safety and Health (NIOSH);
- National Transportation Safety Board (NTSB);
- National Institute for Standards and Technology (NIST);
- Occupational Safety and Health Administration (OSHA);
- U.S. Public Health Service;
- Animal and Plant Health Inspection Service (APHIS);
- U.S. Coast Guard (USCG); and
- U.S. Army Corps of Engineers.

Further, many of these agencies or government administrative bodies have produced key plans that support hazard preparedness and response, some of which are described below.

National Response Framework (NRF)

The National Response Framework (NRF) establishes a comprehensive all-hazards approach to enhance the ability of the United States to manage domestic incidents. The NRF incorporates best practices and procedures from incident management disciplines—homeland security, emergency management, law enforcement, firefighting, public works, public health, responder and recovery worker health and safety, emergency medical services, and the private sector—and integrates them into a unified structure. The NRF forms the basis of how the federal government coordinates with state, local, and tribal governments and the private sector during incidents.[5]

The NRF can be accessed at: http://www.fema.gov/emergency/nrf.

National Contingency Plan (NCP)

The National Oil and Hazardous Substances Pollution Contingency Plan, more commonly called the National Contingency Plan or NCP, is the federal government's blueprint for responding to both oil spills and hazardous substance releases. The first NCP was developed and published in 1968 in response to a massive oil spill from the oil tanker *Torrey Canyon* off the coast of England the year before. More than 37 million gallons of crude oil spilled into the water, causing massive environmental damage. To avoid the problems faced by response officials involved the *Torrey Canyon* incident, U.S. officials developed a coordinated approach to cope with potential spills in U.S. waters. The 1968 plan provided the first comprehensive system of accident reporting, spill containment, and environmental cleanup and established a response headquarters, a national reaction team, and regional reaction teams.

Congress broadened the scope of the National Contingency Plan over the years. As required by the Clean Water Act of 1972, the NCP was revised the following year to include a framework for responding to hazardous substance spills as well as oil discharges. Following the passage of Superfund legislation in 1980, the NCP was broadened to cover releases at hazardous waste sites requiring emergency removal actions. Over the years, additional revisions have been made to the NCP to keep pace with the enactment of legislation. The latest revisions to the NCP were finalized in 1994 to reflect the oil spill provisions of the Oil Pollution Act of 1990, wherein the lessons learned from the 1989 *Exxon Valdez* spill were codified.[6]

The NCP can be accessed at: http://www.epa.gov/OEM/content/lawsregs/ncpover.htm.

National Infrastructure Protection Plan (NIPP)

The National Infrastructure Protection Plan (NIPP) is a national plan to unify and enhance critical infrastructure/key resources (CI/KR) protection efforts through a partnership involving the private sector, as well as federal, state, local, and tribal governments.[7] The NIPP meets requirements set forth in Homeland Security Presidential Directive (HSPD)-7: Critical Infrastructure Identification, Prioritization, and Protection, and provides the overarching approach for integrating the Nation's many CI/KR protection initiatives into a single, national effort.

The NIPP provides the coordinated approach that will be used to establish national priorities, goals, and requirements for CI/KR protection so that federal funding and resources are applied in the most effective manner to reduce vulnerability, deter threats, and minimize the consequences of attacks and other incidents. The NIPP establishes the overarching concepts relevant to all CI/KR sectors identified in HSPD-7, and addresses the physical, cyber, and human considerations required for effective implementation of comprehensive programs. The NIPP specifies the key initiatives, milestones, and metrics required to achieve the Nation's CI/KR protection mission. It also sets forth a comprehensive risk management framework and defines roles and responsibilities for the DHS, Federal Sector-Specific Agencies (SSAs), and other federal, state, local, tribal, and private sector security partners.[8]

The NIPP can be accessed at: http://www.dhs.gov/xlibrary/assets/NIPP_Plan.pdf.

State and Local Governance

The above listing of federal entities is merely a sampling of what exists today, steeped in the U.S. Code, by Executive Orders, or by statute. Similarly, states have enacted numerous laws and regulations that guide the operational practice and standards of performance for commerce, industry, and professional practices. Local jurisdictions also enact municipal codes to complement or strengthen policies, procedures, or performance standards established by federal guidelines or statutes.

Preparedness and Technological Hazards

Preparedness in the domain of technological hazards management must take into account the concept of *forseeability*. There must be an implicit systematic analysis of hazards based on a comprehensive program to identify, monitor, audit, and review the key systems, practices, procedures, and activities of those entities whose operations could result in hazards to the community, the state, or the Nation. Practices which are important to a comprehensive preparedness program include:

Operational Control: Includes the adoption and implementation of procedures and guidance or instructions for safe operation, including maintenance of a plant, its processes, and its equipment.

Management of Change: Includes the adoption and implementation of procedures for planning modifications to or the design of new installations, systems, or processes (also known as configuration management).

Emergency Planning: Includes adoption and implementation of procedures that identify foreseeable emergencies by systematic analysis and to prepare and train, test and exercise, and review and update plans to respond to such emergencies.

Performance Monitoring: Includes adoption and implementation of procedures for the ongoing assessment of compliance with the objectives set by the operator's major accident prevention policy and environmental, safety, and heath (ES&H) protocols (includes investigations and corrective action planning).

Audits and Review: Includes adoption and implementation of procedures for periodic systematic assessment of the accident prevention and the effectiveness and suitability of the ES&H program.[9]

Emergency Planning: Fundamental Building Block of Preparedness

In the current practice of emergency management, each echelon of governance ensures that a current EOP is developed, exercised, and maintained as a fundamental measure in preparedness. A jurisdiction's EOP is a document that:

- Assigns responsibility to organizations and individuals for carrying out specific actions at projected times and places in an emergency that exceeds the capability or routine responsibility of any one agency (e.g., the fire department)
- Sets forth lines of authority and organizational relationships, and describes how all actions will be coordinated;
- Describes how people and property will be protected in emergencies and disasters;
- Identifies personnel, equipment, facilities, supplies, and other resources available (within the jurisdiction or by agreement with other jurisdictions) for use during response and recovery operations; and

- Identifies steps to address mitigation concerns during response and recovery activities.

As a public document, an EOP also cites its legal basis, states its objectives, and acknowledges assumptions. The local EOP focuses on the measures that are essential for protecting the public. These include alert and warning, emergency public information, evacuation, and shelter.

In the U.S. system of emergency management, local government must act first to attend to the public's emergency needs. Depending on the nature and size of the emergency, state and federal assistance may be provided to the local jurisdiction. Emergencies are also the responsibility of state governments, and they play three very important roles:

1. They assist local jurisdictions when capabilities are overwhelmed by an emergency;
2. They themselves respond first to certain emergencies; and
3. They work with the federal government when federal assistance is necessary.

The state EOP is the framework within which local EOPs are created and through which the federal government becomes involved. As such, the state EOP ensures that all levels of government are able to mobilize as a unified emergency organization to safeguard the well-being of state citizens. Thus, the state EOP is of critical importance.

••

Contingency Plans

In addition to the basic plan, specific EOP independent **contingency plans** (or annexes) may be implemented based upon the unique hazards a jurisdiction may face.

Contingency plans typically serve the following objectives:

- Containing and controlling incidents to minimize the effects and to limit damage to population and the natural and built environments;
- Implementing measures necessary to protect human populations and the environment from the effects of major accidents;
- Communicating vital and essential information to the public and to emergency services or authorities in the affected areas; and
- Providing for the reconstitution of services, restoration of infrastructure, and clean-up of the environment following a major accident.

••

Towards National Preparedness

Following the establishment of DHS, officials examined the many developing preparedness programs and initiatives that impact federal, state, and local response communities. Efforts have been underway to consolidate these activities into a unified architecture responsive to all-hazards emergency management best practices. As part of coupling together threat-based risk assessments and capabilities-based planning methodologies, tremendous progress is being seen in defining the target capabilities that local jurisdictions, states, territories, and the federal government need to be better prepared for a range of potential threats and hazards.

HSPD-8: National Preparedness is the keystone in the overarching national preparedness life-cycle and has enabled the definition of a Target Capabilities List (TCL) for state and local governments and has begun to define the common and unique tasks associated with best practices and standards-based emergency response to incidents. The latter set of tasks is evolving; however, this Universal Task List (UTL) offers a set of measuring points for monitoring the effectiveness of planning, training, and exercise programs nationwide.[10]

Notes

Introduction

1. U.S. Department of Homeland Security. 2003. *National Strategy for the Physical Protection of Critical Infrastructures and Key Assets.*

2. U.S. Department of Homeland Security. 2006. *National Infrastructure Protection Plan.*

3. U.S. Department of Homeland Security. 2005. *National Response Plan Brochure.*

Chapter 1

1. U.S. Department of Homeland Security. 2006. *National Infrastructure Protection Plan.*

2. *Oxford Pocket Dictionary of Current English.* New York: Oxford University Press, 2008.

3. Vaughan R., and Pollard, R. *Rebuilding Americas, Volume 1: Planning and Managing Public Works in the 1980s* (pp. 1-2). Washington, DC: Council of State Planning Agencies, 1984.

4. Executive Order 13010 - Critical Infrastructure Protection. 1996, July 17. *Federal Register* 61*(138)*: 37347-37350.

5. Ibid.

6. 107th United States Congress. 2001. *Uniting and Strengthening America by Providing Appropriate Tools Required to Intercept and Obstruct Terrorism Act of 2001 (Public Law 107-56)*, Section 1016(e).

7. Office of Homeland Security. 2002. *National Strategy for Homeland Security*, 31.

8. Moteff, J., and Parfomak, P. 2004. *CRS Report for Congress: Critical Infrastructure and Key Asset Definitions and Identification.* Washington, DC: Library of Congress.

9. Starks, T., and Andersen, M. E. 2004, July 29. Congress, Industry Both in Dismay over Homeland Security's Performance on Critical Infrastructure. *CQ Homeland Security.*

10. U.S. Department of Homeland Security. *Accessing Department of Homeland Security Records through the Freedom of Information Act.* http://www.dhs.gov/xfoia/editorial_0314.shtm.

11. U.S. Department of Homeland Security Office of Inspector General. 2006, June. *Progress in Developing the National Asset Database (OIG-06-04).*

12. National Research Council. July 2002. *Transportation Research Board (TRB) Special Report 27: Deterrence, Protection, and Preparation—The New Transportation Security Imperative.*

13. Ibid.

14. U.S. Army Corps of Engineers Topographic Engineering Center. http://crunch.tec.army.mil/nid/webpages/nid.cfm.

15. U.S. Department of Energy. 2004, April. *Water Energy Resources of the United States (DOE/ID-11111).*

16. Bureau of Transportation Statistics. *T-100 Domestic Market and Segment Data.*

Chapter 2

1. Nyberg, C. 2005, February 7. Pursuing Presidential Directives. *Law Library News.* Seattle, WA: Marian Gould Gallagher Law Library, University of Washington School of Law. http://lib.law.washington.edu/news/2005/Feb7.html.

2. Cadwell, G. 2005, July 1. *Presidential Directive and Where to Find Them.* Washington, DC: Library of Congress Newspaper and Current Periodical Reading Room. http://www.loc.gov/rr/news/directives.html.

3. U.S. Department of Homeland Security. 2008, August 21. *Homeland Security Presidential Directives.* http://www.dhs.gov/xabout/laws/editorial_0607.shtm.

4. Sherman, J. 2006, March 8. President Issues "War on Terror" Directive to Improve Government Coordination. Inside Washington Publishers News Stand. http://defense.iwpnewsstand.com/insider.asp?issue=spclrpt 03092006.

5. Executive Office of the President. 2007, March 26. *The National Strategy for Aviation Security.* Washington, DC. http://www.whitehouse.gov/homeland/aviation-security.html.

6. U.S. Department of Homeland Security. 2007, March 26. *Aviation Transportation System Security Plan: Supporting Plan to the National Strategy for Aviation Security.* Washington, DC.

7. Ibid.

8. Ibid.

9. U.S. Department of Homeland Security. 2007, March 26. *Air Domain Surveillance and Intelligent Integration Plan: Supporting Plan to the National Strategy for Aviation Security.* Washington, DC.

10. U.S. Department of Homeland Security. 2007, March 26. *Domestic Outreach Plan: Supporting Plan to the National Strategy for Aviation Security.* Washington, DC.

11. U.S. Department of Homeland Security. 2007, March 26. *International Outreach Plan: Supporting Plan to the National Strategy for Aviation Security.* Washington, DC.

12. U.S. Department of Homeland Security. 2008, April 8. *Fact Sheet: Our Federal Networks Against Cyber Attacks.* http://www.dhs.gov/xnews/releases/pr_1207684277 498.shtm.

13. Ibid.

14. United States Congress. 2002, November 25. *The Homeland Security Act (HSA) of 2002, Pub. L. No. 107-296,* Section 202. Washington, DC.

15. Ibid.

16. Jaeger, P. T., Bertot, J. C., and McClure, C. R. 2003, July. The Impact of the USA Patriot Act on Collection and Analysis of Personal Information under the Foreign Intelligence Surveillance Act. *Government Information Quarterly, 20*(3), pp. 295–314.

17. United States Congress. 1978, October 25. *The Foreign Intelligence Surveillance Act of 1978, Pub. L. No. 95-511,* Sections 1801–1829, 1841–1846, 1861–1863. Washington, DC.

18. U.S. Department of Justice. 2003. *Domestic Security Enhancement Act of 2003.* Washington, DC. http://www.publicintegrity.org/dtaweb/downloads/Story_01_020703_ Doc_1.pdf.

19. Ibid.

20. GovTrack.us. 2006. *S. 2271[109th]: USA PATRIOT Additional Reauthorizing Amendments Act of 2006.* http://www.govtrack.us/congress/bill.xpd?bill=s109-2271&tab=summary.

21. Ibid.

22. Ibid.

23. Ibid.

24. GovTrack.us. 2006. *S. 3678 [109th]: Pandemic and All-Hazards Preparedness Act.* http://www.govtrack.us/congress/bill.xpd?bill=s109-3678&tab=summary.

25. GovTrack.us. 2006. *H.R. 6061 [109th]: Secure Fence Act of 2006.* http://www. govtrack.us/congress/bill.xpd?bill=h109-6061&tab=summary.

26. GovTrack.us. 2005. *H.R. 3199 [109th]: USA PATRIOT Improvement and Reauthorization Act of 2005.* http://www.govtrack.us/congress/bill.xpd?bill=h109-3199&tab= summary.

27. GovTrack.us. 2004. *S. 2845 [108th]: Intelligence Reform and Terrorism Prevention Act of 2004.* http://www.govtrack.us/congress/bill.xpd?bill=s108-2845&tab=summary.

28. United States Congress. 2006, October 4. *Post-Katrina Emergency Reform Act of 2006, Pub. L. No. 109-295, Title VI – National Emergency Management.* Washington, DC.

Chapter 3

1. U.S. Department of Homeland Security. 2006. *National Infrastructure Protection Plan.* Washington, DC.

2. Ibid.

3. Ibid, p. 20.

4. Ibid.

5. Ibid.

6. Ibid, p. 5.

7. Ibid, p. 17.

8. Ibid, p. 18.

9. U.S Department of Homeland Security. 2008, September 11. *National Protection and Programs Directorate.* http://www.dhs.gov/xabout/structure/editorial_0794.shtm.

10. United States Government Accountability Office. 2007, July 10. *Critical Infrastructure Protection: Sector Plans and Sector Councils Continue to Evolve.* Washington, DC. http://www.gao.gov/new.items/d07706r.pdf.

Chapter 4

1. U.S. Department of Homcland Security. 2008, April. *National Incident Management System (NIMS) – Pre-Decisional DRAFT,* p. 1. Washington, DC.

2. U.S. Department of Homeland Security. 2004, March. *National Incident Management System (NIMS),* p. 6. Washington, DC.

3. Federal Emergency Management Agency. 2008, August 29. *Welcome to the National Integration Center (NIC) Incident Management Systems Division.* http://www.fema.gov/emergency/nims.

4. U.S. Department of Homeland Security. 2008, September 11. *National Preparedness Guidelines.* http://www.dhs.gov/xprepresp/publications/gc_1189788256647.shtm.

5. Federal Emergency Management Agency. 2008, June 27. *Resource Management: Job Titles.* http://www.fema.gov/emergency/nims/rm/job_titles.shtm.

6. Federal Emergency Management Agency. 2007, November 11. *Integrated Public Alert and Warning System (IPAWS).* http://www.fema.gov/emergency/ipaws.

7. Emergency Management Assistance Compact. *What is EMAC?* http://www.emacweb.org/?9.

8. Molino, L. N. *Emergency Incident Management Systems: Fundamentals and Applications,* p. 45. Hoboken, NJ: Wiley Inter Science, 2006.

9. U.S. Department of Homeland Security. 2004, March. *National Incident Management System (NIMS).* Washington, DC.

10. Federal Emergency Management Agency. 2006, October. *Multiagency Coordination Systems: Student Manual,* pp. 1–19. Washington, DC.

11. Firescope. 2005, April. *FIRESCOPE Articles of Organization and Procedures (MACS 410–4).* Riverside, CA.

12. Federal Emergency Management Agency. 2006, October. *Multiagency Coordination Systems: Student Manual,* pp. 2–6. Washington, DC.

13. Molino, L. N. *Emergency Incident Management Systems: Fundamentals and Applications,* p. 71. Hoboken, NJ: Wiley Inter Science, 2006.

Chapter 5

1. Executive Office of the President. 2003, December 17. *Homeland Security Presidential Directive [HSPD]-7: Critical Infrastructure Identification, Prioritization, and Protection.* Washington, DC.

2. Executive Office of the President. 2003, December 17. *Homeland Security Presidential Directive [HSPD]-8: National Preparedness.* Washington, DC.

3. Federal Emergency Management Agency. 2003, December. *FEMA 426: Reference Manual to Mitigate Potential Terrorist Attacks Against Buildings.* Washington, DC.

4. Radvanovsky, R. *Critical Infrastructure: Homeland Security and Emergency Preparedness,* 152. Boca Raton, FL: Taylor and Francis, 2006.

5. Ibid.

6. Ibid.

7. U.S. Department of Homeland Security. 2007. *National Infrastructure Protection Plan: Risk Management Framework.* Washington, DC.

8. American Society for Industrial Security International. 2003. *The General Security Risk Assessment Guideline.* Alexandria, VA.

9. U.S. Food and Drug Administration. 2007, June 14. *Food Defense and Terrorism: CARVER + Shock Software Tool.* http://www.cfsan.fda.gov/~dms/vltcarv.html.

10. Sandia National Laboratories. *Security Risk Assessment Methodologies.* http://www.sandia.gov/ram/index.htm.

Chapter 6

1. U.S. Department of Energy, Energy Information Administration. *Forecasts of International Use to 2020.* Washington, DC.

2. Nakicenovic, N., Grübler, A., and McDonald, A. *Global Energy Perspectives.* Cambridge: Cambridge University Press, 1998.

3. International Energy Annual (2000–2004).

4. International Petroleum Monthly (2005–2006).

5. The House Subcommittee on International Terrorism and Nonproliferation (ITNP). 2005, July 27. *Terrorist Threats to Energy Security.*

6. Canadian Broadcasting Corporation. http://archives.cbc.ca/science_technology/energy_production/clips/13545.

7. U.S. Department of Energy. 2004, December. *Electricity Transmission in a Restructured Industry: Data Needs for Public Policy Analysis.* Washington, DC.

8. American Society for Civil Engineers. 2005. *Report Card for America's Infrastructure.* Reston, VA.

9. U.S. Department of Energy. Retrieved from: http://www.energy.gov.

10. Ibid.

11. Minkel, J. 2008. *The 2003 Northeast Blackout–Five Years Later.* http://www.sciam.com/article.cfm?id=2003-blackout-five-years-later.

12. Report Card for America's Infrastructure. 2005. http://www.asce.org/reportcard/2005/index.cfm.

13. U.S. Energy Information Administration. 2003, August. *Electricity Transmission Fact Sheet.* Washington, DC.

14. Report Card for America's Infrastructure. 2005. http://www.asce.org/reportcard/2005/index.cfm.

15. Ibid.

16. Nuclear Energy Institute. Retrieved from: http://www.nei.org.

17. Energy Information Administration. 2007, March. *Electric Power Monthly.*

Chapter 7

1. U.S. Department of Homeland Security. 2007, May. *Transportation Systems: Critical Infrastructure and Key Resources Sector-Specific Plan as Input to the National Infrastructure Protection Plan.* Washington, DC.

2. Ibid, p. 139.

3. U.S. Department of Homeland Security. 2008, October 17. *National Security Presidential Directive 41 / Homeland Security Presidential Directive 13.* Washington, DC. http://www.dhs.gov/xprevprot/programs/editorial_0597.shtm.

4. U.S. Department of Homeland Security. 2005, September. *The National Strategy for Maritime Security.* Washington, DC.

5. McCarter, M. 2008, May 28. "GAO: Improved Inspections Boost Supply Chain Security." *Homeland Security Today.* http://www.hstoday.us/content/view/3541/128.

6. U.S. Government Accountability Office. 2005, March. *Cargo Security: Partnership Program Grants Importers Reduced Scrutiny with Limited Assurance of Improved Security (GAO-04-404).* Washington, DC.

7. U.S. Department of Homeland Security. 2007, March 26. *National Strategy for Aviation Security.* Washington, DC.

8. U.S. Department of Homeland Security. 2008, March 18. *Postal and Shipping Sector: Critical Infrastructure and Key Resources: Sector Overview.* http://www.dhs.gov/xprevprot/programs/gc_1188412546210.shtm.

9. National Infrastructure Protection Plan: Postal and Shipping Sector. 2007, Summer. *Messenger Courier World.* http://www.mcaa.com/magazine/2007_summer/006.pdf.

Chapter 8

1. Sullivant, J. *Strategies for Protecting National Critical Infrastructure Assets: A Focus on Problem-Solving.* Hoboken, NJ: John Wiley & Sons, Inc, 2007.

2. U.S. Department of Homeland Security. 2008, March 18. *Commercial Facilities Sector: Critical Infrastructure and Key Resources.* http://www.dhs.gov/xprevprot/programs/gc_1189101907729.shtm.

3. U.S. Government Accountability Office. 2006, October. *Critical Infrastructure Protection: Progress Coordinating Government and Private Sector Efforts Varies by Sectors' Characteristics (GAO -07-39).* Washington, DC.

4. U.S. Department of Homeland Security, Homeland Infrastructure Threat Risk Analysis Center. 2007, January 23. *Strategic Sector Assessment: Commercial Facilities (U/FOUO).* Washington, DC.

5. U.S. Department of Homeland Security. 2008, March 18. *Government Facilities Sector: Critical Infrastructure and Key Resources.* http://www.dhs.gov/xprevprot/programs/gc_1189011910767.shtm.

6. George Mason University, School of Law, Critical Infrastructure Protection Program. 2007, July. Inside the Government Facilities Sector. *The CIP Report,* 6(1), pp. 2–3, 10.

7. Ibid.

8. Wright, J. W. *The New York Times Almanac, 2007.* New York: Penguin Books, 2006.

9. U.S. Department of Homeland Security, and U.S. Department of the Interior. 2007, May. *National Monuments and Icons: Critical Infrastructure and Key Resources Sector-Specific Plan as Input to the National Infrastructure Protection Plan.* Washington, DC.

Chapter 9

1. Executive Office of the President. 2004, January 30. *Homeland Security Presidential Directive/[HSPD]-9: Defense of United States Agriculture and Food.*

2. U.S. Department of Homeland Security. 2007, May. *Agriculture and Food: Critical Infrastructure and Key Resources Sector-Specific Plan as Input to the National Infrastructure Protection Plan.* Washington, DC.

3. Ibid.

4. Ibid.

5. Ibid.

6. McGinn, T. 2007, July 9. *Statement for the Record, Tomm McGinn, DMV Director, Food, Agriculture and Veterinary Defense Office of Health Affairs Before the U.S. House of Representatives Committee on Homeland Security Subcommittee on Management, Investigations, and Oversight.* http://www.dhs.gov/xnews/testimony/testimony_1184092241513.shtm.

7. U.S. Department of Homeland Security. 2007. *Water Critical Infrastructure and Key Resources Sector-Specific Plan as Input to the National Infrastructure Protection Plan,* p.18. Washington, DC.

8. Hoover, J. E. 1941. Water Supply Facilities and National Defense. *Journal of the American Water Works Association, 33:11,* p. 1861.

9. Andress, C. 2003, December. *Eliminating Hometown Hazards, Cutting Chemical Risks at Wastewater Treatment Facilities,* p. 14. New York, NY: Environmental Defense.

10. Orum, P. 2007, April 2. *Toxic Trains and the Terrorist Threat, How Water Utilities Can Get Chlorine Gas Off the Rails and Out of American Communities,* p. 23. Washington, DC: Center for American Progress.

11. U.S. Government Accountability Office. 2007, March. *Securing Wastewater Facilities: Costs of Vulnerability Assessments, Risk Management Plans, and Alternative Disinfection Methods Vary Widely (GAO-07-480),* p. 26. Washington, DC.

12. U.S. General Accountability Office. 2002, August. *Water Infrastructure: Information on Financing, Capital Planning, and Privatization (GAO-02-764).* Washington, DC.

13. Ibid.

14. U.S. Environmental Protection Agency. 2001, February. *Drinking Water Infrastructure Needs Survey: Second Report to Congress (EPA 816-R-01-004).* Washington, DC.

15. U.S. Environmental Protection Agency. 2003, August. *Clean Watersheds Needs Survey 2000: Report to Congress (EPA 832-R-03-001).* Washington, DC.

Chapter 10

1. U.S. Department of Homeland Security. 2007, May. *Communications: Critical Infrastructure and Key Resources Sector-Specific Plan as Input to the National Infrastructure Protection Plan.* Washington, DC.

2. Ibid, p. 10.

3. Ibid, p. 19.

4. U.S. Department of Homeland Security. 2007, May. *Information Technology: Critical Infrastructure and Key Resources Sector-Specific Plan as Input to the National Infrastructure Protection Plan.* Washington, DC.

5. Ibid, p. 2.

6. Ibid, pp. 9–10.

7. Ibid, p. 6.

8. Ibid, p. 11.

9. U.S. Department of Homeland Security. 2007, May. *Banking and Finance: Critical Infrastructure and Key Resources Sector-Specific Plan as Input to the National Infrastructure Protection Plan.* Washington, DC.

10. Ibid, p. 13.

11. Ibid, p. 2.

Chapter 11

1. U.S. Department of Homeland Security. http:/dhs.gov.

2. Harrington, M. B., Miller, C. S., and Wang, M. 2005, Spring. "Protecting one of the nation's critical infrastructures: Healthcare." *The Edge.*

3. U.S. Department of Health and Human Services. *Critical Infrastructure Protection: Healthcare and Public Health Sector-Critical Infrastructure Protection.* http://www.hhs.gov/aspr/opeo/cip/index.html.

4. National Law Enforcement Officers Memorial Fund. http://www.nleomf.com.

5. National Volunteer Fire Council. http://nvfc.org.

6. Federal Emergency Management Agency. 2007, September 11. *Principles of Emergency Management Supplement.* Washington, DC.

7. U.S. Department of Homeland Security. http://www.dhs.gov.

8. U.S. Department of Health and Human Services. http://www.hhs.gov.

9. U.S. Department of Transportation. http://www.dot.gov.

10. U.S. Environmental Protection Agency. http://www.epa.gov.

11. Federal Bureau of Investigation. http://www.fbi.gov.

12. U.S. National Guard. http://www.ngb.army.mil/default.aspx.

13. American Red Cross. http://www.redcross.org.

14. U.S. Department of Homeland Security. 2006. *National Infrastructure Protection Plan: Risk Management Framework.* Washington, DC.

15. U.S. Citizen Corps. www.citizencorps.gov.

16. International Association of Chiefs of Police. http://www.theiacp.org.

17. The International Association of Fire Chiefs. http://www.iafc.org.

18. International Association of Emergency Managers. http://iaem.com.

19. National Association of State EMS Officials. http://www.nasemsd.org.

Chapter 12

1. United States Congress. 2002. *Public Health Security and Bioterrorism Preparedness and Response Act of 2002 (Public Law 107-188).* Washington, DC.

2. United States Government. 2001, January. *United States Government Interagency Domestic Terrorism Concept of Operations Plan.* Washington, DC.

3. Federal Emergency Management Agency. *Contemporary CBRNE Threat Profiles.* http://www.fema.gov.

4. Central Intelligence Agency. 2003, May. *Terrorist CBRN: Materials and Effects (CTC 2003-40058).* Langley, VA.

5. Henry L. Stimson Center. *Biological and Chemical Weapons: Responding to Biological and Chemical Threats.* http://www.stimson.org/cbw.

6. Centers for Disease Control and Prevention. *Bioterrorism Agents/Diseases.* http://www.bt.cdc.gov/agent/agentlist.asp.

7. National Academy of Engineering. 2004. *Radiological Attack: Dirty Bombs and other Devices.* Washington, DC. http://www.nae.edu/NAE/pubundcom.nsf/weblinks/CGOZ-646NVG/$file/radiological%20attack%2006.pdf

8. Medalia, J. 2004, April 1. *Terrorist "Dirty Bombs": A Brief Primer (RS21528).* Washington, DC: Congressional Research Service.

9. Sartori, L. 2002. The Effects of Nuclear Weapons. *Physics Today, 36* (3), pp. 32–38, 40–41.

10. National Research Council. *Making the Nation Safer: The Role of Science and Technology in Countering Terrorism.* Washington, DC: The National Academies Press, 2002.

11. Central Intelligence Agency. 2003, May. *Terrorist CBRN: Materials and Effects (CTC 2003-40058).* Langley, VA.

12. Morgenstern, H. *Vehicle Borne Improvised Explosive Device – VBIED: The Terrorist Weapon of Choice.* Miami, FL: Security Solutions International (SSI). http://www.security solutionsint.com.

13. Kopp, C. 1996. The electromagnetic bomb: a weapon of electronic mass destruction. *Air and Space Power Journal: Chronicles Online Journal.* http://www.airpower. maxwell.af.mil/airchronicles/cc/apjemp.html.

14. Taylor, C. D., and Giri, D. V. *High Power Microwave Systems and Effects.* London: Taylor and Francis Group, 1994.

15. Benford, J., and Swegle, J. *High Power Microwaves.* Norwood, MA: Artech House, 1992.

16. Krill, S., and Smith, M. 2002, October. *Threat Assessment 101.* Prepared for the U.S. Department of Homeland Security, Office for Domestic Preparedness. Washington, DC.

17. Ibid.

18. U.S. Department of Homeland Security. 2008, September 23. *Domestic Nuclear Detection Office.* http://www.dhs.gov/xabout/structure/editorial_0766.shtm.

19. Ibid.

20. Ibid.

Chapter 13

1. Center for Research on the Epidemiology of Disasters. http://www.cred.be.

2. Munich Re Group. 2006. *Annual Review: Natural Catastrophes 2005.* Munich, Germany. http://www.munichre.com/publications/302-04772_en.pdf.

3. Ibid.

4. Federal Emergency Management Agency. 2006, June 8. *FEMA Catastrophic Disaster Readiness Program 2006: New Madrid Seismic Zone (NMSZ).* http://training. fema.gov/EMIWeb/edu/06conf/06papers/Jones,%20Melvin%20-%20FEMA%20Cat%20 Disaster%20Plan%20Initiative.ppt.

5. National Drought Mitigation Center. 2006. *What is Drought?* http://drought. unl.edu/whatis/what.htm.

6. Hayes, M. J. 2006. *What is Drought? Drought Indices.* National Drought Mitigation Center. http://drought.unl.edu/whatis/indices.htm.

7. Ibid.

8. Perry, C. A. 2000, March. *Significant Floods in the United States During the 20th Century—USGS Measures a Century of Floods (USGS Fact Sheet 024-00).* Washington, DC: U.S. Geological Survey. http://ks.water.usgs.gov/pubs/fact-sheets/fs.024-00.pdf.

9. Ibid.

10. National Oceanic and Atmospheric Administration, Atlantic Oceanographic and Meteorological Laboratory. *Hurricane Hazards: Storm Surge, Floods, and Winds.* http://www.aoml.noaa.gov/general/lib/stormsurge.html.

11. Miller, M. *The Weather Guide: A Weather Information Companion for the forecast area of the National Weather Service in San Diego (4th Edition).* San Diego, CA: National Weather Service, 2007. http://www.wrh.noaa.gov/sgx/research/Guide/The_ Weather_Guide.pdf.

12. Federal Emergency Management Agency. 2006, April 19. *Dam Ownership in the United States.* http://www.fema.gov/hazard/damfailure/ownership.shtm.

13. Federal Emergency Management Agency. 2008, May 30. *The National Flood Insurance Program.* http://www.fema.gov/about/programs/nfip/index.shtm.

14. Holland, G. J. 1993. *Global Guide to Tropical Cyclone Forecasting.* Melbourne, Australia: Bureau of Meteorology Research Centre. http://www.bom.gov.au/bmrc/pubs/tcguide/globa_guide_intro.htm.

15. Ibid.

16. National Hurricane Center, National Weather Service, National Oceanic and Atmospheric Administration. 2007, August 19. *The Saffir-Simpson Hurricane Scale.* http://www.nhc.noaa.gov/aboutsshs.shtml.

17. U.S. Government. 2006, February. *The Federal Response to Hurricane Katrina: Lessons Learned.* Washington, DC.

18. Ibid.

19. Ibid.

20. Edwards, R. 2008, May 26. *The Online Tornado FAQ: Frequently Asked Questions about Tornados.* Storm Prediction Center, National Weather Service, National Oceanic and Atmospheric Administration. http://www.spc.noaa.gov/faq/tornado.

21. Ibid.

22. Ibid.

23. Ibid.

24. Fenimore, J. 1998. *Personal Communications.* New York State National Guard.

25. National Wildfire Coordinating Group. 2008, March. *Glossary of Wildland Fire Terminology.* http://www.nwcg.gov/pms/pubs/glossary/w.htm.

26. U.S. Geological Survey. 2006, February. *Wildfire Hazards—A National Threat (Fact Sheet 2006-3015).* http://pubs.usgs.gov/fs/2006/3015/2006-3015.pdf.

27. National Weather Service, National Oceanic and Atmospheric Administration. 2005, April 21. *National Weather Service Glossary.* http://www.weather.gov/glossary/index.php?letter=h.

28. Centers for Disease Control and Prevention. 2003, July 3. *Heat-Related Deaths—Chicago, Illinois, 1996–2001, and United States, 1979–1999.* http://www.cdc.gov/mmwr/preview/mmwrhtml/mm5226a2.htm.

29. Changnon, S. A., Kunkel, K. E., and Reinke, B. C. 1996. *Impacts and Responses to the 1995 Heat Wave: A Call to Action. Bulletin of the American Meteorological Society, Volume 77,* pp. 1497–1506.

30. Klinenberg, E. *Heat Wave: A Social Autopsy of Disaster in Chicago.* Chicago: The University of Chicago Press, 1996.

Chapter 14

1. U.S. Geological Survey. 2005, February 10. *2004 Deadliest in Nearly 500 Years for Earthquakes.* http://www.pmel.noaa.gov/tsunami/Faq/e0412_007_deadliest.htm.

2. U.S. Geological Survey. 2008, July 16. *Earthquake Facts.* http://earthquake.usgs.gov/learning/facts.php.

3. U.S. Geological Survey. 1989. *The Severity of an Earthquake.* http://pubs.usgs.gov/gip/earthq4/severitygip.html.

4. Central United States Earthquake Consortium. *About CUSEC.* http://www.cusec.org/about-cusec.html.

5. U.S. Geological Survey. 2008, June 11. *Landslides Hazards Program.* http://landslides.usgs.gov/?PHPSESSID=jnqn7nrkqjvgq18c5mtb8t5hn5.

6. U.S. Geological Survey. 2008, July 16. *Visual Glossary – Tsunami.* http://earthquake.usgs.gov/learning/glossary.php?termID=208.

7. International Tsunami Information Center. 2006, October 8. *About Tsunamis.* http://ioc3.unesco.org/itic/categories.php?category_no=4.

8. Houghton-Mifflin Company. 2006. *Cengage Learning Student Resource Center: Geology Link - Glossary.* http://college.hmco.com/geology/resources/geologylink/glossary/v.html.

9. Siebert, L., and Simkin, T. 2002. *Volcanoes of the World.* Washington, DC: Smithsonian Institution, Global Volcanism Program Digital Information Series. http://www.volcano.si.edu/world.

10. Britt, R. 2000, January 31. *What is a Solar Maximum and What Happens?* http://www.space.com/scienceastronomy/solarsystem/solar_max_sidebar_000131.html.

11. U.S. Climate Change Science Program. 2008, July. *Our Changing Planet,* p. 2. Washington, DC.

12. Ibid, p.5.

Chapter 15

1. Dymon, U. J., and Winter, N. L. *Hazard Mapping and Modeling.* Kent, OH: Kent State University, 1998.

2. Eckerman, I. 2001, August. *Chemical Industry and Public Health: Bhopal as an Example.* Goteborg, Sweden: Nordic School of Public Health.

3. Federal Emergency Management Agency. 2007, May 8. *Community Hazards Emergency Response – Capability Assurance Process (CHER-CAP) Fact Sheet.* http://www.fema.gov/plan/prepare/cher_capfs.shtm.

4. Community Emergency Response Team. http://www.citizencorps.gov/cert.

5. U.S. Department of Homeland Security. 2004, May 15. *National Response Plan.* Washington, DC.

6. Ibid.

7. Environmental Protection Agency. 1994. *National Oil and Hazardous Substances Pollution Contingency Plan.* Washington, DC.

8. U.S. Department of Homeland Security. 2006, May. *National Infrastructure Protection Plan.* Washington, DC.

9. Krejsa, P. 1997, October. *International Decade for Natural Disaster Reduction (IDNDR) Early Warning Program: Report on Early Warning for Technological Hazards.* Geneva, Switzerland: United Nations.

10. Executive Office of the President. 2003, December 17. *Homeland Security Presidential Directive-8: National Preparedness.* Washington, DC.

Bibliography

107th United States Congress. 2001. *Uniting and Strengthening America by Providing Appropriate Tools Required to Intercept and Obstruct Terrorism Act of 2001 (Public Law 107–56)*.

American Red Cross. http://www.redcross.org.

American Society for Civil Engineers. 2005. *Report Card for America's Infrastructure.* Reston, VA.

American Society for Industrial Security International. 2003. *The General Security Risk Assessment Guideline.* Alexandria, VA.

Andress, C. 2003, December. *Eliminating Hometown Hazards, Cutting Chemical Risks at Wastewater Treatment Facilities.* New York, NY: Environmental Defense.

Benford, J., and Swegle, J. *High Power Microwaves.* Norwood, MA: Artech House, 1992.

Britt, R. 2000, January 31. *What is a Solar Maximum and What Happens?* http://www.space.com/scienceastronomy/solarsystem/solar_max_sidebar_000131.html.

Bureau of Transportation Statistics. *T-100 Domestic Market and Segment Data.*

Cadwell, G. 2005, July 1. *Presidential Directive and Where to Find Them.* Washington, DC: Library of Congress Newspaper and Current Periodical Reading Room. http://www.loc.gov/rr/news/directives.html.

Canadian Broadcasting Corporation. http://archives.cbc.ca/science_technology/energy_production/clips/13545.

Center for Research on the Epidemiology of Disasters. http://www.cred.be.

Centers for Disease Control and Prevention. 2003, July 3. *Heat-Related Deaths—Chicago, Illinois, 1996–2001, and United States, 1979–1999.* http://www.cdc.gov/mmwr/preview/mmwrhtml/mm5226a2.htm.

Centers for Disease Control and Prevention. *Bioterrorism Agents/Diseases.* http://www.bt.cdc.gov/agent/agentlist.asp.

Central Intelligence Agency. 2003, May. *Terrorist CBRN: Materials and Effects (CTC 2003–40058).* Langley. VA.

Central United States Earthquake Consortium. *About CUSEC.* http://www.cusec. org/about-cusec.html.

Changnon, S. A., Kunkel, K. E., and Reinke, B. C. 1996. *Impacts and Responses to the 1995 Heat Wave: A Call to Action. Bulletin of the American Meteorological Society, Volume 77,* pp. 1497–1506.

Community Emergency Response Team. http://www.citizencorps.gov/cert.

Dymon, U. J., and Winter, N. L. 1998. *Hazard Mapping and Modeling.* Kent, OH: Kent State University.

Eckerman, I. 2001, August. *Chemical Industry and Public Health: Bhopal as an Example.* Goteborg, Sweden: Nordic School of Public Health.

Edwards, R. 2008, May 26. *The Online Tornado FAQ: Frequently Asked Questions about Tornados.* Storm Prediction Center, National Weather Service, National Oceanic and Atmospheric Administration. http://www.spc.noaa.gov/faq/tornado.

Emergency Management Assistance Compact. *What is EMAC?* http://www.emacweb. org/?9.

Energy Information Administration. 2007, March. *Electric Power Monthly.*

Environmental Protection Agency. 1994. *National Oil and Hazardous Substances Pollution Contingency Plan.* Washington, DC.

Executive Office of the President. 2003, December 17. *Homeland Security Presidential Directive [HSPD]-7: Critical Infrastructure Identification, Prioritization, and Protection.* Washington, DC.

Executive Office of the President. 2003, December 17. *Homeland Security Presidential Directive [HSPD]-8: National Preparedness.* Washington, DC.

Executive Office of the President. 2004, January 30. *Homeland Security Presidential Directive/[HSPD]-9: Defense of United States Agriculture and Food.*

Executive Office of the President. 2007, March 26. *The National Strategy for Aviation Security.* Washington, DC. http://www.whitehouse.gov/homeland/aviation-security.html.

Executive Order 13010 – Critical Infrastructure Protection. 1996, July 17. *Federal Register* 61*(138)*: 37347–37350.

Federal Bureau of Investigation. http://www.fbi.gov.

Federal Emergency Management Agency. 2003, December. *FEMA 426: Reference Manual to Mitigate Potential Terrorist Attacks Against Buildings.* Washington, DC.

Federal Emergency Management Agency. 2006, April 19. *Dam Ownership in the United States.* http://www.fema.gov/hazard/damfailure/ownership.shtm.

Federal Emergency Management Agency. 2006, June 8. *FEMA Catastrophic Disaster Readiness Program 2006: New Madrid Seismic Zone (NMSZ).* http://training.fema. gov/EMIWeb/edu/06conf/06papers/Jones,%20Melvin%20-%20FEMA%20Cat% 20Disaster%20Plan%20Initiative.ppt.

Federal Emergency Management Agency. 2006, October. *Multiagency Coordination Systems: Student Manual.* Washington, DC.

Federal Emergency Management Agency. 2007, May 8. *Community Hazards Emergency Response – Capability Assurance Process (CHER-CAP) Fact Sheet.* http:// www.fema.gov/plan/prepare/cher_capfs.shtm.

Federal Emergency Management Agency. 2007, November 11. *Integrated Public Alert and Warning System (IPAWS).* http://www.fema.gov/emergency/ipaws.

Federal Emergency Management Agency. 2007, September 11. *Principles of Emergency Management Supplement.* Washington, DC.

Federal Emergency Management Agency. 2008, May 30. *The National Flood Insurance Program.* http://www.fema.gov/about/programs/nfip/index.shtm.

Federal Emergency Management Agency. 2008, June 27. *Resource Management: Job Titles.* http://www.fema.gov/emergency/nims/rm/job_titles.shtm.

Federal Emergency Management Agency. 2008, August 29. *Welcome to the National Integration Center (NIC) Incident Management Systems Division.* http://www.fema.gov/emergency/nims.

Federal Emergency Management Agency. *Contemporary CBRNE Threat Profiles.* http://www.fema.gov.

Fenimore, J. 1998. *Personal Communications.* New York State National Guard.

Firescope. 2005, April. *FIRESCOPE Articles of Organization and Procedures (MACS 410–4).* Riverside, CA.

George Mason University, School of Law, Critical Infrastructure Protection Program. 2007, July. Inside the Government Facilities Sector. *The CIP Report, 6*(1), pp. 2–3, 10.

GovTrack.us. 2004. *S. 2845 [108th]: Intelligence Reform and Terrorism Prevention Act of 2004.* http://www.govtrack.us/congress/bill.xpd?bill=s108-2845&tab=summary.

GovTrack.us. 2005. *H.R. 3199 [109th]: USA PATRIOT Improvement and Reauthorization Act of 2005.* http://www.govtrack.us/congress/bill.xpd?bill=h109-3199&tab=summary.

GovTrack.us. 2006. *H.R. 6061 [109th]: Secure Fence Act of 2006.* http://www.govtrack.us/congress/bill.xpd?bill=h109-6061&tab=summary.

GovTrack.us. 2006. *S. 2271[109th]: USA PATRIOT Additional Reauthorizing Amendments Act of 2006.* http://www.govtrack.us/congress/bill.xpd?bill=s109-2271&tab=summary.

GovTrack.us. 2006. *S. 3678 [109th]: Pandemic and All-Hazards Preparedness Act.* http://www.govtrack.us/congress/bill.xpd?bill=s109-3678&tab=summary.

Harrington, M. B., Miller, C. S., and Wang, M. 2005, Spring. "Protecting one of the nation's critical infrastructures: healthcare." *The Edge.*

Hayes, M. J. 2006. *What is Drought? Drought Indices.* National Drought Mitigation Center. http://drought.unl.edu/whatis/indices.htm.

Henry L. Stimson Center. *Biological and Chemical Weapons: Responding to Biological and Chemical Threats.* http://www.stimson.org/cbw.

Holland, G. J. 1993. *Global Guide to Tropical Cyclone Forecasting.* Melbourne, Australia: Bureau of Meteorology Research Centre. http://www.bom.gov.au/bmrc/pubs/tcguide/globa_guide_intro.htm.

Hoover, J. E. 1941. Water Supply Facilities and National Defense. *Journal of the American Water Works Association, 33:11,* p. 1861.

Houghton-Mifflin Company. 2006. *Cengage Learning Student Resource Center: Geology Link – Glossary.* http://college.hmco.com/geology/resources/geologylink/glossary/v.html.

The House Subcommittee on International Terrorism and Nonproliferation (ITNP). 2005, July 27. *Terrorist Threats to Energy Security.*

International Association of Chiefs of Police. http://www.theiacp.org.

International Association of Emergency Managers. http://iaem.com.

The International Association of Fire Chiefs. http://www.iafc.org.

International Energy Annual (2000–2004).

International Petroleum Monthly (2005–2006).

International Tsunami Information Center. 2006, October 8. *About Tsunamis.* http://ioc3.unesco.org/itic/categories.php?category_no=4.

Jaeger, P. T., Bertot, J. C., and McClure, C. R. 2003, July. The impact of the USA PATRIOT Act on collection and analysis of personal information under the foreign intelligence surveillance act. *Government Information Quarterly, 20* (3), pp. 295–314.

Klinenberg, E. *Heat Wave: A Social Autopsy of Disaster in Chicago.* Chicago: The University of Chicago Press, 1996.

Kopp, C. 1996. "The electromagnetic bomb: a weapon of electronic mass destruction." *Air and Space Power Journal: Chronicles Online Journal.* http://www.airpower.maxwell.af.mil/airchronicles/cc/apjemp.html.

Krejsa, P. 1997, October. *International Decade for Natural Disaster Reduction (IDNDR) Early Warning Program: Report on Early Warning for Technological Hazards.* Geneva, Switzerland: United Nations.

Krill, S., and Smith, M. 2002, October. *Threat Assessment 101.* Prepared for the U.S. Department of Homeland Security, Office for Domestic Preparedness. Washington, DC.

McCarter, M. 2008, May 28. "GAO: improved inspections boost supply chain security." *Homeland Security Today.* http://www.hstoday.us/content/view/3541/128.

McGinn, T. 2007, July 9. *Statement for the Record, Tomm McGinn, DMV Director, Food, Agriculture and Veterinary Defense Office of Health Affairs Before the U.S. House of Representatives Committee on Homeland Security Subcommittee on Management, Investigations, and Oversight.* http://www.dhs.gov/xnews/testimony/testimony_1184092 241513.shtm.

Medalia, J. 2004, April 1. *Terrorist "Dirty Bombs": A Brief Primer (RS21528).* Washington, DC: Congressional Research Service.

Miller, M. *The Weather Guide: A Weather Information Companion for the forecast area of the National Weather Service in San Diego (4th Edition).* San Diego, CA: National Weather Service, 2007. http://www.wrh.noaa.gov/sgx/research/Guide/The_Weather_Guide.pdf.

Minkel, J. 2008. *The 2003 Northeast Blackout – Five Years Later.* http://www.sciam.com/article.cfm?id=2003-blackout-five-years-later.

Molino, L. N. *Emergency Incident Management Systems: Fundamentals and Applications.* Hoboken, NJ: Wiley Inter Science, 2006.

Morgenstern, H. *Vehicle Borne Improvised Explosive Device – VBIED: The Terrorist Weapon of Choice.* Miami, FL: Security Solutions International (SSI). http://www.securitysolutionsint.com.

Moteff, J., and Parfomak, P. 2004. *CRS Report for Congress: Critical Infrastructure and Key Asset Definitions and Identification.* Washington, DC: Library of Congress.

Munich Re Group. 2006. *Annual Review: Natural Catastrophes 2005.* Munich, Germany. http://www.munichre.com/publications/302-04772_en.pdf.

Nakicenovic, N., Grübler, A., and McDonald, A. *Global Energy Perspectives.* Cambridge: Cambridge University Press, 1998.

National Academy of Engineering. 2004. *Radiological Attack: Dirty Bombs and other Devices.* Washington, DC. http://www.nae.edu/NAE/pubundcom.nsf/weblinks/CGOZ-646NVG/$file/radiological%20attack%2006.pdf.

National Association of State EMS Officials. http://www.nasemsd.org.

National Drought Mitigation Center. 2006. *What is Drought?* http://drought.unl.edu/whatis/what.htm.

National Hurricane Center, National Weather Service, National Oceanic and Atmospheric Administration. 2007, August 19. *The Saffir-Simpson Hurricane Scale.* http://www.nhc.noaa.gov/aboutsshs.shtml.

National Infrastructure Protection Plan: Postal and Shipping Sector. 2007, Summer. *Messenger Courier World.* http://www.mcaa.com/magazine/2007_summer/006.pdf.

National Law Enforcement Officers Memorial Fund. http://www.nleomf.com.

National Oceanic and Atmospheric Administration, Atlantic Oceanographic and Meteorological Laboratory. *Hurricane Hazards: Storm Surge, Floods, and Winds.* http://www.aoml.noaa.gov/general/lib/stormsurge.html.

National Research Council. *Making the Nation Safer: The Role of Science and Technology in Countering Terrorism.* Washington, DC: The National Academies Press, 2002.

National Volunteer Fire Council. http://nvfc.org.

National Weather Service, National Oceanic and Atmospheric Administration. 2005, April 21. *National Weather Service Glossary.* http://www.weather.gov/glossary/index.php?letter=h.

National Wildfire Coordinating Group. 2008, March. *Glossary of Wildland Fire Terminology.* http://www.nwcg.gov/pms/pubs/glossary/w.htm.

Nuclear Energy Institute. http://www.nei.org.

Nyberg, C. 2005, February 7. Pursuing Presidential Directives. *Law Library News.* Seattle, WA: Marian Gould Gallagher Law Library, University of Washington School of Law. http://lib.law.washington.edu/news/2005/Feb7.html.

Orum, P. 2007, April 2. *Toxic Trains and the Terrorist Threat, How Water Utilities Can Get Chlorine Gas Off the Rails and Out of American Communities.* Washington, DC: Center for American Progress.

Oxford Pocket Dictionary of Current English. New York: Oxford University Press, 2008.

Perry, C. A. 2000, March. *Significant Floods in the United States During the 20th Century— USGS Measures a Century of Floods (USGS Fact Sheet 024–00).* Washington, DC: U.S. Geological Survey. http://ks.water.usgs.gov/pubs/fact-sheets/fs.024-00.pdf.

Radvanovsky, R. *Critical Infrastructure: Homeland Security and Emergency Preparedness.* Boca Raton, FL: Taylor and Francis, 2006.

Report Card for America's Infrastructure. 2005. http://www.asce.org/reportcard/2005/index.cfm.

Sandia National Laboratories. *Security Risk Assessment Methodologies.* http://www.sandia.gov/ram/index.htm.

Sartori, L. 2002. The Effects of Nuclear Weapons. *Physics Today, 36* (3), pp. 32–38, 40–41.

Sherman, J. 2006, March 8. President issues "War on Terror" directive to improve government coordination. Inside Washington publishers news stand. http://defense.iwpnewsstand.com/insider.asp?issue=spclrpt03092006.

Siebert, L., and Simkin, T. 2002. *Volcanoes of the World.* Washington, DC: Smithsonian Institution, Global Volcanism Program Digital Information Series. http://www.volcano.si.edu/world.

Starks, T., and Andersen, M. E. 2004, July 29. Congress, industry both in dismay over homeland security's performance on critical infrastructure. *CQ Homeland Security.*

Sullivant, J. *Strategies for Protecting National Critical Infrastructure Assets: A Focus on Problem-Solving.* Hoboken, NJ: John Wiley & Sons, Inc., 2007.

Taylor, C. D., and Giri, D. V. *High Power Microwave Systems and Effects.* London: Taylor and Francis Group, 1994.

U.S. Army Corps of Engineers Topographic Engineering Center. http://crunch.tec.army.mil/nid/webpages/nid.cfm.

U.S. Citizen Corps. http://www.citizencorps.gov.

U.S. Climate Change Science Program. 2008, July. *Our Changing Planet*, p. 2. Washington, DC.

U.S. Department of Energy, Energy Information Administration. *Forecasts of International Use to 2020*. Washington, DC.

U.S. Department of Energy. 2004, April. *Water Energy Resources of the United States (DOE/ID-11111)*.

U.S. Department of Energy. 2004, December. *Electricity Transmission in a Restructured Industry: Data Needs for Public Policy Analysis*. Washington, DC.

U.S. Department of Energy. http://www.energy.gov.

U.S. Department of Health and Human Services. *Critical Infrastructure Protection: Healthcare and Public Health Sector-Critical Infrastructure Protection*. http://www.hhs.gov/aspr/opeo/cip/index.html.

U.S. Department of Health and Human Services. http://www.hhs.gov.

U.S. Department of Homeland Security, Office of Inspector General. 2006, June. *Progress in Developing the National Asset Database (OIG-06-04)*.

U.S. Department of Homeland Security, and U.S. Department of the Interior. 2007, May. *National Monuments and Icons: Critical Infrastructure and Key Resources Sector-Specific Plan as Input to the National Infrastructure Protection Plan*. Washington, DC.

U.S. Department of Homeland Security, Homeland Infrastructure Threat Risk Analysis Center. 2007, January 23. *Strategic Sector Assessment: Commercial Facilities (U/FOUO)*. Washington, DC.

U.S. Department of Homeland Security. 2003. *National Strategy for the Physical Protection of Critical Infrastructures and Key Assets*. Washington, DC.

U.S. Department of Homeland Security. 2004, March. *National Incident Management System (NIMS)*. Washington, DC.

U.S. Department of Homeland Security. 2004, May 15. *National Response Plan*. Washington, DC.

U.S. Department of Homeland Security. 2005, September. *The National Strategy for Maritime Security*. Washington, DC.

U.S. Department of Homeland Security. 2005. *National Response Plan Brochure*.

U.S. Department of Homeland Security. 2006, May. *National Infrastructure Protection Plan*. Washington, DC.

U.S. Department of Homeland Security. 2006. *National Infrastructure Protection Plan: Risk Management Framework*. Washington, DC.

U.S. Department of Homeland Security. 2007, March 26. *Air Domain Surveillance and Intelligent Integration Plan: Supporting Plan to the National Strategy for Aviation Security*. Washington, DC.

U.S. Department of Homeland Security. 2007, March 26. *Aviation Transportation System Security Plan: Supporting Plan to the National Strategy for Aviation Security*. Washington, DC.

U.S. Department of Homeland Security. 2007, March 26. *Domestic Outreach Plan: Supporting Plan to the National Strategy for Aviation Security*. Washington, DC.

U.S. Department of Homeland Security. 2007, March 26. *International Outreach Plan: Supporting Plan to the National Strategy for Aviation Security*. Washington, DC.

U.S. Department of Homeland Security. 2007, March 26. *National Strategy for Aviation Security*. Washington, DC.

U.S. Department of Homeland Security. 2007, May. *Agriculture and Food: Critical Infrastructure and Key Resources Sector-Specific Plan as input to the National Infrastructure Protection Plan*. Washington, DC.

U.S. Department of Homeland Security. 2007, May. *Banking and Finance: Critical Infrastructure and Key Resources Sector-Specific Plan as Input to the National Infrastructure Protection Plan.* Washington, DC.

U.S. Department of Homeland Security. 2007, May. *Communications: Critical Infrastructure and Key Resources Sector-Specific Plan as Input to the National Infrastructure Protection Plan.* Washington, DC.

U.S. Department of Homeland Security. 2007, May. *Information Technology: Critical Infrastructure and Key Resources Sector-Specific Plan as Input to the National Infrastructure Protection Plan.* Washington, DC.

U.S. Department of Homeland Security. 2007, May. *Transportation Systems: Critical Infrastructure and Key Resources Sector-Specific Plan as Input to the National Infrastructure Protection Plan.* Washington, DC.

U.S. Department of Homeland Security. 2007. *National Infrastructure Protection Plan: Risk Management Framework.* Washington, DC.

U.S. Department of Homeland Security. 2007. *Water Critical Infrastructure and Key Resources Sector-Specific Plan as Input to the National Infrastructure Protection Plan.* Washington, DC.

U.S. Department of Homeland Security. 2008, March 18. *Commercial Facilities Sector: Critical Infrastructure and Key Resources.* http://www.dhs.gov/xprevprot/programs/gc_1189101907729.shtm.

U.S. Department of Homeland Security. 2008, March 18. *Government Facilities Sector: Critical Infrastructure and Key Resources.* http://www.dhs.gov/xprevprot/programs/gc_1189011910767.shtm.

U.S. Department of Homeland Security. 2008, March 18. *Postal and Shipping Sector: Critical Infrastructure and Key Resources: Sector Overview.* http://www.dhs.gov/xprevprot/programs/gc_1188412546210.shtm.

U.S. Department of Homeland Security. 2008, April. *National Incident Management System (NIMS) – Pre-Decisional DRAFT.* Washington, DC.

U.S. Department of Homeland Security. 2008, April 8. *Fact Sheet: Our Federal Networks Against Cyber Attacks.* http://www.dhs.gov/xnews/releases/pr_12076842 77498.shtm.

U.S. Department of Homeland Security. 2008, August 21. *Homeland Security Presidential Directives.* http://www.dhs.gov/xabout/laws/editorial_0607.shtm.

U.S. Department of Homeland Security. 2008, September 11. *National Preparedness Guidelines.* http://www.dhs.gov/xprepresp/publications/gc_1189788256647.shtm.

U.S. Department of Homeland Security. 2008, September 11. *National Protection and Programs Directorate.* http://www.dhs.gov/xabout/structure/editorial_0794.shtm.

U.S. Department of Homeland Security. 2008, September 23. *Domestic Nuclear Detection Office.* http://www.dhs.gov/xabout/structure/editorial_0766.shtm.

U.S. Department of Homeland Security. 2008, October 17. *National Security Presidential Directive 41 / Homeland Security Presidential Directive 13.* Washington, DC. http://www.dhs.gov/xprevprot/programs/editorial_0597.shtm.

U.S. Department of Homeland Security. *Accessing Department of Homeland Security Records through the Freedom of Information Act.* http://www.dhs.gov/xfoia/editorial_0314.shtm.

U.S. Department of Homeland Security. http://www.dhs.gov.

U.S. Department of Justice. 2003. *Domestic Security Enhancement Act of 2003.* Washington, DC. http://www.publicintegrity.org/dtaweb/downloads/Story_01_020703_Doc_1.pdf.

U.S. Department of Transportation. http://www.dot.gov.

U.S. Energy Information Administration. 2003, August. *Electricity Transmission Fact Sheet.* Washington, DC.

U.S. Environmental Protection Agency. 2001, February. *Drinking Water Infrastructure Needs Survey: Second Report to Congress (EPA 816-R-01-004).* Washington, DC.

U.S. Environmental Protection Agency. 2003, August. *Clean Watersheds Needs Survey 2000: Report to Congress (EPA 832-R-03-001).* Washington, DC.

U.S. Environmental Protection Agency. http://www.epa.gov.

U.S. Food and Drug Administration. 2007, June 14. *Food Defense and Terrorism: CARVER + Shock Software Tool.* http://www.cfsan.fda.gov/~dms/vltcarv.html.

U.S. General Accountability Office. 2002, August. *Water Infrastructure: Information on Financing, Capital Planning, and Privatization (GAO-02-764).* Washington, DC.

U.S. Geological Survey. 1989. *The Severity of an Earthquake.* http://pubs.usgs.gov/gip/earthq4/severitygip.html.

U.S. Geological Survey. 2005, February 10. *2004 Deadliest in Nearly 500 Years for Earthquakes.* http://www.pmel.noaa.gov/tsunami/Faq/e0412_007_deadliest.htm.

U.S. Geological Survey. 2006, February. *Wildfire Hazards—A National Threat (Fact Sheet 2006–3015).* http://pubs.usgs.gov/fs/2006/3015/2006-3015.pdf.

U.S. Geological Survey. 2008, June 11. *Landslides Hazards Program.* http://landslides.usgs.gov/?PHPSESSID=jnqn7nrkqjvgq18c5mtb8t5hn5.

U.S. Geological Survey. 2008, July 16. *Earthquake Facts.* http://earthquake.usgs.gov/learning/facts.php.

U.S. Geological Survey. 2008, July 16. *Visual Glossary – Tsunami.* http://earthquake.usgs.gov/learning/glossary.php?termID=208.

U.S. Government. 2001, January. *United States Government Interagency Domestic Terrorism Concept of Operations Plan.* Washington, DC.

U.S. Government. 2006, February. *The Federal Response to Hurricane Katrina: Lessons Learned.* Washington, DC.

U.S. Government Accountability Office. 2005, March. *Cargo Security: Partnership Program Grants Importers Reduced Scrutiny with Limited Assurance of Improved Security (GAO-04-404).* Washington, DC.

U.S. Government Accountability Office. 2006, October. *Critical Infrastructure Protection: Progress Coordinating Government and Private Sector Efforts Varies by Sectors' Characteristics (GAO -07-39).* Washington, DC.

U.S. Government Accountability Office. 2007, March. *Securing Wastewater Facilities: Costs of Vulnerability Assessments, Risk Management Plans, and Alternative Disinfection Methods Vary Widely (GAO-07-480).* Washington, DC.

U.S. Government Accountability Office. 2007, July 10. *Critical Infrastructure Protection: Sector Plans and Sector Councils Continue to Evolve.* Washington, DC. http://www.gao.gov/new.items/d07706r.pdf.

U.S. National Guard. http://www.ngb.army.mil/default.aspx.

United States Congress. 1978, October 25. *The Foreign Intelligence Surveillance Act of 1978, Pub. L. No. 95–511.* Washington, DC.

United States Congress. 2002, November 25. *The Homeland Security Act (HSA) of 2002, Pub. L. No. 107–296.* Washington, DC.

United States Congress. 2002. *Public Health Security and Bioterrorism Preparedness and Response Act of 2002 (Public Law 107–188).* Washington, DC.

United States Congress. 2006, October 4. *Post-Katrina Emergency Reform Act of 2006, Pub. L. No. 109–295, Title VI – National Emergency Management.* Washington, DC.

Vaughan R., and Pollard, R. *Rebuilding Americas, Volume 1: Planning and Managing Public Works in the 1980's.* Council of State Planning Agencies: Washington, DC, 1984.

Wright, J. W. *The New York Times Almanac, 2007.* New York: Penguin Books, 2006.

Index

About the Authors

PAMELA A. COLLINS is Executive Director of the Justice and Safety Center and Professor of Homeland Security at Eastern Kentucky University. She is the co-author of *Women in Law Enforcement*, *Principles of Security and Crime Prevention*, and *Workplace Violence*. She has also published book chapters, book reviews, and several journal articles on security-related topics.

RYAN K. BAGGETT is Director of Homeland Security Programs at the Justice and Safety Center at Eastern Kentucky University, where he directs several federal programs from both the Department of Homeland Security and the Department of Justice. He also serves as adjunct faculty with the Homeland Security department at EKU.

CPSIA information can be obtained at www.ICGtesting.com
Printed in the USA
LVOW04*0009090815

449141LV00007B/87/P

9 780313 351471